STABILITY AND CHANGE ALONG A DIALECT BOUNDARY

STABILITY AND CHANGE ALONG A DIALECT BOUNDARY

The Low Vowels of Southeastern New England

DANIEL EZRA JOHNSON

Publication of the American Dialect Society 95

Supplement to *American Speech*, Volume 85

PUBLICATION OF THE AMERICAN DIALECT SOCIETY

Editor: ROBERT BAYLEY, *University of California, Davis*
Managing Editor: CHARLES E. CARSON, *Duke University*

Number 95
Copyright 2010
American Dialect Society
ISBN: 978-0-8223-6748-2

Library of Congress Cataloging-in-Publication Data

Johnson, Daniel Ezra
    Stability and change among a dialect boundary : the low vowels of south-
    eastern New England / Daniel Ezra Johnson
        p. cm.
    Includes bibliographical references and index
    Revised version of the author's these (Ph.D.)—University of Pennsylva-
    nia, 2007.
    ISBN 978-0-8223-6748-2 (pbk. : alk. paper)
        1. English language—Dialects—Massachusetts. 2. English language—
    Dialects—Rhode Island. 3. English language—vowels. I. Title.
PE3101.M35J64 2010
427'.9744–dc22   2010040347

British Library Cataloguing-in-Publication Data available

CONTENTS

FOREWORD

WILLIAM LABOV, *University of Pennsylvania*

Readers: This is an extraordinary work that you are about to plunge into. Daniel Ezra Johnson has fixed his eye on one of the central problems of linguistic change and variation: how does it come about that phonemes merge and collapse, so that speakers can no longer tell the difference between *cot* and *caught, collar* and *caller, odd ability* and *audibility*? This low back merger is the major factor that differentiates American dialects and determines the future course of sound change. Many scholars have made the low back merger their central topic, but no one has delineated the events more precisely than Johnson has. He has not only studied change in progress, but captured the crucial events almost at the moment they occurred.

Johnson's study is a model of research design and execution. In chapter 3, he first develops an instrument for the school survey, rapidly charting the number of distinctions perceived among the low back vowels. He also includes the important question as to whether *father* and *bother* rhyme, a point badly neglected in the *Atlas of North American English*. Throughout this study, we have data on whether /ah/ differs from /o/ (PALM from LOT) as well as whether /o/ differs from /oh/ (LOT from THOUGHT). The school survey gathers crucial information on the state of the low back vowels in a number of communities, including South Attleboro and Seekonk, two communities near the border between the eastern Massachusetts area, where /o/ and /oh/ are merged, and the Rhode Island area, where /o/ and /ah/ are merged. In these two places, we observe a distinct shift toward the merger of all /o/ and /oh/ (see, for example, figs. 3.10–3.12). Johnson also generates a wealth of data that bear crucially on the influence of the community on in-migrant children, and the relative influence of the mother's versus the father's linguistic system on that of the child.

The reader can have considerable confidence in Johnson's multivariate analyses, since they use mixed models regression, in which the effects of random variables (like individual subjects) are separated from the fixed effects (like gender, age, or community). It is worth noting that Johnson is the author of a statistical package in R—Rbrul—which foregrounds this capacity along with other advantages over other Varbrul programs (see http://www.danielezrajohnson.com/rbrul.html and Johnson's 2009 article on the subject).

In chapter 4, Johnson sets out to trace the geographic boundary between the areas where the LOT and THOUGHT classes are merged and where they are not. He delineates this boundary through short sociolinguistic interviews with 67 seniors and 113 young adults. The end result is the elegant maps in figure 4.3 for the seniors and figure 4.4 for the younger speakers. But surprisingly enough, given the general tendency of mergers to expand, there are very few differences between the two figures. Over two or three adult generations, the line between merged and unmerged systems has remained remarkably stable. There is, however, plenty of room for Johnson to examine with fine-grained acoustic tools the various types of systems involved in the transition areas. The figures in this chapter use a dazzling array of graphic techniques to display these systems, ranging from the three-way system of an 81-year-old man (fig. 4.10) to the complete collapse of the three phonemes in the vowel system of a 19-year-old girl (figs. 4.21 and 4.22).

If Johnson had stopped at this point, we would have had a view of linguistic stability, with a surprisingly small tendency for the low back merger to expand. Fortunately for us, he decided to go further and designed the family study of chapter 5. This involved sociolinguistic interviews with 47 families, recording spontaneous speech and various techniques with minimal pairs. In the crucial transitional town of Seekonk, 14 families with a total of 34 children were interviewed. The results show an explosion of merger among children, which appears as they leave the influence of their parents in favor of their peer groups, sometimes as early as 4 or 5 years of age. Figures 5.2 for Attleboro and 5.3 for Seekonk display this development with remarkable clarity: one can see immediately how the youngest children copy the system of their parents while school-age children follow the pattern of their peers.

Some of the most impressive aspects of this work follow, as Johnson takes up several ways of accounting for this sudden development of the merger. Can the outbreak of merger among local children be the result of in-migration from merged areas? Johnson uses his considerable expertise in the analysis of census data to weigh the evidence for and against this hypothesis. I would urge the reader to follow his argument through to the end, before settling on one interpretation or the other.

But the evidence provided by the school survey has enabled Yang (2009) to develop a model that predicts the percentage of in-migrating children required to produce such a change—in the neighborhood of 20%, and not significantly different from the percentage of children in the Seekonk elementary school who marked all 7 word pairs as the same: 19%.

My appreciation of the main line of research should not tempt readers to jump directly to chapter 3. Johnson's opening chapters provide a masterful review of the history of the vowel systems, the relation of settlement history to the vowel systems of the area, and the evidence for mergers and distinctions in earlier times. This includes an acoustic analysis of ten minutes of the speech of the upper class Bostonian, Henry Wadsworth Longfellow Dana, born in 1881. The result is a clear three-way distinction of the three low back vowels—/o/ in LOT, /ah/ in PALM, and /oh/ in THOUGHT—a system that survives only among the oldest speakers of Johnson's studies. For those of us who are not great scholars, Johnson's chapters 1 and 2 provide a short course in the history of the subject that will save us many trips to the library.

ACKNOWLEDGMENTS

This study is a revision of my 2007 University of Pennsylvania Ph.D. dissertation, for which I was supported by a William Penn Fellowship and a National Science Foundation Graduate Fellowship.

Thank you to my teachers at the University of Pennsylvania and especially to those who formed my dissertation committee: Mark Liberman, Gillian Sankoff, and my advisor and mentor, William Labov.

In addition to Labov, Sharon Ash, Charles Boberg, and their *Atlas of North American English*, this study is indebted to the work of many scholars, especially my predecessors Arvilla Payne and Ruth Herold, dialectological pioneers Hans Kurath, Miles Hanley, and Raven McDavid, and the awe-inspiring Yakov Malkiel and Wilbur Zelinsky.

The school study would have been impossible without the help of administrators Raleigh Buchanan, June Gilch, and Robert Weintraub; the elementary, middle, and high school principals of Attleboro and Seekonk; the teachers who administered the questionnaire, including my friends Rachel Mazor, Emily Tuckman, Sarah Westley, and Michael Williams; and all the students who completed it, combining to reveal subtle patterns of family and peer influence.

Locating the dialect boundary between the Eastern New England and Mid-Atlantic low vowel systems depended on dozens of senior center directors in Massachusetts and Rhode Island, and on many others, notably George Yelle of Norton Historical Society. Thank you to all the senior citizens and young adults, whom I enjoyed talking with so much.

The same goes for the parents and children who welcomed me into their homes so agreeably, even if it was to show that parents and children—and even siblings—can often disagree significantly in their speech.

I was helped immensely in my research by Judith Gray of the Library of Congress, Carol Faber and John Blodgett of the United States Census Bureau, Kevin Lopes of the Massachusetts Executive Office of Transportation, and the librarians at the University of Pennsylvania, Stanford University, M.I.T., and Boston University.

Thank you to Robert Bayley and Charles Carson, my patient and professional editors, as well as to two anonymous reviewers who provided lengthy and constructive criticism. Kyle Gorman prepared the index, and Kate Grandjean checked the text for historical errors.

Regardless of the fate of the "migration hypothesis," the course of this work saw me move among five American states and one English county. Thank you to all of the businesses providing electricity and sustenance, among them Gatehouse Coffee, In-N-Out Burger, Qdoba Mexican Grill, and Starbucks Coffee.

And thank you to my family and friends, who helped me with this work and enriched my life while it was being written. In particular, thanks to Maryam Bakht, Elizabeth Coppock, Bill Haddican, Damien Hall, Nanna Haug Hilton, Uri Horesh, Jason Horger, Sarah Miller, Jennifer Nycz, Dan Paquin, Joanie Sanchez, Sandhya Sundaresan, Laura Whitton, and Molly Williams.

This study is dedicated to my parents, Nicholas Beeching Johnson (3-D) and Susan Bienen Johnson (MAIN).

1. VOWEL MERGERS

THIS STUDY OF DIALECT geography, acquisition, stability, and change examines the low vowels of southeastern New England (Massachusetts and Rhode Island). Because these vowels—represented by Wells's (1982) PALM,[1] LOT, and THOUGHT[2] lexical sets—have undergone several mergers, a review of the nature, causes, and mechanisms of vowel merger is in order.

Historical linguistics texts (Hock 1986; Campbell 2004) treat vowel mergers along with mergers of consonants or tones, without emphasizing the various mechanisms by which similar vowel phonemes can fall together as the same sound, usually creating homonymy between pairs of previously distinct words.

Among modern languages, vowel-rich English and German, as well as French and Yiddish (and their dialects), have provided many examples of this phenomenon, the examination of which has led scholars to develop principles and mechanisms of vowel merger.

One reason why phonemes should not merge is functional: the homonymy created by merger may make comprehension more difficult, hindering communication. On the other hand, the relative ease of pronouncing a language with fewer speech sounds could be a functional argument in favor of merger.

But there is little clear evidence that such functional factors are at play. In the history of Greek, there has been a tremendous amount of vowel merger and loss of lexical contrast. Through fronting, raising, unrounding, and the loss of glides and length distinctions, nine phonemes of Ancient Greek—$\breve{\iota}$ /i/, $\bar{\iota}$ /i:/, $\varepsilon\iota$ /e:/, η /ɛ:/, $\bar{a}$ /a:/, $o\iota$ /oi/, $\upsilon\iota$ /yi/, $\breve{\upsilon}$ /y/, $\bar{\upsilon}$ /y:/—all eventually merged as Modern Greek /i/, in "the most spectacular example" of multiple merger into a single target (Labov 1994, 229). The high front monophthong /i/ is a point of stability, according to Labov's (1994) principles of vowel shifting.

In other cases, multiple vowel merger can occur as one process. When the Classical Latin system of distinctive vowel length collapsed in the transition to Vulgar Latin, regular mergers took place in all varieties, though their number and location differed by area, as shown in table 1.1, derived from R. Hall (1950) and Leonard (1978).

Though the details of these mergers are different, they were all caused by there being, after the loss of Classical Latin's distinctive vowel length, simply too many vowels in too small a phonetic space for them all to remain distinct. Thinking about vowels in terms of their potential crowding in a kind of space—related to the physical space available for the tongue's movements in the mouth—is due to the work of Martinet (1955).

TABLE 1.1

Vulgar Latin Mergers Following Loss of Classical Latin Vowel Length

Classical Latin	French, Spanish, etc.	Romanian	Sicilian	Sardinian
iː	i	i	i	i
i̧	e	e	i	i
eː	e	e	i	e
ȩ	ɛ	ɛ	e	e
a	a	a	a	a
aː	a	a	a	a
o̧	ɔ	o	o	o
oː	o	o	u	o
u̧	o	u	u	u
uː	u	u	u	u
10 distinct vowels	7 distinct vowels	6 distinct vowels	5 distinct vowels	5 distinct vowels

For Martinet, many vowel shifts are a way of avoiding merger; those mergers that do occur are exceptional (Labov 1994, 266). However, another fundamental principle for Martinet is the pressure to achieve symmetry in phonological (sub)systems. Vowel merger can create a more symmetrical system and relieve articulatory crowding at the same time.

1.1. TYPES OF MERGER: APPROXIMATION, TRANSFER, EXPANSION

Most of the vowel mergers mentioned above are of the type known as MERGER BY APPROXIMATION (Trudgill and Foxcroft 1978). These are regular sound changes that occur below the level of conscious awareness. They are lexically abrupt—affecting all relevant words at the same time—and phonetically gradual. For Guy (1990), these are "spontaneous" and "internally induced" changes that stem from language-internal pressures.

In merger by approximation, two vowels can move toward each other, ending up merged in an intermediate position, or one can move while the other remains in place, like Greek /i/, resulting in a merger with the quality of the stationary vowel (Labov 1994, 321).

Another mechanism is MERGER BY TRANSFER (Trudgill and Foxcroft 1978). Here, the primary cause is external—dialect contact—and the change occurs above the level of consciousness (Labov 1994, 321). It is a type of borrowing (Guy 1990). The merger diffuses gradually through the relevant part of the lexicon but is phonetically abrupt: no intermediate forms are observed.[3]

A third mechanism of merger was proposed in Herold (1990). As it is the most relevant for this study, it will be described in detail. Herold discovered a previously unknown area of low back merger (between LOT and THOUGHT) in northeast Pennsylvania and convincingly attributed its origin to a period of heavy foreign immigration.

Foreigners who came to work in the local anthracite coal-mining industry failed to acquire the low back distinction from the native population, who were in a minority. And the immigrants' numbers were so great that not only their children but the natives' children adopted it.

This happened—apparently independently—in most of the anthracite mining towns, one of which Herold studied in depth: Tamaqua, Pennsylvania, population 8,000. Of the 30 natives she interviewed (10 analyzed acoustically), Herold found that speakers aged 74 and older maintained the low back distinction, while those 64 and younger had lost it. Merger thus began community-wide around 1920 and was "completed" (but see below) in just ten years.[4]

Herold developed a theory of individual development to accompany this community-level observation of rapid change. In interaction with merged speakers, those with the distinction stop relying on it to distinguish words, since the usual phonetic cues are absent, or even reversed, in the speech of their interlocutors. And before long, they also stop producing the distinction.[5]

The phonetic range of the younger Tamaqua speakers' merged phoneme was very wide. Acoustically, it covered the combined ranges of both original phonemes. This would not have happened with merger by approximation nor merger by transfer.

Herold coined the term MERGER BY EXPANSION to describe the change in Tamaqua. Unlike merger by transfer, it is a change from below and lexically abrupt. Unlike merger by approximation, it is phonetically abrupt too. Since people who did not speak the local variety natively were crucial in the genesis of the change, it belongs under "imposition" in the typology of Guy (1990).

Figure 1.1 displays the vowels of a Tamaqua father (b. 1907) and son (b. 1942) who display the distinct and merged patterns, respectively. The LOT and THOUGHT clouds were not far separated before the change. Afterward, they are completely intermingled.

In a sense, the merger was "completed within a single generation" (Herold 1997, 185). However, this "completion" left the community divided, not unified. Although the circumstances triggering merger fell into place

FIGURE 1.1

LOT and THOUGHT Plots of a Father and Son from Tamaqua, Pennsylvania
(after Herold 1990, 88–89)

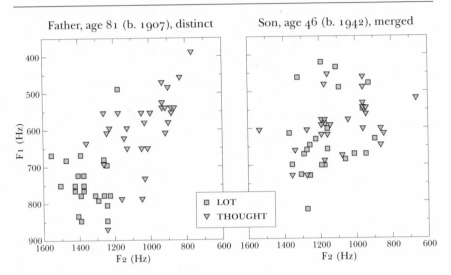

around 1920, the merger did not affect adults who had already acquired the distinction. Nor have older adults been much affected by subsequent contact with younger speakers, such as the 40-plus years the distinct father has presumably spent talking to his merged son.

Herold refers to "speakers" or "people," but by stipulating that it is children who carry out merger by expansion, we explain why the same phonological merger sometimes spreads readily, and sometimes not at all. Children who have initially acquired a vowel distinction are capable of abandoning it upon exposure to (enough) merged speakers, but adults in the same situation will likely retain their distinct patterns for the rest of their lives.

1.2. PRINCIPLES OF MERGER: GARDE AND HERZOG

One of the best-known statements about mergers is called Garde's Principle: "mergers are irreversible by linguistic means" (Labov's [1994, 311] interpretation of Garde's [1961, 38–39] statement, "si deux mots ont été rendus identiques par un changement phonétique quelconque, ils ne peuvent jamais devenir différents par voie phonétique"). If homonymy between a pair of words is irreversible, then a merger of word classes must be too, leading Labov to state that "once two word classes have merged, they cannot be distinguished by any linguistic process" (Labov 1994, 144). This means that once a speech community has completely merged two historically distinct word classes, the usual subconscious processes of sound change cannot separate them later.

If two close word classes are thought to be merged but are actually not, their later separation is no threat to Garde's Principle. The reversal of several cases of falsely believed merger is discussed in Herold (1990, chap. 4) and Labov (1994, chap. 10; see also Maguire 2008).

It is also possible for a true merger to be reversed, but not "by linguistic means." For example, if a speech community were drastically disrupted by large-scale immigration or invasion, the result could certainly be a variety that distinguished two phonemes that the original variety did not.

Changes from above, toward prestigious norms, can be a less dramatic type of externally motivated merger reversal: "Si l'on rencontre des exceptions à cette irréversibilité, ce ne peut être que dans le cas de la forte influence d'une langue littéraire sur un parler" ('If we find exceptions to this irreversibility, it can only be in the case of the strong influence of a literary language on a variety'; Garde 1961, 39). By saying that vowel mergers cannot be reversed "par voie phonétique" ('just anywhere'), Garde meant that Neogrammarian sound change—internal, from below—cannot reverse them, because a type of change that is blind to everything but phonetics cannot affect a pair of homonyms differently. Indeed, the rare instances of merger reversal are usually attributable to factors other than sound change in the strict sense.[6]

A recent investigation in Charleston, South Carolina (Baranowski 2007), has revealed the reversal of a conditioned merger, where two or more vowels have fallen together, but only in certain phonetic environments.[7] In Charleston, the NEAR and SQUARE vowels were pronounced alike by older speakers, but were distinguished again starting around the time of World War II. Since the logic of Garde's Principle applies equally to conditioned mergers, Baranowski notes that Charleston "appears to be a counterexample" (120). Rejecting the idea that the sub-classes were never fully merged, Baranowksi points to the in-migration of many people bearing the distinction. However, the merger seems to have begun to reversing a decade or more before many of these migrants arrived.

Garde's Principle leads to Herzog's Principle: "mergers expand at the expense of distinctions" (Labov 1994, 313). This formulation implies that a merger WILL expand geographically at the expense of an adjacent distinction, although Herzog (summarizing Garde) and Garde himself say that areas of merger can only expand and will never contract.[8] Therefore, contact between a distinct community and an adjacent merged one is predicted to have little or no effect on the merged community, but there may be an effect in the other direction, whereby the merger spreads. If this happens iteratively, all along the length of the isogloss, the area of merger will expand.

There is some disagreement about when mergers should be expected to spread in this contagious manner. For Herzog (1965, 211), "the most significant linguistic factor to limit [the] diffusion [of a change] is the nature of the phonological system with which it comes into contact. If changes emanating from opposite directions are structurally compatible they may overlap." Herzog's prime example of such overlapping mergers is in Yiddish, where the loss of vowel length in the Northeastern dialect—/i = iː/, /u = uː/—converges with the fronting and unrounding of high back vowels in the Central dialect—/u = i/, /uː = iː/ (Herzog 1965, 167, 197). Each process caused merger in its own area, and they overlapped in the intermediate North Central zone, where only one vowel remains of the original four: /i/. Apparently, these two changes were "structurally compatible," although this concept is only vaguely defined. The New England low vowel mergers discussed in this study may be less compatible with each other.

For Garde, there is less expectation that the isoglosses of mergers will spread and overlap. As opposed to the isoglosses of nonphonemic changes, which "passent n'importe où" (62), Garde finds that structural isoglosses tend to form bundles:

> sur chaque frontière linguistique importante paraissent courir des isoglosses distinctives de sens contraire, c-à-d. que la limite d'un groupe d'homonymies réalisées d'un côté de la frontière correspond à la limite d'un autre groupe d'homonymies réalisées de l'autre côté. ['along every important linguistic boundary, there seem to run distinctive isoglosses with opposite orientations, that is to say, the limit of one group of mergers that occurred on one side of the boundary corresponds to the limit of another group of mergers on the other side'; Garde 1961, 58]

To explain why these changes coming from opposite directions tend to face off along the same boundary, Garde (1961, 62) invokes "résistance à l'homonymie, autrement dit le besoin de clarté" ('resistance to merger, otherwise known as the need for clarity'). If this functional explanation is correct, it makes cases like North Central Yiddish—where overlapping mergers have caused extensive homonymy—the exception, not the norm.

Garde notes that the most innovative Slavic languages in terms of segmental phonology are the most conservative prosodically, and vice versa. But it is not structural incompatibility in Herzog's sense that prevents, for example, the merger of /i/ and /y/ (found in South Slavic) from coinciding with the loss of distinctive lexical stress and/or intonation (found elsewhere). After all, many world languages have neither that particular vocalic distinction nor that prosodic one. For Garde (1961, 55–56), varieties are in "equilibrium"; each can undergo different mergers as long as the resulting amount of homonymy is not too great.[9]

Garde and Herzog both emphasize geographic diffusion. They usually assume that an isogloss found in a certain place spread there from somewhere else. This may be justified, especially when there is evidence for the spread, although other isoglosses may develop in situ, at the edges of areas sharing parallel internal developments.

Whether a merger affects a place by internal, structurally motivated evolution, by spreading from an adjacent place (contagious diffusion, Hägerstrand 1953), or by the longer-distance influence of some populous center (hierarchical diffusion), we can still ask why it occurs there when it does—sometimes fairly suddenly and under conditions similar to those associated with vowel system stability in previous generations. What look like stable boundaries between speech communities can collapse; individuals with distinct parents and older siblings can grow up merged.

1.3. SELECTED STUDIES OF LOW BACK MERGER IN THE UNITED STATES

Early dialectological work along the U.S. Eastern Seaboard found the merger of LOT and THOUGHT in two areas, Eastern New England and Western Pennsylvania (Kurath and McDavid 1961). These areas are structurally different: Eastern New England has a distinct PALM vowel, whereas in Western Pennsylvania all three classes are merged.[10]

A national survey of long-distance telephone operators conducted by Labov in 1966 confirmed the merger in Eastern New England and found the Western Pennsylvania merger to extend further east in Pennsylvania and westward into Ohio. A vast third area of merger was revealed in the western United States, including the Great Plains but excluding San Francisco and Los Angeles (Labov 1991; Labov, Ash, and Boberg 2006).[11]

Many local studies have since reported the expansion of the Western area of merger. Terrell (1976) interviewed more than 100 children and teenagers in Orange County, California, and found that none of the white natives, and few of the nonnatives, had a full LOT ~ THOUGHT contrast.[12] Many who had moved from areas of distinction had acquired the merger, "most in less than two years" (Terrell 1976, 355). One boy had moved from New Jersey at age ten, and three years later was "completely indistinguishable from native Californians by his speech" (354).

Minnesota was on the eastern edge of the Western merged area, and Allen (1976, 24; quoted in Wells 1982, 475) reported a "steadily increasing proportion" of university students with the merger there. In Kansas City, right on the telephone survey's merger boundary, Lusk (1976; cited in Majors 2005, 165) reported older speakers as distinct and most younger ones as merged. Gordon (2006) finds the merger in progress among younger speakers in most parts of Missouri. Only the eastern part of the state, around St. Louis, retains the distinction.

As reported in Labov, Ash, and Boberg (2006, chap. 19.5), St. Louis participates to some extent in the Northern Cities Shift, a rotation of several vowels that developed in the twentieth century in a very similar form from New York State to Wisconsin (see Labov, Ash, and Boberg 2006, chap. 14). In the Northern Cities Shift, TRAP is raised in every allophonic environment, and LOT moves forward, sometimes as far as [æ]. This precludes the low back merger, even though THOUGHT can be unrounded and not fully back.

In Oklahoma, also on the eastern edge of the Western merged area, Bailey et al. (1993) show that the low back merger has diffused hierarchically. For speakers born before 1945, substantial merger is mainly restricted to the largest cities, Oklahoma City and Tulsa. Among younger speakers, it is found in most parts of the state.

Other studies documenting the merger on the West Coast are Metcalf (1972) in Southern California and Mills (1980) in the Pacific Northwest. Those finding its advancement elsewhere include Bailey, Wikle, and Sand (1991) and Bernstein (1993) in Texas, Fridland (1998) in Memphis, Tennessee, and Baranowski (2007) in Charleston, South Carolina, cities far from the three core merged areas. Other references are given in the review of low back merger in Thomas (2001, 26–27).

Baranowski (2007) finds that in Charleston, men and women of all social classes are progressing toward merger in parallel. Typical phonetic changes from below are led by women and originate in the interior socio-economic classes (Labov 2001). If mergers in progress escape such gender and class differentiation, it may signal that these phonological restructurings occur even further below the level of conscious awareness than changes such as vowel raising, fronting, and so on.

The above instances of merger involve the unrounding of THOUGHT, so that the merged vowel is approximately [ɑ].[13] Irons (2007) deals with a different phonetic situation, in Kentucky. As will be seen in the next section, the low back merger is now found throughout West Virginia, so the further spread of the merger into northeastern Kentucky, as documented by Irons (2007), is relatively unsurprising. However, in southeastern Kentucky, THOUGHT is traditionally pronounced [ɑɔ] or even [ao], with a back upglide. It is often only the presence of the glide that distinguishes THOUGHT from LOT, as the vowel nuclei are identical. Irons (2007) shows that younger speakers are losing the glide and merging the two vowels. He argues that this is not a further expansion of the Western Pennsylvania/ West Virginia merger. Most of the areas where glide loss was found have low population densities and are far from major transportation routes; for merger to appear there is not expected under contagious or hierarchical diffusion accounts.[14]

1.4. A COMPREHENSIVE LOOK AT MERGER: LABOV, ASH, AND BOBERG (2006)

Labov, Ash, and Boberg's (2006) *Atlas of North American English* considerably advanced our understanding of the geographic distribution of the low back merger and its dynamics in the United States.[15] Based on telephone interviews with 762 speakers, it retraces the three main areas of merger: Eastern New England, Western Pennsylvania (including West Virginia and parts of Kentucky), and the West, where it is still in progress (59).

The merger is most advanced before /n/ (*Don ~ Dawn*), intermediate in *hot ~ caught* and *dollar ~ caller*, and least advanced before /k/ (*sock ~ talk*). A fair number of speakers, particularly in the South, were merged only before /n/. However, these speakers were not clustered in any way that would suggest that the merger expands SPATIALLY on an environment-by-environment basis.

Of Labov, Ash, and Boberg's major dialect areas, the South and Midland are outside the isogloss of regular low back merger, but it is in progress in both areas, although sometimes only as a change from "different" to "close," not "same." In the Mid-Atlantic and Inland North, which have raised THOUGHT and fronted LOT, respectively, maintenance of the distinction is widespread, with no movement toward the merger in apparent time.

In most cases, production—whether the analyst judged the LOT and THOUGHT vowels in a pair to be the same—agreed with "perception"— whether the subject judged the words in question to sound the same (or to rhyme). Where merger was the norm, an equal number of speakers deviated from it in production as in perception. But in the transitional and mainly distinct dialect areas, it was three times as common for perception to lead production: that is, for speakers to judge a pair the same while pronouncing it differently (Labov, Ash, and Boberg 2006, 62).

The merger is particularly active in the Midland, where the cities of Indianapolis, Indiana, and Columbus, Ohio, were examined in detail. Only three speakers there, all over age 40, were fully distinct, and one teenager was fully merged; 30 others showed intermediate patterns (note similar findings for Cincinnati, Ohio, in Boberg and Strassel 1995).

In both Indianapolis and Columbus, *Don ~ Dawn* favored the merger and *sock ~ talk* the distinction. There was no overall difference between men and women, and perception led production four to one among asymmetrical subjects (Labov, Ash, and Boberg 2006, 64).

Labov, Ash, and Boberg adopt Herold's functional explanation of the merger (see §1.1), although these Midland communities are not adopting the merger in the sudden and total fashion that Herold observed in Tamaqua, Pennsylvania. Instead, age groups are heterogeneous, and transitional patterns last for decades.

Assuming that mergers do not retreat, Labov, Ash, and Boberg's findings also contradict previous research in several places. Providence, Rhode Island, is fully distinct according to their data, whereas Kurath and McDavid (1961) had found the merger for all of Rhode Island. This case will be discussed extensively in chapter 2. Labov, Ash, and Boberg also find the distinction in two areas where the 1966 telephone survey had found the merger: (1) central Pennsylvania and northern Ohio and (2) southern Minnesota, eastern South Dakota, and eastern Nebraska.[16]

To summarize, in the dialect areas where the low back merger was already characteristic, it has continued toward completion, and in the case of Western Pennsylvania, it has expanded into an adjacent part of the Midland. However, its expansion across dialect boundaries is not usual, with areas like the Upper Midwest, central Pennsylvania, and Rhode Island remaining distinct, at least until very recently.[17]

In the Midland and the South, the merger is a newer phenomenon. It appears to be developing in parallel across the entire area, replacing more heterogeneous patterns. In the South, it is less advanced, but progressing more quickly than in any other region (Labov, Ash, and Boberg 2006, 59). As in the Midland, the Southern merger is not spreading from any particular point(s) of origin, but is appearing roughly simultaneously in several states.

In much of the South, the merger can only proceed by displacing a system with a back upgliding THOUGHT. In the past, this variety of THOUGHT might have been pointed out as a structural factor giving the South resistance to the low back merger, just as the raised THOUGHT is believed to be in the Mid-Atlantic area (and the fronted LOT in the Inland North).

Since chapter 5 will show that communities on the edge of the Mid-Atlantic area[18]—with raised, ingliding THOUGHT—can yield to the low back merger within a decade, we may wonder whether the Mid-Atlantic and Inland North low vowel patterns really provide protection against the merger, any more than the traditional Southern pattern seems to be doing.

This review of merger gives rise to two general questions. First, when can we expect a merger (or other change) to diffuse from one dialect area to another? The amount and type of contact, whether it is primarily between adults (as Labov 2007 suggests) or also involves the migration of children, and the structural compatibility between the dialects are all relevant here. We must also ask whether a change really has diffused from place A to place B, or whether it simply developed in A at an earlier time and in B, perhaps for similar reasons, at a later time.

Second, what causes the dialects within a dialect area to undergo the same changes (including mergers)? Although this has received less attention than diffusion, it is an equally important question. Internal phonological evolution—transmission and incrementation, in the terms of Labov (2007, 347)—is "the primary source of [linguistic] diversity," although when dialects evolve in parallel, no divergence need result.

The Stammbaum ('family tree') model of linguistic diversification assumes that populations of speakers inherit and pass down the majority of their language faithfully. When innovations occur, divergence arises between dialects if they are no longer in contact. Within each population, innovations diffuse more or less completely. Bloomfield's density principle is a refinement of this: "When any innovation in the way of speaking spreads over a district, the limit of this spread is sure to be along some lines of weakness in the network of oral communication" (1933, 476).

This diffusionist model is challenged by the Midland and Southern low back mergers, and more impressively by the Northern Cities Shift (Labov, Ash, and Boberg 2006, chap. 14.2) and the Southern Shift (chap. 18.3). Whether or not the boundaries of these large areas are "lines of weakness in the network of oral communication"—they are probably not[19]—the practically simultaneous and nearly identical development of these complex shifts, throughout dialect areas hundreds of miles wide, practically rules out an explanation whereby these innovations diffuse; they must be internal processes. But if they are, is their incrementation mainly social or structural? That is, do children learn the direction and speed of changes from observing older members of their communities—the "inherited age vectors" of Labov (2007, 346)—or is linguistic change more deterministic than that?

1.5. THE STUDY OF MERGER ON THREE LEVELS

This study has three main parts. The school survey (chap. 3) will examine constraints on individuals acquiring the low vowels, as revealed by their evaluation of minimal pairs on a questionnaire. The geographic study (chap. 4) will locate and describe the boundary between dialects with different patterns of merger. And the family study (chap. 5) will explore the process of merger as it affects speech communities where the low back merger is recent or ongoing.

When Kerswill (1996, 200) ranks phenomena in a "difficulty hierarchy" with respect to their ease of acquisition—finding that mergers are much easier to acquire than distinctions—the focus is on the individual level. Chapter 3 supports this conclusion, fleshing it out with the details of parental and peer influences.

Herzog's Principle that "mergers expand at the expense of distinctions" is a generalization on the dialect level. Chapter 4 does not find widespread expansion, but a long period of stability followed by expansion in some areas.

Connecting these two is an account of merger at the speech community level. Chapter 5 will describe sudden merger by expansion among children in several speech communities and offer a demographic explanation for why and when the mergers took place.

First, chapter 2 gives background on the study area and the results of previous research on the low vowels in England and New England.

2. THE LOW VOWELS
OF NEW ENGLAND: HISTORY AND
DEVELOPMENT

FOLLOWING ZELINSKY'S (1973) DOCTRINE of First Effective Settlement,[1] section 2.1 focuses on the earliest period of New England history, including the origins of the English settlers and what can be concluded about the low vowels in that period.

Section 2.2 reviews the contributions of the *Linguistic Atlas of New England* (*LANE* 1939–43) and related studies. The best-known publication derived from *LANE*'s data, Kurath and McDavid's (1961) *The Pronunciation of English in the Atlantic States*, tended to oversimplify matters, and rather infamously placed the low back merger in Rhode Island and eastern Connecticut. The reasons for this error, and the literature correcting it, will be reviewed.

Section 2.3 reviews the findings of Labov, Ash, and Boberg (2006) and their relationship to earlier results. Section 2.4 is an auditory and acoustic analysis of the early "Hanley recordings" (S. Hall et al. 2002) from southeastern New England.

Together, these sources suggest a certain interpretation of the historical development of the low vowels in New England, given in section 2.5.

By 1900, two dialect areas had mainly solidified in southeastern New England, with the two largest cities, Boston and Providence, on either side of the divide. Section 2.6 describes the pilot study carried out to locate the boundary between these two dialects.

2.1. THE HISTORY OF THE LOW VOWELS AND THE SETTLEMENT OF (SOUTHEASTERN) NEW ENGLAND

Settlement history is clearly relevant to the linguistic geography of a territory if there are retentions, current features whose distribution can be correlated with settlers' origins. For example, many believe that Eastern New England speech is nonrhotic because its settlers mainly came from southeastern England, a region that led in the loss of postvocalic /r/. The settlers of Appalachia, on the other hand, mainly came from places that were likely rhotic then (northern England) or are still rhotic today (Scotland, Northern Ireland).[2]

However, some view the history of American English more in terms of divergence than retention. According to Dillard (1995, 6), most emigrants spoke a standardized form of English, and any differences that did get imported were "very strikingly leveled" by the eighteenth century, when British travelers noted "how the Americans spoke English of amazing uniformity."

But even if most regional differences developed later on American soil, it is still important to trace settlement patterns. Places with a common settlement history share a linguistic starting point: the output of the same leveling. They may also share lasting cultural ties. Innovations are more likely to have developed in parallel within such settlement areas, or at least to have diffused within them.

It is not fully known where in England the first settlers of New England came from. "In Bradford's 'History of Plymouth Plantation', where he gives a detailed list of the passengers of the Mayflower, there is not one reference to the family origin or home parish of any one of the Pilgrims" (Banks 1930, 12). Historians have reconstructed the origins of some, though not all, of the settlers.

Information on seventeenth-century English regional dialects—assuming they were spoken by at least some of the settlers—is less available. What is known does not appear to shed much light on the low back vowels. The mergers that arose appear to be indigenous American developments.

Better recorded are the patterns in which the land of southeastern New England was taken up in the seventeenth and early eighteenth centuries, as people fanned out from the early coastal settlements and founded new ones in the interior. New towns split off from older ones, and larger towns divided as they grew. At the same time, there was continued immigration from England, as well as mobility within and between the colonies.

2.1.1. THE ORIGINS OF THE FIRST ENGLISH SETTLERS. The original New England colonies, illustrated in figure 2.1, were Plymouth (1620), New Hampshire (1623), Massachusetts Bay (1628), Saybrook (1635), Connecticut (1636), Rhode Island (1636), and New Haven (1638). We will be concerned mainly with Plymouth, Massachusetts Bay, and Rhode Island.[3] Of these, Massachusetts Bay grew the largest and contributed to the settlement of the other two colonies.

2.1.1.1. *Plymouth Colony.* The original Pilgrims, or Separatists, were a congregation from Scrooby, Nottinghamshire. Most were originally from that

FIGURE 2.1

The New England Colonies

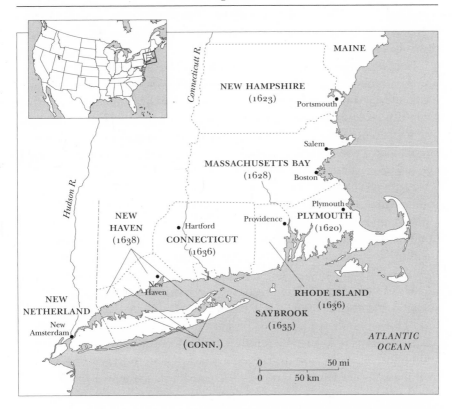

county or adjacent South Yorkshire (Richards 2004, 42). After spending 12 years in the Netherlands, they sailed to found Plymouth in 1620. However, the Separatist congregation comprised only about 40 of the 102 passengers aboard the *Mayflower*; most of the others whose origins are known came from London, Essex, and Norfolk (Banks 1930).[4]

Nearly half the *Mayflower* passengers died during the first winter, but the next 10 years saw several hundred more settlers come to Plymouth. By 1630 an effective settlement had been made, and the colony expanded along the shore and into the interior. The settlers were a mix of Pilgrims from the East Midlands, Londoners, and people from the eastern counties. The eastern component was enhanced over the next decades, as Plymouth attracted immigration from the new Massachusetts Bay colony to the north (Kurath et al. 1939, 68). In 1691, Plymouth was absorbed politically by Massachusetts.

2.1.1.2. *Massachusetts Bay Colony.* Although several settlements preceded it, the founding of Boston in 1630 began a wave of emigration so significant that it has come to be called "The Great Migration." Some 21,000 English settlers, mainly Puritans, came to Massachusetts Bay before the outbreak of the English Civil War in 1640.

Fischer (1989) argues that emigration from "East Anglia" (see n. 4) was the dominant element in the settlement of Massachusetts Bay, effecting a cultural transplant crucial for the history of New England (and other American regions settled from there). But for some historians, "masses of evidence do not fit" Fischer's thesis (V. Anderson 1991, 235), which "has to be qualified in so many ways that its meaning becomes tenuous" (D. Hall 1990, 659).

Fischer (1989, 33) describes 60% of the Great Migration settlers as coming from a nine-county area in the east of England, but Banks (1930, 14) suggests a more even distribution: Norfolk, Suffolk, and Essex, 21.5%; London, Middlesex, Sussex, and Kent, 20%; other counties surrounding London, 11%; Cornwall, Devon, Dorset, and Somerset, 16%; Midlands counties, 9%; and 22.5% from other parts of England, or elsewhere.

The distribution of settlers' origins may have been somewhat different, as Banks was able to trace only 2,646 Great Migration settlers. Emigrants from London and/or lower-class backgrounds would have been harder to trace than most provincials. Another under-recorded group was women and children, who "came from the East of England in larger proportions than men," writes Fischer (1991, 266), tenaciously defending the thesis of an eastern migration.

A more recent project is compiling "comprehensive genealogical and biographical accounts of every person who settled in New England between 1620 and 1643" (R. Anderson 1993), but it is designed for studying individuals. It would be a major undertaking to tabulate this data by English county of origin and New England point of destination.

But it is clear that the regional origins of groups of settlers were correlated with their destinations in Massachusetts Bay. In a 27-town sample, Fischer (1991, 270) concedes there was great variation in the proportion of eastern English origins, from less than 15% in Gloucester and Weymouth to over 70% in Dedham, Hingham, and Watertown.

Settlers with origins in the South and West of England, too, were rare in some places (less than 15% in Boston, Charlestown, and Roxbury) and a majority in others (more than 60% in Dorchester, Gloucester, and Weymouth). And the estimated proportion from London, though never high, reached 20% in Boston and Cambridge, compared with none in Gloucester and Hingham.

The average for the 27 towns is 55% from the East, 27% from the South and West, and 9% from London. Even with Fischer's likely Eastern bias, he acknowledges the regional diversity of Massachusetts Bay settlement.

Assuming that the settlers from different areas spoke differently—which is very likely even if they did not speak broad regional dialects—there must have been a great deal of dialect leveling early in the history of Massachusetts. Any differences between nearby towns like Boston, Dedham, and Dorchester have not survived. There seems to have been leveling within each colony, or at least within the major areas of each colony.

2.1.1.3 *Rhode Island Colony.* The settlers of Rhode Island were a more diverse group, both because the colony was an amalgamation of several settlements and because the liberal policies of the Rhode Island government attracted a wider spectrum of people than were tolerated in Plymouth, let alone in Massachusetts Bay.

After Roger Williams was banished from Massachusetts for his religious views, he founded Providence in 1636 at the head of Narragansett Bay. "A haven for those persecuted elsewhere for their conscientious beliefs," it grew slowly, with settlers from Massachusetts, Plymouth, Connecticut, and directly from England (McLoughlin 1978, 3–17).

In 1638, Anne Hutchinson and a group of allies were banished from Boston, and they began a settlement later called Portsmouth on the northern end of Aquidneck (or Rhode) Island. The next year, part of this group moved to the other end of the island and founded Newport. These settlements grew faster than Providence, though not as quickly as those in Massachusetts Bay (McLoughlin 1978, 18–25).

From the start, there was a rivalry with Massachusetts Bay and a border dispute that was not fully settled until 1862. At the height of it, the Providence and Rhode Island settlements united, beginning in 1647. (During this early period, the eastern shore of Narragansett Bay was disputed, but officially it was Plymouth Colony territory.)

Though it already had a population of Catholics and Jews, Rhode Island's diversity increased with the arrival of the Quakers in the 1650s. This likely brought to Rhode Island some varieties of speech from the North of England, a region poorly represented in Plymouth and Massachusetts Bay. However, the Rhode Island Quakers arrived after an effective settlement was already made.

Once the first effective settlements were made and leveled varieties established in each colony, the regional origins of any new English settlers became less important. The colonial dialects would have developed fairly independently, especially as the colonies were rather isolated from each other throughout the seventeenth century.

As their populations increased, through immigration and natural growth, the colonies expanded geographically, and it is to these internal settlement patterns that we now turn.

2.1.2. THE SETTLEMENT PATTERNS OF SOUTHEASTERN NEW ENGLAND. While Kurath (1928) believed that American regional dialect differences corresponded to and derived from British ones, when it came to delineating the dialect areas within New England, Kurath et al. (1939) referred to internal settlement patterns, not patterns of British origin. Likewise, Bloch (1935) reconstructed the original rhoticity status of 11 New England settlement areas, but did not attempt to link this to settlers' origins or to earlier British dialects, citing a lack of information about both.

Kurath et al. (1939) divide New England into major eastern and western areas. Within southeastern New England, they reconstruct the main thrusts of internal settlement as follows (Plate 1, following p. 240):

(1) from Plymouth: north and south along the coast, then westward into the interior; (2) from Massachusetts Bay: westward into most of the present state of Massachusetts (and northeast Connecticut); (3) from Rhode Island: westward into the interior of the present state, and eastward into original Plymouth territory.

A more detailed description of the settlement patterns involves an understanding of the political boundaries in the region during the colonial period. Where boundaries were disputed, a more complex pattern of settlement resulted.

The boundary between Plymouth Colony and Massachusetts Bay, a diagonal line running southwest from the ocean to the Rhode Island border (see figure 2.1), was established in 1640. The line is now the boundary between Massachusetts's Norfolk County and Plymouth and Bristol counties.

Rhode Island's northern boundary was long disputed but never moved significantly. On the other hand, it eastern boundary—in conflict first with Plymouth, then with Massachusetts—has undergone significant changes (see figure 2.2).

In 1746, King George II awarded Rhode Island the town of Cumberland in the northeast corner of the state, and the towns of Bristol, Warren, Tiverton, and Little Compton on the eastern shore of Narragansett Bay. These places had been settled under the auspices of Plymouth, though not all their settlers had come from there.

In 1862, a smaller adjustment occurred, when Massachusetts received the northern end of Tiverton in exchange for the western half of Seekonk,

FIGURE 2.2

Disputed Border between Plymouth and Rhode Island Colonies

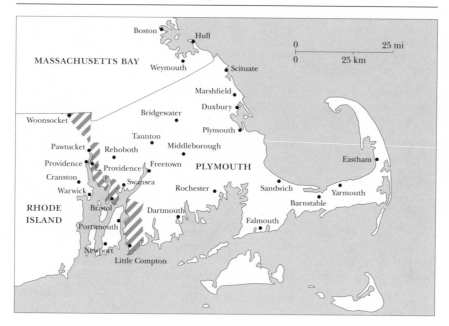

which became East Providence, Rhode Island. The city of Pawtucket, Massachusetts, was also transferred, becoming the east side of Pawtucket, Rhode Island.

Since it is along the modern Massachusetts–Rhode Island boundary that this study was conducted, it is important to understand how the three settlement currents came together near the borders of their respective territories.

Table 2.1 shows the "family tree" of the study area of chapter 4. There are 40 communities: 29 in present-day Massachusetts, 11 in Rhode Island. In the leftmost columns the original towns are in bold, towns that split from them are in normal type, and further divisions are in italic and small type. The dates in the center columns show that some "daughter" places were settled much earlier than they were incorporated, sometimes just as early as their parent towns.

The rightmost column gives information on the origins of the first settlers of each place. We see that two early Plymouth Colony settlements that produced many daughter towns in the study area did not have predominantly Plymouth settlers. Taunton was settled by a group mainly from Devon and Somerset in southwest England. Rehoboth, the parent town of Attleboro and Seekonk (a focus of chapter 5), was settled from several Mas-

TABLE 2.1

Settlement History of the Study Area of 40 Cities and Towns

Colony & Town/City	Code	Incorp.	Settled	Settled From
MASSACHUSETTS BAY				
Mendon	ME	1667	1660	Mass. (Braintree, Weymouth)
Bellingham (part)	BH	1719	1713	
Uxbridge	UB	1727	1662	
Blackstone	BS	1845	1662	
Millville	MV	1916	1662	
Wrentham	WR	1673	1669	Mass. (Dedham)
Bellingham (part)	BH	1719	•1713	
Foxborough (part)	FB	1778	1704	Mass. (Dorchester)
Franklin	FK	1778	1660	Mass. (Dedham)
Plainville	PV	1905	1661	
Douglas	DO	1775	1721	Mass. (Sherborn, Natick)
PLYMOUTH (MASS. BAY after 1691)				
Taunton	TA	1639	1638	Eng. (Taunton) via Ply. & Mass.
Norton	NT	1711	1669	Taunton North Precinct
Mansfield	MF	1775	1659	
Dighton	DI	1712	1678	Taunton South Purchase
Berkley	BK	1735	1638	
Rehoboth	RE	1645	1644	Mass. (Weymouth etc.), Ply.
Swansea	SW	1667	1667	
Warren	WA	1717	1676	
Barrington	BA	1770	1676	
Somerset	SO	1790	1677	
Attleboro	AB	1694	1662	Rehoboth North Purchase
Cumberland	CL	1747	1662	
Woonsocket (part)	WS	1867	1695	
N. Attleborough	NA	1887	1669	
Seekonk	SK	1812	1644	
Pawtucket (part)	PT	1828	1644	
E. Providence	EP	1862	1644	
Dartmouth	DM	1664	1650	Plymouth, R.I.
Little Compton	LC	1682	1675	
Tiverton	TI	1694	?	
Westport	WP	1787	1670	Plymouth, R.I. (Portsmouth)
New Bedford	NB	1787	1640	
Fairhaven	FH	1812	1670	
Acushnet	AC	1860	1659	
Middleborough		1669	1660	Plymouth
Lakeville	LV	1853	1717	
Freetown	FT	1683	1659	Plymouth (Scituate, Marshfield)
Fall River	FR	1803	1670	
PROVIDENCE (RHODE ISLAND after 1647)				
(Gloucester)		1713	1706	Providence
Burrillville	BV	1806	1706	
(Smithfield)		1731	1636	Providence
N. Smithfield	NS	1871	1672	
Woonsocket (part)	WS	1871	1695	
(Lincoln)		1871	1650	
Central Falls	CF	1895	?	
(N. Providence)		1765	1636	Providence
Pawtucket	PT	1874	1655	

sachusetts and Plymouth towns, but largely from Weymouth, which had a high proportion of West Country settlers.

For the most part, later-incorporated towns drew their population from their parent towns. Taunton grew and spawned Norton, Dighton, and Berkley; Swansea, Attleboro, and (later) Seekonk were set off from Rehoboth.[5] Uxbridge, Blackstone, and Millville, however, were not secondary settlements; they were settled around the same time as the rest of Mendon.

If linguistic divisions closely corresponded to settlement patterns, we would expect a clear boundary to follow the northern border of Rhode Island, where communities derived from Providence (Burrillville, North Smithfield) abut ones detached from Mendon in Massachusetts Bay (Uxbridge, Blackstone, Millville).

We might also see a difference between the Wrentham daughter towns derived originally from Dedham, a strongly east-of-England settlement, and those derived from Taunton, Rehoboth, and Dorchester, which had more West Country settlers. This would be a line between Wrentham and Plainville on the west, Foxborough and Mansfield on the east.

Linguistic boundaries might be more unclear along the eastern shore of Narragansett Bay, where communities like Dartmouth (Kilpatrick 1937, 49) and Westport (Kurath et al. 1939, 179) had a mixed Plymouth and Rhode Island settlement history. In Somerset, Swansea, and Seekonk, the majority of the settlers were probably from Rehoboth, but some would have come from Rhode Island. Kilpatrick (1937, 49) even suggests that the East Bay developed a culture distinct from the rest of individualistic Rhode Island, due to the "stabilizing influences of communitarian Plymouth."

Little Compton, Tiverton, Warren, Barrington, and Cumberland also likely had some original Rhode Island settlement, as well as being part of that state for the last 250+ years. If Cumberland were still like its parent town of Attleboro, this would truly be a testament to the doctrine of First Effective Settlement. (But as we will see, it is not.)

Chapter 4 will show that current linguistic boundaries match these predictions in the north, where a phonological boundary runs along the settlement (and state) line. In the east, the line runs further into Massachusetts than expected. And instead of always dividing settlement subareas, it cuts through two of them (Dartmouth and Rehoboth).

2.1.3. THE LOW VOWELS OF ENGLISH IN THE SEVENTEENTH CENTURY. Settlers' origins and settlement history could have relevance for any dialect feature. This study focuses on the low vowels, so we examine their status at the time of settlement, starting with the developing standard variety. Even if some emigrants used broad English regional dialects, they might have spoken more standardly in the dialect contact situation they now found themselves in. Others, due to their geographical or social origins, probably spoke this developing standard natively.

2.1.3.1. *Low Vowels in the Development of British Standard English: E. J. Dobson.* The low vowels were undergoing substantial change in England during the seventeenth century; they had not arrived at the configuration PALM [ɑː], LOT [ɒ], THOUGHT [ɔː] found in present-day southern British English, including Received Pronunciation (RP) (Wells 1982, 119). What follows recapitulates the most important changes described in Dobson (1957).

Many words in our PALM, LOT, and THOUGHT sets had the Middle English vowels *ă*, *ŏ*, and *au*, respectively, but the correspondence is not always one-to-one. Middle English *ă* was always [a], but in the seventeenth century it underwent a split. In most environments (TRAP) it stayed short, but in syllables closed by /r/ (START) or one of the front voiceless fricatives /f/, /s/, or /θ/ (BATH), it lengthened.

"Pre-R Lengthening" was widespread, but only some dialect areas, including southern England and Eastern New England, underwent the "TRAP-BATH Split" (Wells 1982, 199–206). As with nonrhoticity, Eastern New England's similarity to the British standard can be attributed to settlement history and/or to later contact.

Several other phonetic environments also caused *ă* to lengthen. The word *father* lengthened in almost all dialects of English. In lengthening *rather*, Eastern New England again tends to agree with the mother country.

In RP, lengthened *ă* ended up backed to [ɑː] while unlengthened *ă* was fronted to [æ]. Although their earlier phonetics are much debated, the most important thing is the length difference. In any given dialect, the words that have lengthened *ă* form part of our PALM class (see chap. 1, n. 1).[6] This includes many foreign borrowings with [a] in the original language (e.g., *Obama*) (see Boberg 1997).

The changes undergone by *ă* in the seventeenth century were paralleled by *ŏ*, pronounced [ɔ] in Middle English. In most environments (LOT), *ŏ* remained short, but it lengthened before tautosyllabic /r/ (NORTH) and before /f/, /s/, and /θ/ (CLOTH). The lengthening of *ŏ* before /r/ happened almost everywhere. Before the fricatives, the "LOT-CLOTH Split" would survive in America but eventually die out in England (Wells 1982, 204). In southern England, the CLOTH ~ THOUGHT merger was either never complete (Dobson 1957), or it reversed through dialect contact (Wells 1982). The two word classes are largely in complementary distribution (exceptions like *sauce* are rare), perhaps easing a reversal. Other words with *ŏ* lengthened, such as *broad*, and in some dialects, *on* and/or *gone*. Lengthening before /ŋ/ has been almost universal in American dialects; before /g/ it has been very irregular.

Words with unlengthened *ŏ* form our LOT word class. In most English dialects, including RP, LOT lowered but remained rounded: [ɒ]. But an unrounded [ɑ] also developed in the South of England.[7]

Words with lengthened *ŏ* form part of our THOUGHT class.[8] The rest of this class derives from *au*, a diphthong that arose in early Middle English from *ă* before /g/, /h/, or /w/ (e.g., *law, taught, claw*) or from French *au* and *ao* (e.g., *laud, fawn*). Circa 1400, *au* developed from *ă* in syllables closed by /l/ (e.g., *palm, half*) or /x/ (e.g., *thought*) and in French borrowings before /m/ or /n/ (e.g., *dance, lawn*) (Dobson 1957, 553–56).

As Standard British English developed, all these subclasses had [au] in the fifteenth century, backing to [ɑu] in the sixteenth century, and [ɒu] in the seventeenth century (Dobson 1957, 783). That evolution was a dead end, but over the same period, a competing development was a monophthongization that resulted in *au* merging with lengthened *ŏ* (NORTH, CLOTH, *broad*, etc.). Dobson places this monophthong at [ɔː] in the seventeenth century, which would make the same realization, as found today in RP, conservative. Others suggest [ɑː] for lengthened *ŏ* (from [ɑ] for unlengthened *ŏ*), with *au* monophthongizing to [ɑː]. Any backing and rounding would have occurred only later, perhaps in parallel with the backing of PALM from [aː] to [ɑː].

In syllables closed by /m/ (*palm*), /f/ (*half*), /v/ (*halve*), and /nC/ (*dance*), *au* also monophthongized, but wound up further front—call it [aː]—falling in with lengthened *ă* (START, BATH, *father*, etc.), and completing our PALM class.

This alternate monophthongization from *au* to [aː] made lengthened *ă*, previously a mere allophone, into a separate phoneme, with contrasts like *aunt ~ ant, palm ~ Pam* (Dobson 1957, 536). The number of minimal pairs remained small if postvocalic /r/ was retained, but its loss created a huge number like *cart ~ cat*.

Outside Eastern New England, American English presents a puzzle: words like *dance* and *half* do not have the expected PALM vowel. For *dance*, this may derive from an early variant with *ă*, not *au* (Dobson 1957, 555). The case of *half* is more problematic: the change of *ă* to *au* before /l/ long predated American settlement, so *half* and *calf* should have developed like *palm* and *calm*. Why American dialects escaped this regular development "has not been satisfactorily explained" (Wells 1982, 143).

Tables 2.2–2.6 summarize the developments from Middle English into the modern period, where the results are given for RP, Eastern New England (e.g., Boston), and Western New England (e.g., New Haven). The develop-

TABLE 2.2
Pronunciation of Low Vowel Word Classes:
Late Middle English (Fifteenth Century)

ă	ŏ	au
[a]	[ɔ]	[au]
TRAP	LOT	THOUGHT
BATH	CLOTH	PALM
father	*broad*	*half*
START	NORTH	*dance*

TABLE 2.3
Pronunciation of Low Vowel Word Classes:
Developing Standard British English (Sixteenth–Seventeenth Century)

[æ]~[a]	[aː]	[ɔ]~[ɒ]	[ɔː]	[au]~[ɒu]
(BATH)	(BATH)	LOT	(THOUGHT)	(THOUGHT)
	(PALM)	(CLOTH)	(CLOTH)	(PALM)
TRAP	*(half)*		*(half)*	*(half)*
(dance)	*(dance)*		*(dance)*	*(dance)*
(father)	*(father)*	*(broad)*	*(broad)*	
	START		NORTH	

TABLE 2.4
Pronunciation of Low Vowel Word Classes:
Standard British English (Modern RP)

[æ]	[ɑː]	[ɒ]	[ɔː]
TRAP	BATH	LOT	THOUGHT
	PALM	CLOTH	*broad*
	half		
	dance		
	father		
	START		NORTH

TABLE 2.5
Pronunciation of Low Vowel Word Classes:
Eastern New England (Modern Boston)

[æ]	[aː]	[ɒː]
TRAP	PALM	THOUGHT
(BATH)	(BATH)	*broad*
(half)	*(half)*	LOT
	father	CLOTH
[ɛ̣ə]	START	NORTH
dance		

TABLE 2.6
Pronunciation of Low Vowel Word Classes:
Western New England (Modern New Haven)

[æ]	[ɑ]	[ɔ̞ə]
TRAP	LOT	THOUGHT
BATH	PALM	*broad*
half	*father*	CLOTH
[ẹ̞ə]	[ɑɹ]	[ɔɹ]
dance	START	NORTH

ments are shown for eight of Wells's (1982) lexical sets: TRAP, BATH, PALM, START, LOT, CLOTH, THOUGHT, and NORTH, and for *father, half, dance,* and *broad,* which show different origins and/or evolutions.

Dobson (1957) never mentions any merger involving unlengthened ŏ, which fell from [ɔ] to [ɒ] and/or [ɑ] while [ɔː] was developing from *au.* But because of their phonetic closeness, the LOT ~ THOUGHT merger was at least conceivable in the seventeenth century. On the other hand, the new PALM class, being [aː], was not close enough phonetically to LOT for a merger to be plausible.

Another factor inhibiting any merger in the seventeenth century was the alternate pronunciations these vowels retained in the speech of older or more conservative speakers. For PALM words like *palm* itself, this was [ɔː] or [ɒu]; for the BATH and START subsets, it was [a]. For LOT, the conservative pronunciation was [ɔ]; and for THOUGHT, it was [ɒu]. These sounds are phonetically very far apart, even more so than the innovative pronunciations.

Since Dobson (1957) is based on the testimony of contemporary orthoepists, phoneticians, and spelling reformers, one would expect some mention of a merger among these word classes if there had been any such trend. However, Dobson's focus was on the development of the London standard; he did not take into account purely regional developments.

2.1.3.2. *Low Vowels in English Regional Dialects: Joseph Wright.* Using *The English Dialect Grammar* (Wright 1905), we can see the phonetic developments of the low vowel word classes in nineteenth-century English regional dialects. Following Garde, any merger that existed at the time of American settlement would still be observable.

West Somerset is one of the only locations showing a wholesale lengthening of Middle English ŏ to [ɔː] (with conversion of Wright's phonetic alphabet to IPA) in, for example, *stop, cot,* and *flock* as well as in, for example, *broth* and *lost* (Wright 1905, 73–74). In this same dialect, the usual THOUGHT class appears either as [ɔː] in, for example, *thought* and *talk*, or as [ɑː] in, for example, *brought, saw*. The same [ɑː] is found in, for example, *path, hard,* and *half.*

So there are two low vowels where the standard has three, but differences of phonemic incidence, like *saw* appearing as a PALM word, makes it slightly misleading to call the situation in West Somerset—where many of the settlers of Taunton in Plymouth Colony originated (§2.1.2)—a LOT ~ THOUGHT merger.

In the adjacent West Country county of Dorset—whence came many of the settlers of Dorchester in Massachusetts Bay—we find three low vowels. Despite much lengthening, a LOT category still exists. And though words like *talk* have joined the PALM class, a distinct THOUGHT class remains, for example, *thought* itself.

Between West Somerset and Dorset, both inventory and incidence are different. Differences in incidence alone might lead to merger in a situation of dialect contact, although here the most confusion is between PALM and THOUGHT (which never merge in American dialects without LOT as well).

The records for northeast Norfolk and east Suffolk, in East Anglia, show similar developments to RP. They both have three low vowel categories, although the incidence of THOUGHT is not always standard. Table 2.7 summarizes the evidence of these dialects and the standard for the most common sources of the modern low vowels. Since eastern and southwestern emigrants were the most numerous settlers of early New England and an early standard was probably also spoken, the table should give some idea of the components of the dialect mixture.

TABLE 2.7

Evolution of Low Vowel Word Classes in West Country
and East Anglian Dialects (from Wright 1905)

	Late ME Source	RP	NE Norfolk	E Suffolk	Dorset	W Somerset
START	*ă + r*	[ɑː]	[ɑː]	[ɑː]	[ɑː]	[ɑː]
HALF	*au + f*	[ɑː]	[ɑː]	[ɑː]	[ɑː]	[ɑː]
LOT	*ŏ + t*	[ɒ]	[ɒ]	[ɒ]	[ɒ]	[ɔː]
CLOTH	*ŏ + θ*	[ɒ]	[ɒ]	[ɒ]	[ɔː]	[ɔː]
THOUGHT	*ŏ + x*	[ɔː]	[ɔː] ~ [ʌu]	[oː] ~ [ʌu]	[ɔː]	[ɔː]
TALK	*au + k*	[ɔː]	[ɔː]	[ɔː]	[ɑː]	[ɔː]
LAW	*au*	[ɔː]	[ɔː]	[ɔː] ~ [ɑː]	[ɑː]	[ɑː]
Vowels	–	3	3	3	3	2

Except for the development in, for example, *saw*, the two-vowel pattern in West Somerset is quite similar to Eastern New England's. However, even though Taunton, Massachusetts, was settled largely from Somerset, it seems unlikely that this regional dialect was responsible for the much larger area of low back merger in Eastern New England.

Contact between dialects, rather than any single one, may have contributed to the low back merger. For instance, the CLOTH set was likely merged with THOUGHT in the West Country dialects, while in the East Anglian varieties it may never have split from LOT. The mixture of these systems could have caused confusion and abandonment of the LOT ~ THOUGHT distinction, although as we shall see, this merger was not complete until some 250 years after settlement.

Based on a 1930s dialect survey, Kurath and Lowman (1970, 25–26) reported the LOT ~ THOUGHT merger across the entire southwest of England as "an unrounded low vowel [ɒ ~ ɑ], varying in length.... In this dialect area *hawk* rimes with *lock* and *bought* with *lot.*"[9]

But Wright, a generation earlier, had not encountered this large merged area—West Somerset was exceptional—nor did the *Survey of English Dialects* (Orton et al. 1962–71) a generation later. Leaving aside the CLOTH set, Wright and Orton et al. consistently distinguish THOUGHT from LOT by length, if not by vowel quality as well. Nor does Wakelin (1988) question the length distinction.

Especially considering Kurath's handling of the same alleged merger in Rhode Island (§2.2), we can tentatively overrule his analysis here and suppose that English dialect speakers generally distinguished LOT and THOUGHT in the early twentieth century—and thus, by Garde's Principle, did so in previous centuries as well.

As far as the Western New England or "General American" merger of PALM and LOT is concerned, we have no report of it in England at any period, so it seems even safer to say it did not form part of the repertoire(s) of the first emigrants to New England.

2.2. THE *LINGUISTIC ATLAS OF NEW ENGLAND* AND OTHER STUDIES

2.2.1. EARLY EVIDENCE. Three types of early New England evidence will not be reviewed here: nonstandard spellings in official records (Orbeck 1927); observations made by travelers, whose description of sounds is often hard to interpret; and manuals of correct spelling and/or pronunciation, whose degree of independence from an English standard is unknown.

But the spelling reformer Michael Barton, born 1798 in Dutchess County, New York, is too relevant to overlook. As noted in Labov (1994, 317, n. 8), Barton "criticizes [English orthoepist] Walker 'in making the sound of *o* in *not*, and *a* in *far* to be different,'" suggesting that the "General American" merger of PALM and LOT could be heard just outside of (western) New England, in the early nineteenth century.[10]

Somewhat earlier, the extensive descriptions made by Noah Webster (b. 1758 in Hartford, Conn.) reflected a robust three-way distinction. Its persistence can be seen from the self-reports of two later linguists. Charles Grandgent, born in 1861 and whose dialect "was formed in Boston and Cambridge," uses three different symbols for the low vowels in a transcription of his own speech (1891, 199). William Moulton, born in Providence in 1914, describes his PALM and LOT as "two low central vowels that are identical in quality and differ only in quantity," while his THOUGHT is distinct from both (1990, 126).

2.2.2. *LINGUISTIC ATLAS OF NEW ENGLAND* (*LANE*).

In the early 1930s, the *Linguistic Atlas of New England* (*LANE* 1939–43) interviewed 413 people, including 11 in the study area, most of them born between 1850 and 1875. Nine field-workers, each working in a different area, manually recorded the phonetic forms of 814 words and phrases from each informant.

Kurath et al. (1939, 8–13) make a primary division between Eastern and Western New England. Within Eastern New England, Rhode Island is part of the Narragansett Bay Area, while the towns to the north fall into the Worcester Area (e.g., Mendon) or the Boston Area (e.g., Foxborough). Due to its mixed vocabulary, Bristol County, Massachusetts—which covers much of the study area—is placed in both the Narragansett Bay Area and the Plymouth Area.

Regarding the low back vowels, Kurath et al. (1939, 3) make a surprising statement:

> The rounded vowel [ɒ] of Eastern New England ... is losing ground. [It] has been extensively replaced by an unrounded variety in the Eastern Margin and in such cities as Providence.... As a result of this trend, some Easterners now have distinct phonemes in *rod, crop* and in *off, law, salt.*

This must be seriously doubted. The low back merger is intact today in the northern part of the Eastern Margin (central Massachusetts, western New Hampshire), while further south it was likely never present. Rachel Harris, a purportedly unreliable field-worker, investigated all the *LANE* communities in eastern Connecticut and Rhode Island, and all but one in Bristol County, Massachusetts (Kurath et al. 1939, 41). The isogloss drawn for [ɒ] in *rod* (chart 8) follows the field-worker boundary. Harris worked in one community in the western area, Hebron, Connecticut, and her *LANE* transcript shows [ɒ] in *rod* there too.

Harris came from Haverhill, in Essex County, Massachusetts, and she had the low back merger in her own speech (McDavid 1981, 23). She may have had difficulty hearing the distinction in Rhode Island. She was given the worst rating for "freedom from systematization according to the phonemic system of the field worker's own speech" (Kurath et al. 1939, 53).

2.2.3. "THE SPEECH OF RHODE ISLAND": RACHEL KILPATRICK NÉE HARRIS. The controversy over Harris and the low vowels of Providence has been discussed in the literature (see §2.2.6), but the doctoral dissertation she wrote under her married name (Kilpatrick 1937) has received little attention. It discusses the stressed vowels and diphthongs of Rhode Island and adjacent parts of Connecticut and Massachusetts—that is, in her own *LANE* records.

Her phonemic approach was innovative for American dialectology of the day—neither Kurath et al. (1939) nor *LANE* has anything like her map 29, which displayed whether speakers have "the same phoneme in *lot* and *law*"—but Kilpatrick's interpretation of her own records is untrustworthy. She reports the low back merger for most Rhode Islanders, even though her data sometimes shows the distinction quite clearly.

For example, speaker 104.2 from East Providence has [ɑ] in *crop, fox, frog, John,* and *rods,* while *cloth, loft, long, loss, jaundice, launch,* and *laundry* occur with [ɒ] (Kilpatrick 1937, maps 30–36). This is a perfectly ordinary "General American" distinction between LOT and CLOTH = THOUGHT. Yet somehow, this speaker is said to have the same phoneme in *lot* and *law*.

2.2.4. "SHORT *O* IN THE SPEECH OF NEW ENGLAND": MARGARET CHASE. In another little-known thesis based on *LANE* data, Chase (1935) analyzed the low vowels in about half of New England.[11] Despite its title, "The Derivatives of Middle English Short *o* in the Speech of New England," it deals with all three word classes.

Along the coast from southern Maine to Essex County, Massachusetts, Chase finds a clear two-vowel system, PALM ≠ LOT = THOUGHT. This pattern will be called Eastern New England (ENE). In western Connecticut and western Vermont, an equally clear conclusion is reached: a two-vowel system where PALM = LOT ≠ THOUGHT. This pattern will be called Mid-Atlantic/Inland North (MAIN).

In the Connecticut Valley (west-central Massachusetts and north-central Connecticut), the THOUGHT class has [ɔ] and the LOT class has [ɑ], while the PALM class "is recorded more frequently with [a] than with [ɑ]" (Chase 1935, 61). This probably means that some speakers have the MAIN pattern with PALM = LOT, but most retain a three-way distinction, PALM ≠ LOT ≠ THOUGHT (abbreviated 3-D). In eastern Massachusetts (around Boston and Plymouth), Chase also finds a mixture of systems. The PALM phoneme is distinct for everyone, but some distinguish LOT and THOUGHT (3-D) while others do not (ENE).

Chase (1935, 18) sees the 3-D pattern as innovative, the result of dialect contact, but Garde's Principle requires that it be the most conservative system. This would square with section 2.1.3, where we saw that seventeenth-century settlers of New England would likely have had a version of the 3-D system.

2.2.5. *THE PRONUNCIATION OF ENGLISH IN THE ATLANTIC STATES.* Kurath and McDavid (1961) also derived their New England data from *LANE.* Kurath and McDavid's text usually agrees with Chase (1935), but their individual speakers' synopses do not always agree with their text.

2.2.5.1. *Kurath and McDavid's (1961) Text.* According to the text, all of eastern New England, including Rhode Island and eastern Connecticut, has the ENE pattern of low vowels in cultivated speech (and map 15 shows it for all social classes):

E[arly] M[oder]n E[nglish] /ær/ appears as the free vowel /a/ ... and this /a/ occurs also to some extent in *laugh, bath, glass, can't, aunt,* and occasionally in *dance, France.* EMnE short /o/ and /aʊ/ are completely merged in a free vowel /ɒ/. [8]

In most of western New England the MAIN pattern is indicated:

[EMnE] /aʊ/ becomes /ɔ/ ... /o/ splits into /ɑ/ and /ɔ/, and this /ɔ/, as in *cough, frost, dog, long,* is merged with the /ɔ/ derived from EMnE /aʊ/.... Earlier /ær/ becomes /ɑr/, the vowel being subsumed under the /ɑ/ from earlier /o/. [8]

Kurath and McDavid's text do not mention any 3-D patterns near Boston, but they agree with Chase that they exist in the Lower Connecticut Valley and the New Haven area, where:

Cultured speakers in urban areas usually have two unrounded low vowels, a free low-front to low-central vowel /a/, as in *car, barn, father, palm, half, aunt,* and a checked low-central to low-back vowel /ɑ/, as in *crop, rod, John, college* ... some speakers have [a] rather consistently, some fluctuate between [a] and [ɑ], others have predominantly [ɑ]. [14]

2.2.5.2. *Kurath and McDavid's (1961) Speaker Synopses.* In the speaker synopses, Kurath and McDavid transcribe seven potential PALM words, three LOT words, and four THOUGHT words, for 17 cultured speakers in New England (31–47). For PALM, these are *aunt, barn, father, garden, glass, half,* and *palm;* for LOT, *college, crop,* and *John;* for THOUGHT, *daughter, frost, law,* and *water.*

Each speaker's vowels are sorted into two or three phonemic categories, but the data often supports a distinction where the editors show a merger. Only three speakers are explicitly presented as 3-D, but six more may well have been.

For the part of western New England where the text described the MAIN system, only the speaker from Litchfield, Connecticut, shows that pattern clearly. For the Burlington, Vermont, speaker, PALM has long [ɑ·], LOT has plain [ɑ], and THOUGHT has [ɔ] or [ɔᵛ]. This suggests a 3-D system, though not as clear as the one indicated as such in Pittsfield, Massachusetts.

In the area where the text identified variation between MAIN and 3-D, the speaker from Northampton, Massachusetts, is shown with a clear 3-D system. But the Deerfield, Massachusetts, and New Haven, Connecticut, speakers are likely 3-D too, with [a·] or [a⁼·] for PALM, [ɑ] or [ɒ] for LOT, and [ɔ] or [ɔ·] for THOUGHT. The 3-D pattern is also suggested in Springfield, Massachusetts, and Middletown, Connecticut, with PALM and LOT differing by length.

In eastern New England, the transcriptions from Nobleboro, Maine, Portland, Maine, Concord, New Hampshire, and Billerica, Massachusetts, support the text's diagnosis of ENE. But the speaker from Boston is shown with a clear 3-D pattern, and the data from Plymouth also suggests 3-D: [a·] for PALM, [ɒ] for LOT, and [ɔ] or [ɔᵛ] for THOUGHT.[12]

The three remaining synopses are of speakers transcribed by Harris, in Providence, Rhode Island, Newport, Rhode Island, and New London, Connecticut. They usually have [a] for PALM, and a range of phones from [ɒᶜ] to [ɔᵛ] for LOT and THOUGHT, but without a consistent difference between those two classes.

The synopses show that in most parts of New England,[13] at least some speakers had PALM ≠ LOT ≠ THOUGHT. These three-way distinct speakers were not all elderly, either. Several were in their 40s, having been born around 1890. Where this 3-D pattern was found in western New England, LOT was closer to PALM, sometimes distinguished only by length. In eastern New England, LOT was closer to THOUGHT.

These 3-D patterns may be the late stages of two mergers by approximation, one of which was bringing the PALM ~ LOT merger (and MAIN system) to western New England, the other bringing the LOT ~ THOUGHT merger (and ENE system) to eastern New England.

2.2.6. RESOLVING THE PROVIDENCE CONTROVERSY: WILLIAM MOULTON AND RAVEN I. McDAVID, JR. Moulton's (1990) self-report showed the 3-D system could be acquired in Providence, Rhode Island, by someone born as late as 1914. His is the western type of 3-D, where PALM is longer than LOT, and THOUGHT clearly further back and rounded.

Moulton (1968) discusses the error in *LANE* and Kurath and McDavid (1961) in which Providence was said to have the LOT ~ THOUGHT merger. Calling the *LANE* field-workers "hopelessly and humanly incompetent at transcribing phonetically the low and low back vowels they heard from their informants," Moulton (1968, 464) argues that linguists should leave the recording to their audio equipment, and ask subjects which sounds rhyme.

This is unfair: the low vowels were admittedly challenging (Chase 1935, 4), but most *LANE* field-workers seem to have handled them adequately. Even Harris was not "hopeless," but she was the only field-worker with the LOT ~ THOUGHT merger herself. And listening to audio recordings (see §2.4) of two *LANE* informants from Providence, McDavid (1981) confirms that they did have a LOT ~ THOUGHT distinction.

McDavid then reviews the *LANE* data for informant 80.4 and shows that Harris actually did transcribe LOT and THOUGHT differently. Despite a wide range of symbols for both phonemes, LOT was most often [ɒ], and THOUGHT [ɔ]. The words in Kurath and McDavid's (1961) synopsis were an unlucky sample that did not reflect the usual distinction. McDavid (1981, 23–26) concludes that "Harris's phonetics were tolerably minute ... [her] *LANE* transcriptions come off very well." Harris was thus sometimes able to hear and transcribe a distinction that she could not consciously recognize. For like Kurath and McDavid (1961), Harris considered all four of *LANE*'s Providence speakers to have the LOT ~ THOUGHT merger (Kilpatrick 1937).[14]

McDavid (1981, 26) asks, "Why should Providence retain a contrast that has been lost in Boston?" He cites Rhode Island's history of "individualism and dissent," its local pride "contribut[ing] to the preservation of speechways distinct from those of Boston."

But the LOT ~ THOUGHT distinction has been preserved throughout the Mid-Atlantic and Inland North; Providence simply happens to be at the edge of this region. And without understanding why eastern Massachusetts underwent the merger, we cannot say why—or, really, if—Rhode Island resisted it. Furthermore, if we focus on PALM ~ LOT, it is Boston that retained a distinction which Providence lost; would a similar cultural explanation then make sense?

Both McDavid (1981, 26) and Herold (1990, 108–9) find it surprising that phonemic differences should exist between nearby communities in modern times in the United States. We may have to concede that easy intercommunication between places—"the present-day influences of easy travel, radios, and talking-pictures" (Chase 1935, 3)—does not necessarily level dialect differences between them.

2.3. MORE RECENT STUDIES

2.3.1. *DICTIONARY OF AMERICAN REGIONAL ENGLISH* (*DARE* 1985–). Carver (1987) draws lexical dialect boundaries within New England based on *DARE* data, collected 1965–70 from speakers born around 1900. Map 2.4 shows Rhode Island to have fewer characteristically New England words than Massachusetts. A heavy line runs east-west along the state boundary, separating informants in Douglas and Uxbridge, Massachusetts, from one in Burrillville, Rhode Island. A lighter north-south line through Bristol County divides New Bedford, Massachusetts, from Little Compton, Rhode Island. Together, these follow the same dialect boundary as will be seen in chapter 4.

An auditory analysis of "Arthur the Rat" passages read by *DARE* informants (American Languages 2009) revealed three possible 3-D patterns in our eastern area, one in Mendon (b. 1894, female) and two in Douglas (b. 1889, male; b. 1892, female) along with several clear ENE patterns: in Boston (b. 1892, female; b. 1899, male), New Bedford (b. 1886, male), Plymouth (b. 1891, female), and Uxbridge (b. 1895, male).

In the western area, there were clear 3-D patterns in Bristol, Rhode Island (b. 1884, female), and Little Compton, Rhode Island (b. 1884, female; b. 1910, female), as well as MAIN patterns in Hope, Rhode Island (b. 1904, male) and Westerly, Rhode Island (b. 1897, male). The *DARE* recordings deserve further analysis, but these findings are in line with the earlier Hanley recordings, discussed in section 2.4, as well as the oldest living speakers described in chapter 4.

2.3.2. CHARLES BOBERG. In the *LANE* and *DARE* era, the 3-D system had not fully yielded to MAIN in western New England. Much more recently, drawing on the 1992–99 Telsur telephone interviews that are also the source material for Labov, Ash, and Boberg (2006), Boberg (2001) shows the MAIN system prevailing in Connecticut. Springfield, Massachusetts, had been MAIN, but phonetic approximation may signal the onset of three-way merger there.

The LOT ~ THOUGHT merger has more thoroughly affected western Vermont, with seven speakers showing a clear merger and only one elderly speaker maintaining the distinction. In Wetmore (1959, 18), by contrast, the low back distinction is reported throughout western Vermont.

It is not explicitly stated whether the merger there involves the PALM class as well. One would expect so, if it evolved from a MAIN system, in which PALM and LOT were already merged. Burlington's system is said to resemble the Canadian ones to the north, which are 3-M. And Rutland's merged vowel is [ɑ], not [ɒ], making merger with PALM likely there too.

2.3.3. *THE ATLAS OF NORTH AMERICAN ENGLISH.* Labov, Ash, and Boberg (2006, chap. 16.4) make it more clear that the 3-M system has developed in Burlington and Rutland. PALM is fronted by at least 100 Hz before /r/, but other PALM words have the same vowel as LOT; *father* rhymes with *bother.* If Eastern New England's LOT ~ THOUGHT merger spread to western Vermont (Boberg 2001), the PALM ~ LOT distinction did not.

Labov, Ash, and Boberg (2006) identify clear MAIN systems in Springfield, Massachusetts (along with one 3-M speaker), across Connecticut, and from six speakers in Providence, Rhode Island. Acoustic analysis was conducted on three of these—the oldest born around 1940—and no PALM ~ LOT distinction was found, although the Telsur methodology might not have identified such a distinction if it was based only on length; indeed, "the PALM-class was not the focus of direct elicitation" (230).

In eastern Massachusetts (Boston, Worcester), New Hampshire, and Maine, the PALM ~ LOT distinction is clear (map 16.5), and the LOT ~ THOUGHT merger mainly so (map 16.3). Of the 29 informants, 22 show a total low back merger, while the others' were incomplete in either perception or production. Given the antiquity of the low back merger in this region, it is likely that these informants exhibit it stably in ordinary speech.

To summarize, we have evidence that a three-way-distinct low vowel pattern (3-D) once existed in most parts of New England, including eastern Massachusetts and Rhode Island. In the twentieth century, the typical system became ENE in eastern Massachusetts (with the LOT ~ THOUGHT merger) and MAIN in Rhode Island (with the PALM ~ LOT merger). A phonological boundary developed from a phonetic difference, as the next section will help show.

2.4. THE HANLEY RECORDINGS:
VOICES FROM *LANE*

From 1932 through 1934, Miles Hanley and colleagues revisited about
half of the *LANE* informants interviewed several years previously, as well as
some others.[15] For each speaker, they recorded one or more 10-minute alu-
minum discs, using a recording apparatus that fit—barely—in the back of a
car (S. Hall et al. 2002). Although the discs contain a lot of noise, strained
conversation, and silence, most are adequate for auditory, and some for
acoustic, analysis.[16]

2.4.1. MAINE. As noted in section 2.2.5.2, Maine and New Hampshire
are the only New England states with no evidence of a three-way-distinct
(3-D) low vowel system in Kurath and McDavid (1961), which is curi-
ous given their generally conservative dialects. An auditory investigation
of two Hanley recordings from Maine supports the ENE configuration:
PALM ≠ LOT = THOUGHT.

No Hanley recording exists of the two cultured Maine speakers whose
synopses appear in Kurath and McDavid (1961). But for *LANE* informant
356 from Biddeford, Maine (born c. 1855), the auditory impression is
similar to Kurath and McDavid's synopsis from Portland. The PALM phoneme is roughly [ɑ], while LOT and THOUGHT words both occur with a back
rounded vowel close to [ɔ].

For informant 352.1 from York, Maine (b. 1890), PALM appears as
[a], while the low back vowels vary over a larger phonetic range centered
around [ɒ]. For example, *morning* was as front as [ɑ], while the vowel of
long was close to [ɔ]. Within each word class, there were large differences
in vowel quality and duration, depending on phonological context. The
speaker produced eight examples of LOT and THOUGHT in the environment
before word-final /t/: *lot* and three tokens of *not* for LOT; *bought*, *caught*, and
two tokens of *thought* for THOUGHT. With, for example, *lot* rounded and
caught fronted, these produced the auditory impression of merger.

Instrumental measurement revealed overlapping formant ranges. For
LOT, F1 ranged from 766 to 860 Hz (mean 816 Hz); THOUGHT was between
756 and 821 Hz (mean 783 Hz). For F2, LOT was between 1163 and 1318 Hz
(mean 1249 Hz), while THOUGHT ranged from 1167 to 1268 Hz (mean
1218 Hz). Although both formants differed in the direction expected if
there were a LOT ~ THOUGHT distinction, the differences in means are only
31 and 33 Hz and are not statistically significant according to one-tailed
t-tests ($p(F1) = .14$; $p(F2) = .24$). Merger is likely, though more tokens
might have been able to confirm a vestigial distinction.[17]

2.4.2. CAMBRIDGE AND PLYMOUTH, MASSACHUSETTS. If Henry Wadsworth Longfellow Dana of Cambridge, Massachusetts, had been in *LANE*, he would have been a "cultured informant." Born in 1881 and educated at Harvard, he was descended on his father's side from early settlers of Cambridge; his maternal grandfather was the poet Longfellow. Although only ten minutes long, his recording suggests that the Boston upper class retained a clear 3-D pattern at this time.

Dana's PALM was a long, low, unrounded vowel varying from front [aː] to central [ɑː]. His LOT was shorter, usually a lightly rounded, back [ɒ], sometimes an unrounded, central [ɑ]. THOUGHT words had a raised, rounded back [ɔ ~ ɔː].

An acoustic analysis confirms that there are three distinct word classes. In fact, as figure 2.3 shows, there is hardly any overlap in formant values among the three word classes (with 7 tokens of PALM, 11 of LOT, and 13 of THOUGHT). Dana's categories are so distinct that even without measuring rounding or length, we can see that he has a 3-D system. The PALM class is significantly fronter than the LOT class. The mean F2 value for PALM is 1401

FIGURE 2.3
Henry Wadsworth Longfellow Dana (b. 1881, Cambridge, Mass.):
Tokens, Means, and ±1 Standard Deviations

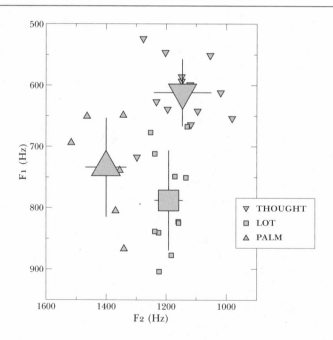

Hz (standard deviation 67), and for LOT, it is 1192 Hz (s.d. 44). A *t*-test shows that the F2 difference of 209 Hz is statistically significant ($p < 0.001$). The THOUGHT class is significantly higher than the LOT class. The mean F1 value for THOUGHT is 612 Hz (s.d. 54), and for LOT it is 788 Hz (s.d. 81). This F1 difference of 176 Hz is also statistically significant ($p < 0.001$).

Although the categories are roughly equally spaced in F1 and F2, Dana's usually rounded LOT sounds closer to THOUGHT—with which it would soon merge in the Boston area—than to his long, sometimes quite fronted PALM.

Another Hanley recording, speaker 112.2 from Plymouth, Massachusetts (born c. 1890), definitely had a distinct PALM, while LOT and THOUGHT were quite close together.[18] PALM was distinguished by length and fronting, [aː]; LOT varied between [ɑ] and [ɒ]; while THOUGHT sounded higher and backer on the whole, often rounded and sometimes offgliding, [ɒə]. Comparing F1 before final /t/, using seven LOT tokens (mean 726 Hz, s.d. = 52) and five THOUGHT tokens (mean 677 Hz, s.d. = 26), gives a small, marginally significant difference of 49 Hz ($p = 0.03$).

2.4.3. PROVIDENCE, RHODE ISLAND. For informant 80.4 from Providence (born c. 1890), *LANE*, Kurath and McDavid (1961), and even the fieldworker Harris (Kilpatrick) herself reported the low back merger, but McDavid (1981) reviewed the case and found evidence for a distinction, in his own auditory impressions as well as in Harris's full transcriptions.

My own auditory analysis finds that the speaker's THOUGHT is not even close to the other low vowels, being realized as a fully rounded [ɔ]. The question instead becomes whether PALM and LOT are distinct. The LOT word class occupies a wide phonetic range, from a front-central [ɑ̈] to a far-back, lightly rounded [ɒ] reminiscent of RP. The PALM class has a long vowel that takes up an even wider range, from a rather front [aː] to a far-back, unrounded [ɑː]. Because of these overlapping ranges, instead of formant measurements, the apparent difference in duration was pursued instrumentally.

From the 20-minute recording, 14 PALM and 19 LOT words, reasonably balanced prosodically and phonetically, were selected. The length of the fully voiced portion of the vowels was measured. The LOT tokens had an mean duration of 136 ms (s.d. = 50), while the PALM tokens had a mean of 191 ms (s.d. = 48). A *t*-test shows that this large difference, illustrated in figure 2.4, is significant ($p = .003$).

Providence informant 80.4's speech does not give the impression that any of the low vowels are nearing the point of merger. Indeed, neither does the self-description of Moulton (1990), born a quarter-century later.

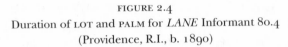

FIGURE 2.4

Duration of LOT and PALM for *LANE* Informant 80.4

(Providence, R.I., b. 1890)

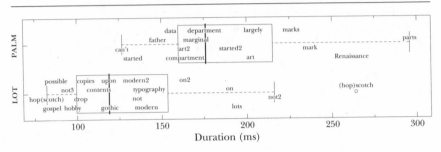

2.4.4. OTHER EASTERN MASSACHUSETTS. This section will discuss the status of LOT and THOUGHT based on an auditory review of the Hanley recordings from those parts of eastern Massachusetts where they are merged today.

Besides H. W. L. Dana (Cambridge, b. 1881), discussed in section 2.4.2, a clear low back distinction (3-D) was observed from the linguist Charles Grandgent (Cambridge, b. 1862), confirming his self-report (see §2.2.1); *LANE* informant 114, born c. 1860, from Rochester; *LANE* informant 152.1, born c. 1862, from Weston; and a non-*LANE* speaker, born c. 1864, from Worcester.

These four places have no geographical or historical connection. In fact, for each place where the distinction was found, the merger was also observed nearby. Across the river from Cambridge, even the oldest Boston speaker (150.2, born c. 1848) showed a possible merger, and several younger Bostonians, born from 1858 on, were definitely merged (ENE pattern).

Directly east of Rochester, in Marion, the merger was heard from informant 210.1 (b. 1853). East of Worcester, Shrewsbury speaker 204.1 (born c. 1854) was merged. And in Weston, informant 152.2 (born c. 1873) was also judged merged (the distinct Weston speaker was 12 years older).

On Martha's Vineyard, a linguistically conservative island (Labov 1963) where, for example, the loss of postvocalic /r/ had made no headway, two *LANE* informants—122.1 from West Tisbury (born c. 1873) and 123.1 from Edgartown (born c. 1857)—had a clear low back merger.

We see that in eastern Massachusetts, speakers born in the period 1850–75 can exhibit either 3-D or ENE low vowel systems. Thereafter, primarily the ENE pattern is found. Since we find 3-D in and near Boston at the same time as, or even later than, clear instances of ENE on usually conservative Martha's Vineyard (and Cape Cod), the change does not appear to have diffused hierarchically from Boston, as might have been expected.

Rather, the LOT ~ THOUGHT merger developed simultaneously, if irregularly, across the eastern Massachusetts Bay and Plymouth settlement areas. It did not develop in Rhode Island, even in areas which are much closer to and more accessible from Boston than, for example, Martha's Vineyard, where it did occur.

2.5. EVOLUTION OF THE LOW VOWELS OF (SOUTHEASTERN) NEW ENGLAND

In most parts of New England, we have seen evidence that the original system of low vowels was 3-D: PALM ≠ LOT ≠ THOUGHT. This fits well with what we know of English English in the seventeenth century, when such a system had only recently developed from earlier patterns.

The New England 3-D systems we have heard can be divided into two types. In the eastern one, PALM is a distinct, fairly front vowel; LOT and THOUGHT are back and closer to each other, distinguished by some combination of length, height, and/or rounding. In the western 3-D system, including Rhode Island (pace *LANE* and Kurath and McDavid 1961), PALM and LOT are central, unrounded and distinguished chiefly by length, while THOUGHT is a quite distinct rounded back vowel.

Although all three word classes differ between eastern and western 3-D systems, we can make a connection to seventeenth-century English (§2.1.3) by suggesting that the first dialects to coalesce in Massachusetts Bay and Plymouth had a more conservative back rounded LOT, not far phonetically from the new monophthongal THOUGHT. In Rhode Island—and western New England proper—a dialect formed with a more innovative LOT, unrounded and more central, which became the short counterpart of PALM.

It is not clear how this proposed difference in LOT might relate to the regional (and social) origins of the first effective settlers. While many settlers' origins are known—the eastern and southwestern English counties provided the majority—little is known for certain about the dialects they spoke or what their versions of standard English might have been like.

Still, we can distinguish between two scenarios: retention and divergent leveling. A retention theory holds that important linguistic differences resulted from differences in backgrounds—regional, social, or simply temporal—between the settlers of eastern and western New England. Retention is the avowed perspective of Bloch (1935) in his reconstruction of early New England rhoticity patterns, even though he does not "attempt to go back beyond the colonial stage" (180) to account for the origin of the differences.[19]

For the low vowels, the regional-retention approach does not apply straightforwardly. Southwestern English dialects feature fronted unrounded LOT, but Eastern Massachusetts, with its back rounded LOT, actually seems to have had more settlement from the Southwest than other colonial areas. However, the even higher level of East Anglian (and other eastern) settlement could have been what contributed a conservative LOT to the Eastern Massachusetts mix.

A divergent leveling theory suggests that dialect differences between the settlers of the two areas were less important. Indeed, on such a view, within-colony variation probably exceeded between-colony variation. But for whatever reasons—perhaps including chance—the leveling processes in each area had different outcomes, which were then carried throughout each colony as it developed and expanded.[20]

If Fischer (1989, 270) was correct to say that "Connecticut and Rhode Island were broadly similar (not identical) to the [Massachusetts] Bay Colony in the English origins of their founders," divergent leveling is one way to account for the dialect differences that developed. But whether these differences originated in England (retention) or shortly after settlement (divergent leveling), in each area a different merger eventually took place, reducing the inventory of low vowels from three to two. In the east, LOT merged with THOUGHT, creating the ENE pattern as early as the mid-nineteenth century in Eastern Massachusetts, and maybe even earlier in New Hampshire and Maine. In the west, PALM merged with LOT somewhat later, creating the MAIN pattern.[21]

I suggest that the communities in each area were affected by one of these two mergers for internal (structural) reasons, not because of diffusion. For one thing, the geographic pattern of LOT ~ THOUGHT merger in the Hanley recordings does not show a spread from Boston.[22]

Chapter 4 will show the line between MAIN and ENE patterns basically following the settlement boundary between Rhode Island and Massachusetts Bay/Plymouth. But a few towns are on the "wrong side" of the line, as if they shifted allegiance from one area to the other after settlement.

As long as both dialects were 3-D—phonetically different, but phonologically identical—such shifts would be unproblematic; they would not involve the reversal of any merger. But after LOT merged with either PALM or THOUGHT, the resulting MAIN and ENE areas would have been divided by a much more impervious linguistic boundary. Given Herzog's Principle, any influence across the line could only lead to three-way merger, never to a shift in the boundary.

2.6. THE PILOT STUDY: LOCATING THE DIALECT BOUNDARY

An earlier pilot study set out to determine the location of the boundary between the MAIN and ENE patterns, by concentrating on LOT and THOUGHT. The first phase, conducted in 2002 with the assistance of Joanie Sanchez, asked local people in public libraries—often the librarians themselves—to read five minimal pairs of the type *cot ~ caught*. We judged whether each pair sounded the same or different, and the same question was put to the informants.

The low back merger was identified in the following southeastern Massachusetts communities: Bellingham (1 subject), Dartmouth (1), Middleborough (2), New Bedford (1), North Attleborough (1), Plymouth (2), Raynham (1), Taunton (2), and Wareham (2). In these places, vowel productions were almost universally judged merged; most subjects' perceptions agreed.[23]

In northeastern Rhode Island—Providence (4 subjects), Pawtucket (1), Cumberland (1), and Woonsocket (1)—the low back distinction was universal, with not a single judgment of "same" in perception or production. This is similar to Labov, Ash, and Boberg's (2006) finding that the low back distinction was categorical in Providence, while in the merged areas of New England, there was some variation in perception or production for some speakers.

Across the Massachusetts state line to the north, Blackstone (1) agreed with Rhode Island, as did Fall River (1), Somerset (2), and Rehoboth (2), across the line to the east.

Both Attleboro and Westport, Massachusetts, had one speaker with a clear merger and one with a clear distinction.[24] In Attleboro, this difference had a potential geographic correlate: a 30-year-old woman from South Attleboro, a neighborhood adjacent to Rhode Island, showed the distinction; a 50-year-old man from the other side of the city showed the merger.

The possibility of a linguistic boundary cutting through a municipality was an exciting one, and the second phase of the pilot study—carried out in 2004—pursued it. However, the results were not consistent with a strict geographical division. Distinct, intermediate,[25] and merged responses were obtained in both "regular" Attleboro and South Attleboro.

The pilot study suggested that speakers' low vowels are generally predictable from geography but that there may be other factors influencing them as well. Chapter 3 will address questions on the individual level, with data from a survey of schoolchildren in Attleboro and other communities.

3. THE SCHOOL SURVEY

Dialect geography tells us that where a person grows up is an important factor determining the way he or she speaks as an adult. But the importance of other factors, such as parental influence, has also long been recognized.

By choosing informants from established local families, projects like *LANE* made the dialectal influences of parents and peers overlap as much as possible, reducing the need to ask which is more important. But that question gains relevance to the extent that today's young parents are more mobile and more children are growing up with peers whose dialects differ from their mothers' and fathers'.

Because the "independent variables" potentially influencing the low vowel system of a speaker tend to be correlated—for example, a person's mother and father often come from the same place—only a large sample can determine their relative significance. This was achieved by means of the school survey, a written questionnaire administered to over 2,000 young people with the help of teachers in several sites in New England and New York.

The questionnaire was a simple instrument that directly asked students to decide whether seven LOT ~ THOUGHT minimal pairs sounded "same" or "different" (§3.2). Two items probed the status of PALM ~ LOT by asking whether pairs of words rhymed. The survey also gathered basic demographic information about each student, as well as a history of schools attended.

The survey responses were analyzed using mixed-effects logistic regression, treating Item and Subject as random effects and variables like parents' origin and previous and current peers' dialect as fixed effects. The analysis determined the size and significance of these effects.

3.1. DIFFICULTY OF SECOND DIALECT ACQUISITION

The "irreversibility of merger" (Labov 1994, chap. 11) is a principle usually stated at the level of the speech community or higher, but such a consequence would be unlikely if individuals could unmerge word classes easily. On the other hand, the rapid spread of various mergers, such as the American low back merger (Labov, Ash, and Boberg 2006, §9.1), strongly suggests that individuals can learn them.

On the difficulty hierarchy of Kerswill (1996, 200), learning new oppo-sitions is labeled "most difficult" and can only happen from age 3 to 13.[1] Mergers, conversely, can be acquired throughout the lifespan. However, not many studies have specifically addressed how hard it is to learn vowel distinctions or how easy it is to merge.

Chambers (1992) studied six children who had moved from Canada to England around two years before. Two, aged 7 and 11 on arrival, had acquired the low back distinction well, pronouncing at least 8 of 10 word pairs differently. None of the others, who moved between ages 10 and 14, pronounced more than one pair differently.

Sankoff (2004) followed a speaker from Yorkshire, in the North of England, who had no distinction between FOOT and STRUT at age 7. He moved to Oxford (in the South) at age 16 and had learned to separate the classes fairly well by age 28.

Payne (1976, 1980) studied the acquisition of several linguistic vari-ables by children who had moved to King of Prussia, Pennsylvania, a Phil-adelphia suburb. One of these tasks was similar to unmerging a merged vowel; two involved learning a certain subtype of merger.

Payne's out-of-state children essentially failed to learn the Philadelphia-area "short-a pattern," a complex split between lax [æ] and tense [æ̃ː ~ iːə]. This split is partially phonologically predictable (tense before front voice-less fricatives), but also has lexical exceptions (lax before /d/, but tense in mad, bad, glad).[2]

Of 34 out-of-state children, only one (3%) completely acquired the Philadelphia short-a pattern, although six others (18%) had substantial success. By contrast, among the children of local parents, 34 of 36 (94%) learned the complete pattern (Payne 1976, 209). This complex phonologi-cal pattern seems to require learning at a very early age, from parental input. As Payne (1980, 174) puts it, "unless a child's parents are locally born and raised, the possibility of his acquiring the short-a pattern is extremely slight even if he were to be born and raised in King of Prussia." By contrast, the simpler phonetic variables were more readily acquired from peers.

The other two phonological variables did not show the same degree of difficulty of acquisition. These are conditioned mergers in Philadelphia English: the raising of, for example, more to merge with Moore, and the back-ing of, for example, merry to merge with Murray. The out-of-state children did better at learning these mergers than they did at learning the short-a pattern.

Payne's overall conclusion is that phonological features of a second dia-lect are harder to acquire than phonetic ones, but this should be amended to state that certain phonological features—namely, mergers—are easy to acquire, perhaps almost as easy as phonetic features.

With the school survey, there was little opportunity to test the difficulty of unmerging LOT and THOUGHT, because the students with merged parents almost never had distinct peers. Students with distinct parents and merged peers were more common, so it was possible to examine the constraints on the merger's acquisition.[3]

While certainly learnable, mergers do not simply spread like wildfire; subjects differ in their degree of acquisition. The literature can oversimplify this and also overstate the primacy of peer over parental influence: "young children, almost universally, pick up their accents from their peers"; "kids get their accents from their peers" (Barbara Partee and Susan Ervin-Tripp; quoted in O'Brien 1992, 1). The survey results, like Payne's, are much more nuanced.

The school survey data does not contain information on peer networks or other measures of popularity, on social class, or on other potentially relevant variables. Knowing about these would have reduced the leftover variation assigned to the Subject random effect and possibly sharpened the estimation of other effects.

The survey returned many intermediate responses (e.g., *cot ~ caught* is marked "same," but *tock ~ talk* is "different"). This could reflect merger in production in one phonological environment but not another, as in the Midland (Labov, Ash, and Boberg 2006, 64), but that is not the only possibility.

First, some students, even if fully merged or fully distinct, might be uncomfortable marking each item the same way. Like on a history quiz, they might doubt that all the "correct answers" would be the same.

Intermediate responses could also reflect the tendency for perception to lead production, signaling incipient merger in the community (Labov 1994, 319), and perhaps in the individual as well. On the other hand, such responses could also convey the tension between an individual's merged production patterns, which do match his/her peer group, and underlying distinct representations learned earlier from parents. In other cases, intermediate responses might accurately represent the production patterns of children whose low back vowels are actually partially merged and partially distinct, on a phonological or lexical basis.

With all these possible sources of intermediacy, there were still regular patterns in the Item random effect. If a child marked 2 of 7 LOT ~ THOUGHT minimal pairs "different," it was not random which pairs those would be, even if it was unclear just what such a response meant.

While the school survey data does not have as clear an interpretation as production data from an interview, it has been collected from many more people than most sociolinguistic studies reach. Even if some subjects' responses are almost worthless, the very large total number of subjects allows us to ask, and to some extent answer quantitatively, questions that have so far been approached only qualitatively, if at all.

3.2. THE INSTRUMENT

The survey instrument is shown in figure 3.1. It asked for each student's name, gender, age, current and previous schools, parents' origins, and other demographic information. As the survey items were completed in a classroom setting, students and teachers were discouraged from pronouncing the key words out loud and influencing one another. Each item consisted of two short sentences to be read silently, each using one of the words from a target pair. Students circled "same" or "different" to indicate how the target pair sounded to them.

The first two items were designed to eliminate subjects who were likely to give inaccurate answers on the other items. Since *barn* and *born* are pronounced differently in the eastern United States, anyone who marked the pair "same" would be unlikely to accurately recognize more subtle differences in sound. Only 2% of subjects actually "failed" this item.

The second item was the opposite case: *pause* and *paws* are pronounced identically in all dialects of North American English, so subjects who said they sounded "different" would be likely, probably under the influence of spelling, to misidentify other identically pronounced pairs. Thirteen percent of subjects, many younger children, were eliminated by this item.

The next pair contrasted the singing term *la* for PALM with *law* for THOUGHT. These should sound different unless they are both merged with LOT. The three-way-merged pattern is expected to occur among some young people, especially in situations of contact between the two two-way mergers. But perhaps because of the marginal status of *la* as a word, this pair was actually marked "different" even by some speakers with the three-way merger. The next seven items all inquired about LOT ~ THOUGHT pairs. Alphabetically, these were: *collar ~ caller, cot ~ caught, Don ~ Dawn, Moll ~ mall, Otto ~ auto, tock ~ talk,* and *tot ~ taught.*

The items *cot ~ caught* and *tot ~ taught* turned out to be the best predictors of the remaining items, though they were not consistently marked more "same" or "different" overall.

FIGURE 3.1
The School Survey Instrument

First Name:		Male / Female	Age:	School:

List all the other SCHOOLS you went to before this one. Include kindergarten, pre-K, etc.

	Name of School	Location of School (City/Town/State)	Grade(s) Attended
1.			
2.			
3.			
4.			

Be as specific as you can.	List any SIBLINGS you have.
	Brother or Sister? Age
Where did your MOTHER grow up?	1.
Where did your FATHER grow up?	2.
	3.

Circle your race (one or more):   WHITE   HISPANIC   AFRICAN-AM.   ASIAN   OTHER

Does anyone in your family ever speak ANOTHER LANGUAGE besides English?
If so, WHO is it and WHAT LANGUAGE do they speak?

- Sometimes two words MEAN different things, and they are different in SPELLING too, but they SOUND exactly the same. Not just close, but EXACTLY the same sound.

- A grizzly BEAR isn't the same thing as BARE skin, but the two words sound the same. To MEET somebody is different frome eating MEAT, but the words sound the same.

- Sometimes people disagree about what sounds the same. So what do YOU think? Circle "same" or "different" for these 10 pairs of words. There are no wrong answers!

1. farm animals sleep in the BARN – he was BORN in 1990	same	different
2. press this button to PAUSE – cats lick their PAWS	same	different
3. in singing you go "fa la la la LA" – don't break the LAW	same	different
4. the boys' name is DON – and the girls' name is DAWN	same	different
5. Emily CAUGHT the ball – a small bed is called a COT	same	different
6. a boy named OTTO – another word for a car is an AUTO	same	different
7. a nickname for Molly is MOLL – you shop at the MALL	same	different
8. students learn what they are TAUGHT – eat a tater TOT	same	different
9. the clock goes "tick TOCK" – teenagers like to TALK	same	different
10. a shirt has a COLLAR – a phone has CALLER i.d.	same	different
• Do these words rhyme? 11. my FATHER – don't BOTHER	rhyme	don't rhyme
12. the boy's name is TOMMY – one kind of meat is SALAMI	rhyme	don't rhyme

The pairs *tock ~ talk* and *collar ~ caller* were more often rated "different" than the others. We can understand this, if some subjects pronounce the /l/ in *talk*, or think they should. And for variably rhotic subjects, the morpheme *-er* in *caller* could generally retain its /r/ more than the last syllable of the monomorpheme *collar*, not to mention that the survey had *collar* sentence finally, but a linking /r/ in *caller ID*. The different morphological structure could also lead to different syllabifications, and thus different realizations of /l/ in the two words, which could differentiate them by itself or by affecting the stressed vowels.

However, it is less clear why subjects rated *Moll ~ mall* and *Otto ~ auto* "same" more often than the other pairs, other than a possible effect of initial position in *auto*.

The survey then asked if *father ~ bother* and *salami ~ Tommy* rhymed.[4] Though intended to probe the same PALM ~ LOT contrast, these rhyming questions were answered differently by 27% of subjects, more disagreement than was found for most "same/different" pairs—though even the most concordant pair of pairs, *cot ~ caught* and *tot ~ taught*, were marked differently by 17% of subjects.

The survey was administered by obtaining the permission of school administrators in some places, individual teachers and parents in others. The teachers who oversaw the completion of the questionnaires instructed the students that participation was voluntary. By every indication, the great majority of students in each class did complete the form.

3.3. THE SAMPLE

After eliminating surveys that said *barn ~ born* sounded the same or *pause ~ paws* sounded different, as well as obviously joking responses (e.g., father from "North Pole"), a total of 1,562 surveys remained, from four principal communities, as shown on figure 3.2.

The largest source, with 1,013 surveys, was Attleboro, Massachusetts, a city of 43,000 (2005 Census estimate). The pilot study had placed Attleboro—35 miles southwest of Boston, 12 miles northeast of Providence—on the boundary between MAIN and ENE low vowel systems and even identified a possible difference between South Attleboro and the rest of the city. To find out how children reflected that difference, the survey was administered to the fourth, eighth, and twelfth grades. These are the highest grade levels of Attleboro's five elementary schools, three middle schools, and one high school, respectively.

South Attleboro children were found to no longer maintain the low back distinction, so the survey was extended to an adjacent town where it might still be more intact. In Seekonk, Massachusetts—a town of 14,000 located just 5 miles east of Providence and, like South Attleboro, sharing a border with Rhode Island—208 of the fourth, eighth, and twelfth graders completed the survey.

In the ENE area of low back merger, Brookline, Massachusetts, (pop. 55,000), an inner suburb of Boston, provided 227 responses from twelfth

FIGURE 3.2
Location of Primary School Survey Data Sources

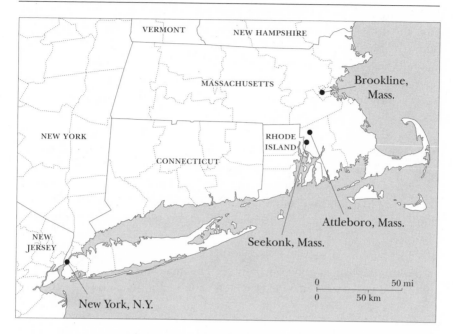

graders. And in New York City (pop. 8,143,000), a part of the MAIN area where the low back distinction is strong among adults (Labov, Ash, and Boberg 2006, 59), 114 tenth and eleventh graders at two high schools also completed it.

In addition to these primary sources, a Massachusetts college class provided 35 responses.

3.4. ACCURACY

It is not obvious how accurate the survey data is, or how to interpret it, although the resemblance to minimal-pair tests (Labov 1994, 353–56) is clear. In such tests, the linguist's impression (or subsequent instrumental analysis) of whether sounds are the same or different is called "production" data. The subject's own judgment is known as "perception" data.

Speakers may produce a distinction that they do not perceive; this is typical of mergers in progress and a defining feature of near-mergers (a type of small yet stable distinction). However, this pattern was not typically observed in the in-person interviews for this study.

Speakers can also produce near-identical forms in a minimal-pair test, yet claim they are different. This was occasionally observed in in-person interviews, most often from young children. Such a discrepant pattern suggests the subject makes no distinction in natural speech (Herold 1990, 17), but with only the written response, it cannot be identified.

Speakers can also perform differently on minimal pair tests than they do in natural speech, by using a "borrowed prestige pronunciation" (Labov, Yaeger, and Steiner 1972, 232) or shifting toward an incoming norm (Labov 1994, 355).

Conflict between the dialect of current peers and that acquired earlier from parents may account for many of the cases where perception does not match production. The influence of orthography will usually favor the perception of distinctions rather than mergers. And as noted, students treating the survey like a school quiz might have been less invariant (more random?) in their responses than ones accurately following their production intuitions.

Fortunately, 31 survey subjects were interviewed in person, where some of the same minimal pairs were tested. This makes it possible to compare their production of the low back vowels to the judgments indicated on the form. Figure 3.3 gives the result.

3.4.1. ADULTS' ACCURACY. We look first at the nine adult speakers: three mothers from the family study, and six of my own friends and family. Seven of the nine are 100% distinct in production and marked 7 of 7 pairs "different" on the survey. One is 100% merged in production and marked 7 of

FIGURE 3.3

The Low Back Vowels: Survey Responses versus Speech Production

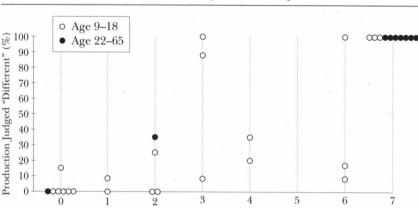

7 pairs "same." These eight adults have completely retained the pattern of where they grew up, even though at least four of them have had extensive contact with the opposite pattern, through residence and/or marriage, for over 20 years.

The other adult, a mother from Wooster, Ohio, was intermediate on both tasks. Reading the word pairs embedded in sentences, her vowels were distinct or very close; but when presented with the bare words out of context, she pronounced them identically. Averaging these judgments, she was 35% distinct in production. On the survey, she marked 2 of 7 pairs "different," or 29%. Her intermediacy is not surprising as she grew up on the northern edge of the Midland, where similar behavior is widespread (Labov, Ash, and Boberg 2006, 62–64).

For adults, then, survey performance seems to accurately reflect linguistic productions.

3.4.2. CHILDREN'S ACCURACY. The 22 children in this comparison—14 from Seekonk, six from Attleboro, and two from Brookline—behaved differently from the adults. They were more variable in production and, at the same time, less accurate in reflecting their production patterns on the survey.

Eight children were 100% merged in production. On average, these children marked 0.6 of 7 items "different" on the survey: five scored a 0, one scored a 1, and two scored a 2. Five children were 100% distinct in production, and they marked 6.0 items "different" on average. One child scored a 3—our best example of merger perception leading production (Labov, Ash, and Boberg 2006, 62)—one a 6, and three a fully distinct 7.

So while most were accurate, some of the children who were categorical in production were variable on the survey. Children who were intermediate in production were, so to speak, even more intermediate on the survey. A group of four, rated between 8% and 15% distinct in production, averaged 2.5 out of 7 on the survey (36% "different"), while another group of four, rated between 17% and 35% distinct in production, averaged 4.0 (57% "different"). Assuming a merger in progress, these children's productions are leading their perceptions. One Seekonk 10-year-old was rated as low as 8% distinct in production, but still marked 6 of 7 pairs "different" on the survey.

Only one child was more consistent on the survey than in production, while 13 were less consistent on the survey—that is, closer to the midpoint of 3.5. The more intermediate children were in production, the more their survey scores tended to deviate from their production levels.

Some children who are categorical in production sometimes allow various other factors to supersede that grammar in making choices on the school survey, but these other factors seem to have more influence on speakers who are intermediate or "unsure" in production.

Bresnan (2007) found that for sentences strongly predicted to appear in one of two possible syntactic constructions, subjects had strong preferences in the same direction. However, for sentences with weaker predictions, subjects tended to have no preferences, rather than simply weaker ones. In tasks where subjects consciously reflect on their choice of linguistic forms, they may not discriminate very sensitively, tending rather toward categories of 0%, 50%, and 100% (equivalent to "no," "I don't know," and "yes"). In tasks measuring subjects' actual linguistic performance with respect to the same choices, a much finer, gradient pattern is observed.

A more generous interpretation of the school survey suggests that when its measurements departed from subjects' productions, this did not always make them less worthwhile. Imagine two children growing up in Boston, where the low back merger is the norm; one of them has local parents while the other's are from New York. Both children may be indistinguishably merged in everyday speech, but the child with the distinct family, who likely acquired the distinction himself in infancy, may well have performed differently on the survey, perhaps by marking just one or two (more) items "different."

3.5. FACTORS AFFECTING VOWEL INVENTORY:
LOT AND *THOUGHT*

3.5.1. MIXED-EFFECTS LOGISTIC REGRESSION. The factors influencing subjects' responses to the LOT ~ THOUGHT items were assessed with mixed-effects logistic regression, implemented using the lmer( ) function (from the lme4 package) in the statistical software environment R (Bates, Maechler, and Dai 2008; Baayen, Davidson, and Bates 2008). lmer( ) uses the Laplace approximation to maximize the likelihood of models fitting the probability p of a binary response with an equation of the following form:

$$\text{logit}(p) = \ln(p/(1-p)) = X\beta + Zb, \; b \sim \mathcal{N}(0, \sigma^2)$$

The log-odds of the response depends on both fixed effects and random effects. The fixed effects (β) are the traditional independent variables, factors whose levels are fixed and repeatable. A good example of a fixed effect is gender, which has a small number of levels, each of which could be sampled again, in repeating or extending an experiment.

The random effects (b) are factors whose levels are not necessarily repeatable. A typical random effect is that of Subject, where each participant constitutes a unique level sampled from a larger population. Each subject's effect is assumed to be drawn from a normal distribution with a mean of zero; the larger the effect, the larger the standard deviation.

In modeling a fixed factor, we estimate the effect of each specific level on the response. For a random factor, we are more interested in estimating the overall amount of variation. However, the model still gives estimates of the effects of each individual level of a random factor (called best linear unbiased predictors, or BLUPs).

Although the same seven LOT ~ THOUGHT items were answered by each subject, Item was also treated as a random effect, allowing inference to be made about other potential word pairs.

The chief advantage of treating Subject as random is that individual subject effects can be modeled at the same time as between-subject fixed effects. The method provides more accurate size and significance estimates for the fixed effects of most interest—parents' and peers' backgrounds—than if the data's by-subject grouping were most ignored (Johnson 2009).

Regression coefficients will be expressed as log-odds differences between factor levels. As the natural logarithm of an odds ratio, a given change in log-odds does not correspond to any fixed increase or decrease in probability. A log-odds increase of $+1$ multiplies the odds by e^{+1}, approximately 2.7. If the odds were already 2:1 in favor of the response "different," they would now be 5.4:1 in favor; the probability would increase from 0.67 to 0.84. But if the odds in favor of "different" had been 10:1 (probability 0.91), they would now be 27:1 (probability 0.96).

In terms of survey scores out of seven items, a change from 3 of 7 to 4 of 7 would correspond to $+0.58$ in log-odds, while a change from 3 of 7 to 6 of 7 would be $+2.08$.

Each subcommunity (for example, the Attleboro twelfth grade) was initially analyzed in a separate regression, in order not to assume that the same factors significantly affect low vowel inventory everywhere (§3.5.3–10). A combined analysis was then performed, including interactions between the most important factors (§3.5.11–12).

3.5.2 MASSACHUSETTS STATE COLLEGE (MS15). With only 35 responses, the data set from "Massachusetts State College" is small enough to discuss directly, without regression. Figure 3.4 shows the pattern of subject scores. The distribution has a mean of 1.29 and is highly skewed: 49% of subjects scored a fully merged 0 of 7; only 12% scored above the midpoint. This campus—located in the ENE dialect area, with most of its students from there—is a mainly merged environment.

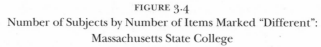

FIGURE 3.4
Number of Subjects by Number of Items Marked "Different":
Massachusetts State College

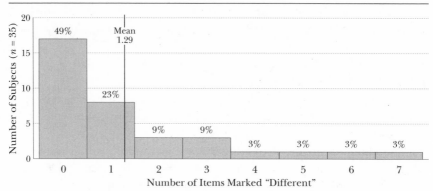

The three highest-scoring students grew up in areas with the low back distinction and had parents from there too, though they have lived in merged surroundings for several years: one from New Jersey, who moved three years ago, scored a 7; one from New York State, who moved five years ago, scored a 6; one from western Massachusetts, who moved four years ago, scored a 5.

Two other students also grew up in distinct areas, but had low scores. One was from Somerset, Massachusetts; his mother from (merged) Pittsburgh, Pennsylvania, likely has much to do with his low score of 2. The other lived as a child in (distinct) northern Illinois. She attended high school in a merged part of Massachusetts, where her parents were also from. She scored a 0.

Setting aside a student who grew up in a part of central Massachusetts where the dialect boundary has not been established (an "unresolved origin"), 29 remain with origins in merged areas. Their scores were distributed as follows: 15 with 0; eight with 1; two with 2; three with 3; and one with 4.

Neither parental origin nor gender distinguished the higher-scoring students in this subgroup. But we note that the items *collar* ~ *caller* and *tock* ~ *talk* were marked "different" 16 times between them, while the other five items were marked "different" only nine times (see §3.2). By taking into account subjects' origins, looking to their parents' origins in some cases, and being aware of these item effects, the MS15 responses can be quite satisfactorily explained.[5]

3.5.3. BROOKLINE, MASSACHUSETTS, TWELFTH GRADERS (BR12). The data from Brookline, Massachusetts, consists of 227 responses from twelfth graders. Figure 3.5 shows BR12 with a similar distribution of subject scores to MS15. Almost half (42%) are fully merged, with a steep decline, and fairly few (18%) are on the distinct side of the midpoint; the mean score was 1.72.

The regression models for BR12 considered the following fixed factors, listed with the baseline level italicized:[6] Gender (*male*, female); Origin (*Brookline*, distinct, merged, other); Mother (*distinct*, merged, other); and Father (*distinct*, merged, other).

The Origin factor represents where the subject spent their earliest childhood, based on the information given for preschool, kindergarten, and elementary school. The Mother and Father factors are based on where the subject's parents were reported to have grown up.

Only places whose low back vowel status was known with some certainty were treated as "merged" or "distinct"; when in doubt, the assignation was always to "other." So Maine, New Hampshire, most of eastern Massachusetts (following chap. 4), western Pennsylvania, Hazleton, Pennsylvania (following Herold 1990), Canada, and Scotland were coded "merged." The Mid-Atlantic (part of southeastern Massachusetts, Rhode Island, Connecticut, metropolitan New York City and Long Island, New Jersey, southeastern Pennsylvania, Delaware, and Maryland) and Inland North (upstate New York, northern Ohio, Michigan, northern Indiana, northern Illinois, and eastern Wisconsin), as well as England, South Africa, and Australia, were all coded "distinct."

When we compare a regression model with the fixed factors of Gender, Origin, Mother, and Father (and the random factors of Subject and Item)

FIGURE 3.5

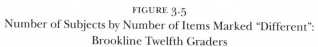
Number of Subjects by Number of Items Marked "Different":
Brookline Twelfth Graders

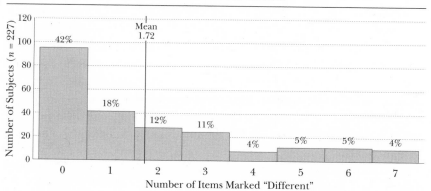

to the same model without Gender, we find that Gender is not significant by a likelihood-ratio χ^2 test: $p = .28$.[7] Nor is Gender significant if it is added as the only fixed factor ($p = .49$); we will therefore drop Gender.

The other three factors are all significant if they are added alone (Origin: $p = .0004$; Mother: $p = .0006$; Father: $p = .005$), but if each is dropped in turn from the full model, Father does not show significance (Origin: $p = .005$; Mother: $p = .02$; Father: $p = .22$).

This chapter will demonstrate that mothers and fathers each have an independent effect on their children. But because the mother's effect is greater, and because both parents often come from the same place—the agreement between the two factors as measured by Cohen's κ is 0.445—statistical significance is not always achieved for both parents.

Another consequence of this correlation is that the coefficients for Mother and Father are less reliable. If we only included Mother, then that effect would certainly be larger, but also less comparable to other models where both parents reach significance. For comparability's sake, we will discuss the model with both Mother and Father (and Origin). For similar reasons of comparability, we will always compare models including both Subject and Item random effects, even though Item did not reach significance with one or two of the smaller data sets (Subject always did).

We can measure the contribution of the fixed between-subject factors by observing how adding them decreases the size of the Subject random effect, which accounts for residual between-subject variation. For the BR12 null model with no fixed effects, the Subject effect's standard deviation is 2.129. Adding Origin, it drops to 2.034; with Mother, it drops to 1.973; and with Father, it drops to 1.953.

Only 16% of the between-subject variance (the square of the standard deviation) is accounted for by adding all three fixed factors. This means that there is still substantial unexplained individual variation within each cell or combination of fixed effects. For example, the 22 natives of Brookline with both parents from distinct dialect areas still spanned the full range of scores from 0 to 7.

Table 3.1 gives the regression results, with the levels of each factor ordered from highest coefficient estimate (favoring "different") to lowest (favoring "same"). Highlighted levels are significantly ($p < .05$) different from the baseline, according to a Wald Z-test.

Compared to the 138 students native to Brookline, the 9 with distinct Origin were much more distinct on the survey (+1.911 log-odds). The highest scores in this group were from those who had moved more recently, but one student who had moved from near Philadelphia before fifth grade—that is, seven years previously—still scored a 5.

TABLE 3.1
Model without Interactions for Brookline Twelfth Graders

Factor	Subjects	Coefficient	Wald p-Value
Origin			
distinct	9	+1.911	.01
other	32	+1.177	.01
merged	48	+0.974	.01
Brookline	138	0.000	—
Mother			
other	115	+0.175	.68
distinct	57	0.000	—
merged	55	−1.084	.03
Father			
distinct	65	0.000	—
other	117	−0.222	.59
merged	45	−0.892	.09
Item			
collar ~ caller	227	+0.424	
tock ~ talk	227	+0.398	
Moll ~ mall	227	+0.173	
Otto ~ auto	227	+0.147	
Don ~ Dawn	227	+0.069	
tot ~ taught	227	−0.145	
cot ~ caught	227	−0.312	
Subject			
maximum	1	+4.062	
> +1 std. dev.	30	> +1.953	
< −1 std. dev.	2	< −1.953	
minimum	1	−2.533	

Intercept: −1.941; log-lik.: −706; d.f.: 10; subject std. dev. (null): 2.129.

Subjects whose Origin was "other" (+1.177) or merged (+0.974) were more similar to the Brookline natives, but still significantly more distinct. It makes sense for the miscellaneous "other" group to be intermediate, but there is no obvious reason why subjects who had moved from merged places, mainly other towns near Boston, would be less merged than Brookline natives.

Under Mother, the "merged" level is significantly lower (−1.084) than the baseline of "distinct." Controlling for subjects' own backgrounds, there remains a difference in their LOT ~ THOUGHT response probability associated with their mother's dialect. The modeled effect of a merged father (−0.892) is slightly smaller and does not reach significance.

Table 3.2 illustrates the parental effects using mean scores for a subset of Brookline natives. Each parent has an effect, but they do not combine linearly; if either parent is merged, the other seems to have less effect. This point will be taken up in section 3.5.12.

The magnitude of the Item effect for BR12 was smaller than the fixed effects. As in MS15, the items *collar ~ caller* (+0.424) and *tock ~ talk* (+0.398) were most often marked "different." *Cot ~ caught* (−0.312) was most often marked "same," with *tot ~ taught* (−0.145) following behind it. The seven items ranged from 18% to 30% "different" (25% overall).

Table 3.1 also indicates the span of the Subject effect, with standard deviation 1.953: the largest positive effect (+4.062) was for a Brookline native with parents from eastern Massachusetts, who nevertheless scored a 5, while the largest negative effect (−2.533) was for a student with parents from New York and New Jersey, who herself lived in Buffalo until fourth grade, yet scored a 0.

3.5.4. ATTLEBORO, MASSACHUSETTS, TWELFTH GRADERS (AB12). Attleboro's 281 twelfth graders marked 27% of items "different" for a mean score of 1.92, slightly higher than Brookline's 1.72. Comparing figure 3.6 with figure 3.5 shows that AB12 has fewer fully merged subjects (28%) than BR12

TABLE 3.2

Mean 0–7 Scores for Native Brookline Twelfth Graders by Parents' Origin

	Distinct Mother	*Merged Mother*
Distinct Father	2.00 (N = 22)	0.20 (N = 10)
Merged Father	0.50 (N = 8)	0.71 (N = 17)

FIGURE 3.6

Number of Subjects by Number of Items Marked "Different":
Attleboro Twelfth Graders

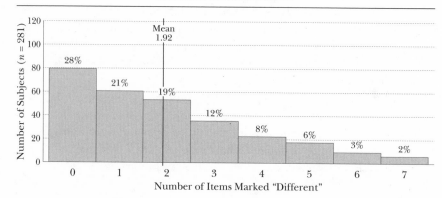

and more intermediate ones, with a more gradual decline from merged toward distinct. The difference between the BR12 and AB12 distributions is significant even by the fairly conservative Mann-Whitney test ($p = .03$).

The AB12 distribution is closer to what would happen if subjects actually treated each item as an independent probabilistic choice. So the model fits better, and we see in table 3.3 that the Subject random effect is smaller than for BR12 even before we add the fixed effects (1.318) and shrinks more when we add them (1.110, or 29% reduction in variance). However, the AB12 data still shows much individual variation.

Again, Gender is not a significant predictor ($p = .54$), while Origin ($p = .002$) and Mother ($p = .004$) clearly are. The Father effect is smaller

TABLE 3.3
Model without Interactions for Attleboro Twelfth Graders

Factor	Subjects	Coefficient	Wald p-Value
Origin			
distinct	24	+1.241	.0002
South Attleboro	61	+0.433	.07
rest of Attleboro	125	0.000	—
other	44	−0.004	.99
merged	27	−0.249	.45
Mother			
distinct	52	0.000	—
other	142	−0.655	.009
merged	87	−0.931	.0008
Father			
distinct	51	0.000	—
other	139	−0.294	.59
merged	91	−0.601	.04
Item			
collar ~ caller	281	+0.242	
tock ~ talk	281	+0.148	
cot ~ caught	281	+0.052	
Moll ~ mall	281	+0.040	
tot ~ taught	281	+0.028	
Don ~ Dawn	281	−0.082	
Otto ~ auto	281	−0.144	
Subject			
maximum	1	+2.373	
> +1 std. dev.	31	> +1.110	
< −1 std. dev.	9	< −1.110	
minimum	1	−1.526	

Intercept: −0.489; log-lik.: −1039; d.f.: 11; subject std. dev. (null): 1.318.

than that of Mother, in the same direction, and likely real but not indepen-dently statistically significant ($p = .14$).

Compared with the baseline of subjects from the rest of the city, those Attleboro natives who had grown up in South Attleboro, as identified by elementary and middle school attendance, were only slightly more distinct (+0.433, n.s.). Thus, these twelfth graders only displayed a vestige of the linguistic difference between the two sections of the city that exists for older speakers.

Movers to Attleboro from a distinct city or town were more likely to respond "different" (+1.241); those with merged or other origins were not significantly different from the baseline.

The AB12 Mother effect is clear: compared to subjects with distinct mothers, those with "other" (−0.655) or merged mothers (−0.931) marked more items "same." The difference between distinct and merged mothers is almost the same as in BR12 (−1.084). While the Father effect did not reach significance as a whole, the difference between merged and distinct fathers is estimated at −0.601, not far from BR12's −0.892.

Like table 3.2 for BR12, table 3.4 for AB12 suggests that fathers and mothers have a parallel effect and that the mothers' effect is greater. Again, if one parent is merged, the status of the other makes less difference.

It is remarkable that parental patterns this clear can be observed in high school seniors, who have had peer influences for 12 or more years. Even the powerful adolescent peer group (Eckert 1989) does not com-pletely overwhelm earlier influences on vowel inventory. An anonymous reviewer wonders if the details of phonetic realization are more completely subject to peer influence, while matters of phonological inventory, as well as morphosyntactic and lexical variables, may be affected by a wider range of factors.

As far as Item effects are concerned, *collar ~ caller* (+0.242) and *tock ~ talk* (+0.148) are once again the most often "different," though to less of a degree. *Otto ~ auto* is now the pair most often marked "same" (−0.144).

The Subject effect has a much narrower span, ranging from +2.373 for a boy who had just moved from Norway—where British English is often

TABLE 3.4

Mean 0–7 Scores for Native Attleboro Twelfth Graders by Parents' Origin

	Distinct Mother	Merged Mother
Distinct Father	3.54 ($N = 13$)	1.75 ($N = 4$)
Merged Father	2.25 ($N = 12$)	1.43 ($N = 40$)

taught—and scored a 7, much higher than most subjects with "other" Origin and parents, to −1.526 for a subject from South Attleboro with Rhode Island parents, who nevertheless scored a fully merged 0 (scores from 3 to 5 were typical for students with similar backgrounds).

3.5.5. ATTLEBORO, MASSACHUSETTS, EIGHTH GRADERS (AB8). Attleboro's 402 eighth graders took the survey in their last year of middle school, of which the city has three. One of them, Coelho, is located in South Attleboro. The distribution of responses is shown in figure 3.7. The mean score is only 1.31, with almost half the subjects responding as fully merged and very few at the distinct end of the spectrum. Attleboro eighth graders are, on the whole, slightly more merged than their twelfth-grade counterparts; a Mann-Whitney test gives $p = 6 \times 10^{-6}$ as the chance these two sets of subject scores are drawn from equally merged populations.

Once again, the predictors Origin ($p = .0002$) and Mother ($p = .0007$) clearly reach the significance threshold, while Father does not ($p = .11$), and Gender clearly does not ($p = .58$). The coefficient estimates for AB8, given in table 3.5, are very similar to those for AB12. So is the behavior of the Subject random effect, which has a standard deviation of 1.369 without the fixed effects and 1.194 with them (24% reduction in variance).

Natives of South Attleboro, nearly all of whom were attending Coelho Middle School there, were not significantly more distinct (+0.090, n.s.) than the baseline group from the rest of the city. This shows the continued fading away of the Attleboro/South Attleboro distinction. The effect of having moved from a distinct community is still strong (+1.914).

FIGURE 3.7

Number of Subjects by Number of Items Marked "Different":
Attleboro Eighth Graders

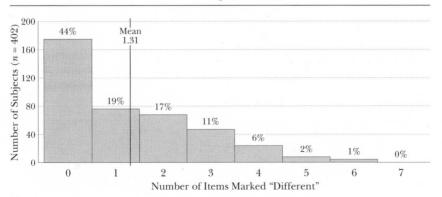

TABLE 3.5
Model without Interactions for Attleboro Eighth Graders

Factor	Subjects	Coefficient	Wald p-Value
Origin			
distinct	15	+1.914	1×10^{-6}
merged	33	+0.153	.63
South Attleboro	58	+0.090	.72
rest of Attleboro	208	0.000	—
other	88	−0.012	.96
Mother			
distinct	66	0.000	—
other	232	−0.826	.0006
merged	104	−1.075	.0002
Father			
distinct	71	0.000	—
other	236	−0.176	.47
merged	95	−0.600	.04
Item			
tock ~ talk	402	+0.713	
collar ~ caller	402	+0.581	
Moll ~ mall	402	+0.490	
tot ~ taught	402	−0.009	
cot ~ caught	402	−0.189	
Don ~ Dawn	402	−0.232	
Otto ~ auto	402	−0.232	
Subject			
maximum	1	+2.804	
> +1 std. dev.	38	> +1.194	
< −1 std. dev.	1	< −1.194	
minimum	1	−1.208	

Intercept: −1.081; log-lik.: −1213; d.f.: 11; subject std. dev. (null): 1.369.

Children of mothers with an unknown dialect background ("other," −0.826), and children of known merged mothers (−1.075) were more merged than children of distinct mothers. On top of this, a merged-father effect does show up, but it is smaller (−0.600). The cross-tabulation in table 3.6 confirms this pattern of parental influence.

Each cell of table 3.6 has a lower mean score than the corresponding cell of table 3.4. In part, this is due to AB12's South Attleboro subjects scoring higher than AB8's: 2.34 versus 1.44. But AB12 subjects of every origin scored higher than their AB8 counterparts. This suggests that in the AB12 milieu, some merged-background students had learned something of the distinction from the minority of distinct students.

TABLE 3.6

Mean 0–7 Scores for Native Attleboro Eighth Graders by Parents' Origin

	Distinct Mother	*Merged Mother*
Distinct Father	2.58 (*N* = 24)	0.83 (*N* = 6)
Merged Father	1.67 (*N* = 6)	0.70 (*N* = 37)

A similar pattern of Item effects appears, though with a greater magnitude than in AB12 and BR12: *tock ~ talk* is at +0.713, *collar ~ caller* at +0.581, and *Moll ~ mall* at +0.490, favoring "different," with *Don ~ Dawn* and *Otto ~ auto* favoring "same" at −0.232. While it makes sense that younger children might have been more affected by the shortcomings of the various items, the regularity of these effects is surprising. For example, of the subjects who marked just one item "different," 74% (56/76) chose one of the three favoring items.

The AB8 subject effects pattern similarly as in AB12. While the most frequent subject adjustment is a small negative one (for subjects who scored a 0 when predicted to score near 1), the larger individual adjustments are positive, in the direction of the distinction. This makes sense for a subcommunity that overall is one of the most merged we have seen.

3.5.6. ATTLEBORO, MASSACHUSETTS, FOURTH GRADERS (AB4). The 330 responses from Attleboro fourth graders came from the city's five elementary schools. Figure 3.8 shows that AB4 responded similarly to AB8. The mean is slightly higher (1.55 for AB4, 1.31 for AB8), but the difference is not significant (Mann-Whitney, *p* = .08).

FIGURE 3.8

Number of Subjects by Number of Items Marked "Different":
Attleboro Fourth Graders

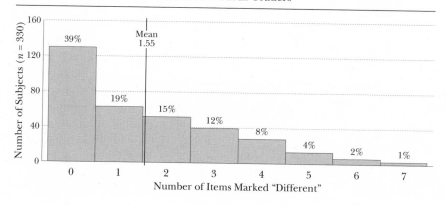

After dropping Gender (p = .76) from the model, testing the other three fixed factors shows that the Origin variable is significant (p = .006), but the Mother (p = .26) and Father (p = .99) variables are not. The standard deviation of the Subject effect is 1.411 without fixed factors, decreasing to 1.367 with Origin included and to 1.361 with Mother and Father included (only a 7% reduction in variance). Table 3.7 shows the model.

Subjects who came to Attleboro before or during elementary school from a distinct community were more likely to be distinct (+1.347, p = .006), but those who moved from a merged community were no more likely to be merged (+0.016, n.s.). In a reversal, subjects with South Attleboro origins (as

TABLE 3.7
Model without Interactions for Attleboro Fourth Graders

Factor	Subjects	Coefficient	Wald p-Value
Origin			
distinct	13	+1.347	.006
other	141	+0.353	.11
merged	32	+0.016	.96
rest of Attleboro	112	0.000	—
South Attleboro	32	−0.629	.11
Mother			
distinct	55	0.000	—
other	205	−0.007	.98
merged	70	−0.464	.19
Father			
distinct	53	0.000	—
merged	65	−0.016	.97
other	212	−0.017	.95
Item			
collar ~ caller	330	+0.195	
tot ~ taught	330	+0.098	
Don ~ Dawn	330	+0.098	
cot ~ caught	330	+0.087	
Moll ~ mall	330	+0.065	
tock ~ talk	330	+0.021	
Otto ~ auto	330	−0.194	
Subject			
maximum	1	+3.031	
> +1 std. dev.	41	> +1.361	
< −1 std. dev.	1	< −1.361	
minimum	1	−1.586	

Intercept: −1.765; log-lik.: −1111; d.f.: 11; subject std. dev. (null): 1.411.

measured by elementary school attendance) were marginally more merged (–0.629, p = .11) than natives of the rest of the city. The biggest difference about the AB4 model is the absence of significant parent effects, although merged mothers do show a weak, nonsignificant effect (–0.464, p = .19) in the expected direction. Table 3.8 suggests the usual parent effects may be operating among Attleboro natives, but that they are smaller in size (cf. table 3.4 for AB12 and table 3.6 for AB8).

If anything, one might have expected to see larger parent effects among these fourth-grade students, who have had peers for fewer years and who are more dependent on their parents than eighth and certainly twelfth graders. One possible explanation is that younger children are less accurate on the survey, and subtle effects are lost in the noise. However, this would likely result in a much larger residual Subject effect, something that is not seen for AB4. The Item effects for AB4 are noticeably smaller than for AB8, which is also surprising as one might expect younger children to be more likely to be influenced by orthography. Rather, they seem to be treating the seven items more equally than any other group.

3.5.7. SUMMARY OF BROOKLINE AND ATTLEBORO RESULTS. Table 3.9 summarizes the regression models for Brookline and Attleboro. BR12 has the most intersubject variation; and even after adding the fixed effects of Origin, Mother, and Father, it has the most subject variation left over. With AB12 and AB8, the fixed effects make the most impact on the model, leaving the smallest amount of unexplained subject variation. The fixed effects make little improvement to the AB4 model.

TABLE 3.8
Mean 0–7 Scores for Native Attleboro Fourth Graders by Parents' Origin

	Distinct Mother	Merged Mother
Distinct Father	1.83 (N = 12)	0.00 (N = 3)
Merged Father	0.40 (N = 4)	0.88 (N = 16)

TABLE 3.9
Summary of Models for Brookline and Attleboro

Community	N	Mean	Subject s.d. (total)	Subject s.d. (residual)	% Reduction in Variance	Item s.d.
BR12	227	1.72	2.129	1.953	16%	0.292
AB12	281	1.92	1.318	1.110	29%	0.163
AB8	402	1.31	1.369	1.194	24%	0.402
AB4	330	1.55	1.411	1.361	7%	0.149

AB4 and AB12 have the least Item variation, AB8 the most. Table 3.10 shows that in three of the four communities, *collar ~ caller* was the item most often marked "different," and it was in second place in AB8. In the three Attleboro communities, *Otto ~ auto* was the item most often marked "same," while in BR12 it was in the middle of the pack.

Subjects who had moved to the mainly merged environments of Brookline or Attleboro from a distinct dialect area always marked more items "different" than their peers, receiving a coefficient ranging between +1 and +2 log-odds. The number of distinct in-movers was small, which may explain the variability in these coefficients.

The effect of a merged mother was consistently close to −1, and that of a merged father between −0.6 and −0.9, except in the AB4 data where the parental effects were much smaller and not statistically significant.

The eighth- and twelfth-grade subjects showed the influence of both peers and parents, an important result, though we do not know if their speech would also reflect both influences.

3.5.8. NEW YORK CITY HIGH SCHOOL STUDENTS (NY11). Unlike the above communities, which were mainly merged, the average response from 114 New York City high school students—103 eleventh graders at Brooklyn Tech High School and 11 tenth graders at a Jewish private school in Manhattan—was 69% "different," with a mean score of 4.81.

The score distribution for NY11 is shown in figure 3.9. It looks roughly like the mirror image of figure 3.5 for BR12. The New York distribution falls rapidly from its peak on the right—36% fully distinct—levels off somewhat, and then there is a small second peak at the left end of the spectrum, as 9% of subjects gave a fully merged response.

As before, there was no detectable effect of Gender on the responses ($p = .82$). And, unfortunately, there were no in-movers from merged areas, so it was not possible to evaluate whether they were acquiring the distinction in New York.

TABLE 3.10
Summary of Principal Effects for Brookline and Attleboro

Community	Distinct Origin	Merged Mother	Merged Father	Most Often "Different"
BR12	+1.911	−1.084	−0.892	*collar ~ caller*
AB12	+1.241	−0.931	−0.601	*collar ~ caller*
AB8	+1.914	−1.075	−0.600	*tock ~ talk*
AB4	+1.347	−0.464	−0.016	*collar ~ caller*

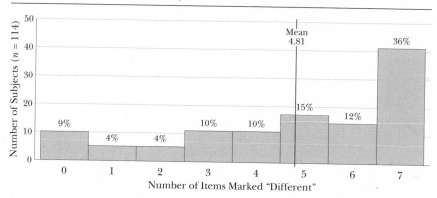

FIGURE 3.9

Number of Subject by Number of Items Marked "Different":
New York City Tenth and Eleventh Graders

Dividing students' origins into three categories showed that the 35 subjects from Queens were marginally more merged (-1.281, $p = .04$) than the 48 from Brooklyn; the remaining 31 were intermediate.[8]

There were no merged fathers and only one merged mother, so these variables were coded as distinct versus "other." Almost all distinct parents were from New York City; almost all "other" parents were from foreign countries.

Mother was not significant ($p = .87$), but Father was: compared to subjects with distinct fathers, those with "other" fathers were much more merged (-2.734, $p = .003$). The greater importance of fathers (also seen in table 3.11) may relate to NY11's subjects' being two-thirds male (see section 3.5.13 for further discussion).

With its large positive intercept ($+4.520$), the regression model given in table 3.12 predicts that subjects with distinct parents will almost always mark LOT ~ THOUGHT items "different." Indeed, 11 subjects in this cell scored a perfect 7, while 1 scored a 0.

TABLE 3.11

Mean 0–7 Scores for Native New York City Tenth and Eleventh Graders
by Parents' Origin

	Distinct Mother	*"Other" Mother*
Distinct Father	6.42 ($N = 12$)	6.11 ($N = 9$)
"Other" Father	2.33 ($N = 3$)	4.54 ($N = 90$)

TABLE 3.12
Model without Interactions for New York City Tenth and Eleventh Graders

Factor	Subjects	Coefficient	Wald p-Value
Origin			
Brooklyn	48	0.000	—
other	31	–0.392	.54
Queens	35	–1.281	.04
Mother			
distinct	15	0.000	—
other	99	–0.169	.87
Father			
distinct	21	0.000	—
other	93	–2.734	.003
Item			
cot ~ caught	114	+1.002	
tot ~ taught	114	+0.307	
tock ~ talk	114	+0.099	
collar ~ caller	114	–0.101	
Don ~ Dawn	114	–0.481	
Otto ~ auto	114	–0.603	
Moll ~ mall	114	–1.422	
Subject			
maximum	1	+2.657	
> +1 std. dev.	6	> +2.350	
< –1 std. dev.	15	< –2.350	
minimum	1	–6.171	

Intercept: +4.520; log-lik.: –369; d.f.: 7; subject std. dev. (null): 2.561.

This one surprisingly merged subject was assigned the very large Subject effect of –6.171. Smaller, but still large subject effects were common in this model (std. dev. 2.350). In the group of students with "other" (foreign) parents, there is a great deal of variation. Even among those who have always lived in New York, many do not seem to have acquired the low back distinction. Whether they can be said to be leading a merger is another matter.

The Item effects are also the largest thus far, perhaps no coincidence as English was often not the native language, and they appear in a very different order. The "canonical" pairs cot ~ caught (+1.002) and tot ~ taught (+0.307) were preferably marked "different" in New York City; they had favored "same" in Brookline and were neutral in Attleboro.

Otto ~ auto (–0.603) favored "same" in New York, like in Attleboro. Moll ~ mall (–1.422), which tended to favor "different" elsewhere, greatly

favored "same" here. These results suggest that if there is a merger in progress, it is favored before final /l/ and disfavored before final /t/. At the least,
the differences in Item effects between communities show that it is not
universal phonological factors that are guiding subjects to mark items differently.

3.5.9. SEEKONK, MASSACHUSETTS, TWELFTH, EIGHTH, AND FOURTH GRAD-
ERS (SK12, SK8, SK4). The 109 responses from twelfth graders in Seekonk,
Massachusetts, represented two-thirds of the high school senior class, the
same proportion of high school seniors as in Attleboro. But there was a
much lower response rate—therefore, a less representative sample—in the
grades where the school administration required parental permission: only
27 eighth graders and 72 fourth and fifth graders responded (the survey
was given to the fifth grade by mistake at one school).

Because of these relatively small numbers, regression analysis will be
performed on all the Seekonk data together, using Grade as a separate variable. Grade is expected to be a significant predictor, since there is obvious
change between the twelfth, eighth, and fourth grades.

SK12 (figure 3.10) is even more distinct than NY11. The mean score
was 5.28 (75% "different"); 46% scored a 7 while only 21% were in the
merged half of the spectrum. Like Attleboro, SK12 had very few subjects
who completely disagreed with the majority pattern; such "dissent" was
more common in Brookline and especially New York, though even there it
was not common.

The pattern of SK8 scores (figure 3.11) appears very different. The
mean is lower, at 3.67 (Mann-Whitney $p = .0006$), and the score distribu-

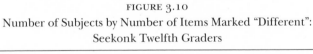

FIGURE 3.10
Number of Subjects by Number of Items Marked "Different":
Seekonk Twelfth Graders

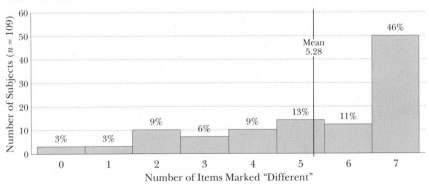

FIGURE 3.11

Number of Subjects by Number of Items Marked "Different":
Seekonk Eighth Graders

tion is fairly flat, which indicates a mixture of merger-favoring and distinc-
tion-favoring subjects (if all subjects responded with 50% probability, then
scores of 3 and 4 would be the most common).

In SK4 (figure 3.12), the mean is lower again: 2.57 (Mann-Whitney
$p = .026$), with most scores coming from all across the merged half of the
spectrum (0–3).

Chapters 4 and 5 will show that native Seekonk speakers in their twen-
ties and older preserve the low back vowel distinction. The above results
suggest that SK12 largely does so as well, but that the low back merger is
characteristic of some children in SK8 and most children in SK4. Still, SK4
is not as merged a group as those in Brookline and Attleboro.

FIGURE 3.12

Number of Subjects by Number of Items Marked "Different":
Seekonk Fourth and Fifth Graders

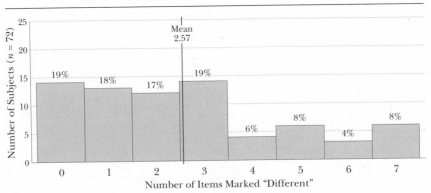

Because there is community change in Seekonk, the regression analysis to a degree becomes a process of identifying the leaders of change (and the trailers). It would be helpful to have more social information here, including such about peer groups, but we do not.

A combined analysis assumes that factors operate the same way across grade levels, which they may not. We have seen the seven Item effects change across communities. Parental effects were much smaller in AB4 than AB8 and AB12; this could be a general trend. And a factor like "distinct Origin" might mean little in SK12 where most natives are distinct, but SK4 subjects who had moved from more solidly distinct communities, especially recently, might behave differently than their peers. Such complications will be swept under the rug as we perform a joint regression, made necessary by the smaller size of the data sets.

Removing three subjects who did not report their gender, Gender emerges as a significant predictor for the first time ($p = .02$). The other fixed factors are also significant: Origin ($p = .04$), Mother ($p = .0007$), Father ($p = .03$), and Grade ($p = 2 \times 10^{-14}$).

Under Grade, we see a statistical confirmation of what the mean scores showed: SK12 is the most distinct, SK8 is considerably more merged (-1.745), SK4 even more so (-2.641).

Subjects with distinct Origin were slightly more distinct, but the difference was not significant ($+0.296$, n.s.). This makes sense when we recall that most of the baseline Seekonk subjects were in twelfth grade and mainly distinct themselves. On the other hand, the small number of subjects with merged Origin were much more merged than the Seekonk natives. Their coefficient, -2.554, is the largest (in absolute size) that we have seen under Origin. In Brookline and Attleboro, distinct Origin always received a positive coefficient against the mainly merged native baseline, but it never exceeded $+2$.

Subjects with a merged Mother (-1.832) or Father (-1.670) gave a more merged response than the majority with distinct parents. Like that for Origin, the Seekonk parental effects are larger than those observed in Brookline and Attleboro.

While females lead many sound changes, they have not been found to do so for mergers (see chap. 1). However, no previous study has measured the degree of merger of so many subjects in a community undergoing change. For that reason, the school survey could potentially register a smaller Gender effect than previous studies could have. In the Seekonk data, female subjects were slightly more merged than males (-0.659).

The Item effects are in the same order as in NY11, except for *Don ~ Dawn*, which slightly favored "same" in NY11, but is most "different"

(+0.470) in Seekonk. *Don ~ Dawn* is tied for second-most "different" Item in SK12 and SK8 and is the most "different" in SK4. This suggests that *Don ~ Dawn* behaves conservatively with respect to the merger in progress, a pattern that might arise if some subjects know older people named *Don* and/or *Dawn*, and attend to or remember the realizations of those names more carefully than common nouns or other words.

The "canonical" pairs *cot ~ caught* (+0.406) and *tot ~ taught* (+0.375) also favor "different," while *Otto ~ auto* (−0.634) and *Moll ~ mall* (−0.665) favor "same." The magnitude of the effects is not as large as NY11, but their position appears to be a signature of mainly distinct places, just as having *collar ~ caller* and *tock ~ talk* most "different" was a hallmark of mainly merged places.

The total between-subject variation was high (s.d. = 2.343) which makes sense, since the Seekonk data was a mixture of heterogeneous grade levels. Controlling for grade, the Subject effect fell to 1.943 (a 31% decrease in variance). Taking that as a baseline, adding the other fixed factors reduced it to 1.617 (also a 31% decrease). Comparing table 3.13 to table 3.9, we see that the Seekonk subjects, with their merger in progress, were a fairly diverse group, but that the fixed effects also made a large difference in predicting their scores.

For all four fixed factors—Origin, Mother, Father, and Gender—the effect sizes were larger than in Attleboro and Brookline. To explain this, we might note that in Seekonk the merger is in progress and suggest that while it is ongoing, subjects are naturally more different from one another and perhaps more differentiated according to relevant factors.

This may well be true for Gender, but for Origin and the parental factors there is another explanation, which hinges on Seekonk being a mainly distinct community while Attleboro and Brookline are mainly merged. Recall that either parent's low back vowel status matters more if the other parent is distinct and less if the other parent is merged; this follows from it being easier to acquire the merger than the distinction. By the same token, one's parents will make more of a difference if one's peers are distinct, and former peers (the Origin factor) will be more important if current peers are distinct.

3.5.10. COMPARISON ACROSS COMMUNITIES. In sections 3.5.3–3.5.9 separate mixed-effect logistic regressions were performed for each subcommunity's survey data. These treated Subject and Item as random effects and evaluated the fixed effects of Origin, Mother, Father, and Gender. The Origin effect, reflecting differences between in-movers and subjects native to the place in question, was the strongest. The other widely important factors

TABLE 3.13
Model without Interactions for Seekonk, Massachusetts

Factor	Subjects	Coefficient	Wald p-Value
Grade			
12th	106	0.000	—
8th	27	–1.745	3×10^5
4th (and 5th)	72	–2.641	5×10^{-15}
Origin			
distinct	71	+0.296	.35
other	33	+0.182	.70
Seekonk	94	0.000	—
merged	7	–2.554	.02
Mother			
distinct	131	0.000	—
other	52	–1.017	.01
merged	22	–1.832	.0004
Father			
other	56	+0.027	.95
distinct	137	0.000	—
merged	12	–1.670	.01
Gender			
male	89	0.000	—
female	116	–0.659	.02
Item			
Don ~ Dawn	205	+0.470	
tot ~ taught	205	+0.406	
cot ~ caught	205	+0.375	
tock ~ talk	205	–0.057	
collar ~ caller	205	–0.331	
Otto ~ auto	205	–0.634	
Moll ~ mall	205	–0.665	
Subject			
maximum	1	+3.104	
> +1 std. dev.	13	> +1.617	
< –1 std. dev.	22	< –1.617	
minimum	1	–2.924	

Intercept: +2.724; log-lik.: –707; d.f.: 13; subject std. dev. (null): 2.343.

were those of Mother's and Father's origins. But these parental influences were unexpectedly smaller for the youngest subjects, AB4 and SK4.[9]

Table 3.14 displays a selection of the above effects, intended to show trends and patterns across communities. As above, statistically significant

TABLE 3.14
Selected Effects (in Log-Odds) Compared across Communities

	BR12	AB12	AB8	AB4	NY11	SK12 SK8 SK4
N	227	281	402	330	114	106 27 72
Mean	1.72	1.92	1.31	1.55	4.81	5.28 3.67 2.57
Distinct origin (vs. native)	+1.911	+1.241	+1.914	+1.347	0.000 (Brooklyn)	+0.296
Merged origin (vs. native)	+0.974	−0.249	+0.153	+0.016	−1.281 (Queens)	−2.554
Merged mother (vs. distinct)	−1.084	−0.931	−1.075	−0.464	−0.169 ("other")	−1.832
Merged father (vs. distinct)	−0.892	−0.601	−0.600	−0.016	−2.734 ("other")	−1.670
Female gender (vs. male)	−0.351	−0.115	−0.096	+0.061	−0.126	−0.659
Most "different" item	collar ~ caller	collar ~ caller	tock ~ talk	collar ~ caller	cot ~ caught	Don ~ Dawn
Most "same" item	cot ~ caught	Otto ~ auto	Otto ~ auto	Otto ~ auto	Moll ~ mall	Moll ~ mall

$(p < .05)$ fixed effects are highlighted. Note that real effects close to zero may not be "significant," and even real effects far from zero may not be "significant" if insufficient data support them.

The positive effect of distinct origin is clear in Brookline and Attleboro, and the negative effect of merged origin is even larger in Seekonk. There were no in-movers from merged areas into New York, so the effect of Queens versus Brooklyn origin is shown instead.

Brookline behaves as though it is more merged than the known-merged places people move from, which is unexplained. There is no significant effect of merged origin in Attleboro or of distinct origin in Seekonk (again, New York lacked data). This makes sense, if Attleboro is considered a merged community itself (other than the diminishingly "independent" South Attleboro), so subjects who moved from neighboring places, mainly closer to Boston, would encounter a similar peer environment on arrival in Attleboro.

A parallel explanation would cover SK12, which makes up more than half of the Seekonk data set. Seekonk twelfth graders are essentially a distinct community, and children moving into it from other distinct communities would not be expected to show any greater degree of distinction. On the other hand, for Seekonk fourth graders, many of whom are merged, we observe a modest coefficient of +0.591 for distinct origin. This does not reach significance, though it presumably would with more data.

The Origin effect stands in for early community and peer influences and seems to be fairly well behaved. Many subjects reflected these early influences despite many years in the survey community. Others partially accommodated to the local norm, and others fully. On average, there is an effect of about +1.5 log-odds on the response of a distinct-origin person who has spent several years in a mainly merged school system.

The reverse question, of whether subjects who start their lives merged can learn the distinction under peer influence, cannot be addressed equally well with this data. Compared to 61 distinct-origin subjects in Attleboro and Brookline, there were no merged-origin subjects in New York and only seven who moved to Seekonk. Of these seven subjects, three were twelfth graders, and therefore had mainly distinct peers. After living in Seekonk for between 2 and 10 years, they scored 0, 2, and 2 on the survey. The sample is small, but we see why the merged-origin coefficient is large; these subjects show little evidence of learning the distinction, so they stand out. Certainly not all, but many, of the distinct movers to Attleboro and Brookline learned the merger better than these merged movers to Seekonk learned the distinction.

The effects of merged (vs. distinct) parents are quite constant from community to community. The Father effect is usually somewhat smaller than the Mother effect. In Seekonk, where many peers would have the distinction, the parental effects are larger. As noted, this is because the merger is easier to learn than the distinction. Merged peers in places like Brookline and Attleboro do a better job at undoing the "inherited" differences between children than distinct peers do in places like Seekonk.

The effect of female gender is not significant in Brookline, Attleboro, and New York, although we note that it is negative (favoring merger) in four of five data sets. In Seekonk, females do significantly favor the merger in progress, although the effect is small. If this is surprising, it is only because such an effect may not have been noticeable previously.

The Item effect clearly behaves differently across communities. In the mainly merged communities of Brookline and Attleboro, *collar ~ caller* was most "different," except in AB8, where it was runner-up to *tock ~ talk*. On the other hand, in the mainly distinct communities of New York and Seekonk, the pairs *cot ~ caught* and *tot ~ taught* favored "different," edged out by *Don ~ Dawn* in Seekonk as it underwent the merger.

The items that favored "same" were *cot ~ caught* (and *tot ~ taught*) in Brookline, but consistently *Otto ~ auto* in Attleboro. The pair *Otto ~ auto* was marked "same" second most often in New York and Seekonk, too, but there *Moll ~ mall* favored "same" even more.

It would be interesting to dissect these patterns further to discover whether they have more to do with the different items being better or worse tools for investigating subjects' (more consistent) phonologies or whether the Item effects actually reflect phonological conditioning of the low back vowels, perhaps especially when they are merging.

3.5.11. A COMBINED MODEL. As long as we account for the different patterns of Item effects, a combined regression analysis of all communities' data allows a more precise estimation of the fixed effects. We create a new variable, Current Peers, which takes the value "distinct" for the New York and Seekonk high school students, "other" for Seekonk's fourth and eighth graders, and "merged" for the Attleboro, Brookline, and Massachusetts State College subjects.

Under the Origin variable, natives of Brookline and Attleboro are now being coded as "merged," except for twelfth graders from South Attleboro, who are "other." Seekonk natives in fourth and eighth grades are also "other," while those in twelfth grade are "distinct." Native New Yorkers are "distinct," except those from Queens, who are coded here as "other."

The data remains unbalanced; because of where the survey was administered, most subjects have merged current peers. And most movers have gone from distinct to merged areas, rather than the other way; this seems to be a real demographic pattern in the region.

Table 3.15 shows the results of a mixed-effects regression performed on these 1,597 subjects. Because of the larger number of subjects, all effects are significant at a much higher level than before. Compared to each "distinct" level, each "merged" level has a clear negative effect on the response—favoring "same"—while the "other" level has the expected intermediate effect.[10]

The largest difference between "distinct" and "merged" (−1.952 log-odds) is for Current Peers, which reflects the community where the subject now attends school. This is followed by Origin (−1.562), where a subject lived in earlier years. The effect of Mother (−0.970) is smaller than either of these, and that of Father (−0.576) is the smallest of the four.

Of course, these four variables are not independent. The substantial correlation between Mother and Father (Cohen's $\kappa = 0.529$) arises because people are more likely to marry people from nearby communities. The even higher correlation between Origin and Current Peers ($\kappa = 0.652$) exists because most children have not moved between dialect areas (if at all), so their earlier peers match their current ones from the point of view of the low back vowels.

TABLE 3.15
Combined Model without Interactions for 1,597 Subjects

Factor	Subjects	Coefficient	Wald p-Value
Mother			
distinct	382	0.000	—
other	849	−0.452	.0008
merged	366	−0.970	2×10^{-9}
Father			
distinct	405	0.000	—
other	856	−0.282	.03
merged	336	−0.576	.0005
Origin			
distinct	253	0.000	—
other	492	−1.065	2×10^{-10}
merged	852	−1.562	$< 2 \times 10^{-16}$
Current peers			
distinct	223	0.000	—
other	99	−1.697	4×10^{-6}
merged	1275	−1.952	2×10^{-11}

Intercept: +2.303; log-lik.: −5319; d.f.: 13.

Despite these correlations, the number of subjects is high enough to be quite sure that each of these four variables has its own effect on the response, as table 3.15's Wald *p*-values indicate. And the standard errors of these estimates are small enough that we can trust this assessment of their relative size.

The two peer effects are larger than the two parental effects, but not overwhelmingly so. The Father effect is between one-half and two-thirds as large as the Mother effect.

Current Peers yields the largest effect size here, seeming to imply that peers from late childhood and adolescence have a larger linguistic effect than those from earlier years. But because of the imbalance in migration patterns (see table 3.16), when Origin and Current Peers do not match, it is almost always Current Peers that are merged. So while we may indeed have more evidence that mergers tend to win out over distinctions, the data is

TABLE 3.16
1,070 (of 1,597) Subjects, Cross-Tabulated by Origin and Current Peers

	Distinct Origin	Merged Origin
Distinct Current Peers	158	4
Merged Current Peers	66	842

not balanced enough to assess the relative importance of early versus late peer influence.

3.5.12. INTERACTION BETWEEN FACTORS. None of the above models contained interaction terms; they assumed that effects such as Mother and Father combine linearly. But cross-tabulations like table 3.4 suggest that these factors interact; for example, the effect of Father is more pronounced when Mother is distinct. A model with interactions would have a positive interaction term for merged Mother–merged Father, mitigating the combined effect of the negative coefficients for each parent.

Interactions were found between Mother and Father (p = .02), Mother and Origin (p = .04), Father and Origin (p = .006), and Origin and Current Peers (p = .01). Table 3.17 shows the most important coefficients from a model including these interactions, using the same data as section 3.5.11.

The "main effect" terms have larger magnitudes in table 3.17 than in table 3.15. They now represent the effect size when the other factors are "distinct." In that case, the Origin effect (−4.205) is the largest, followed by

TABLE 3.17
Excerpt from Model with Interactions for 1,597 Subjects

Factor	Subjects	Coefficient	Wald p-Value
Mother			
distinct	382	0.000	—
merged	366	−2.552	1×10^{-5}
Father			
distinct	405	0.000	—
merged	336	−2.326	.0004
Origin			
distinct	253	0.000	—
merged	852	−4.205	4×10^{-5}
Current Peers			
distinct	223	0.000	—
merged	1275	−1.708	2×10^{-6}
Mother & Father			
merged	206	+0.945	.02
Mother & Origin			
merged	266	+1.063	.07
Father & Origin			
merged	253	+1.645	.02
Origin & Current Peers			
merged	842	+1.965	.06

Intercept: +2.708; log-lik.: −5299; d.f.: 29.

roughly equal parental effects (Mother: −2.552, Father: −2.326), with Current Peers smallest (−1.708).

The positive interaction terms reflect the fact that the merger can be learned more easily than the distinction, so any merger-favoring factors decrease the importance of the other factors. Having two merged parents makes a child more merged than having one, but not twice as much. Conversely, two distinct parents impart the distinction much better than one alone does.

In the case of Current Peers, we see an interaction term (+1.965) large enough to cancel out the main-effect term (−1.708). This suggests that distinct current peers have no strong effect on subjects who had merged peers earlier in childhood; however, this result is based on a small number of subjects. Many more subjects moved in the other direction, and we can see that merged current peers definitely do have a medium-sized effect on subjects whose original peers were distinct.

Table 3.18 assesses the predictions made by two models. Both include the fixed factors—of which the most common combinations not involving "other" are shown—and their interactions, as well as Item effects. One model has a random Subject effect, the other does not. The models' predictions are compared with the actual mean score for the group. Even the model without Subject effects does a good job of predicting the mean scores of the different groups.

When Mother is distinct, we see a Father effect in the expected direction (compare rows DDMM and DMMM). When Mother is merged, Father appears to have a reverse effect (MMMM vs. MDMM), as a distinct father leads to an even more merged response. Section 3.5.13 will explore this further, concluding that for boys, having a distinct father makes them more distinct, but suggesting that a distinct father may actually make girls more merged.

TABLE 3.18

Models' Predictions versus Observed Means for Common Factor Combinations

Mother/Father/ Origin/Current	Predicted Mean w/o Subject Effect	Predicted Mean w/Subject Effect	Observed Mean	No. of Subjects
DDDD	6.02	6.14	6.12	73
DDDM	4.66	4.79	4.69	16
DDMM	2.06	2.14	2.16	68
DMMM	1.44	1.45	1.50	34
MMMM	1.00	0.94	0.98	155
MDMM	0.88	0.71	0.69	29

The model with individual Subject effects naturally has better predictions for group means, but also deals explicitly with the data's overdispersion, meaning that subjects are more different from one another than they would be under a simpler model's assumptions.

To illustrate this, consider the group of 155 subjects with "merged" for all four factors, whose observed mean score is 0.98 out of 7. Assuming there were no Subject and Item effects, such a mean score would correspond to a response probability of $0.98/7 = 0.14$.

Now, if each subject answered each item randomly with a 14% chance of answering "different" each time, the distribution of the resulting scores would be 35% 0s, 40% 1s, 19% 2s, and 6% 3s or higher. But the actual distribution of subject scores for the MMMM group is much more dispersed: 54% 0s, 16% 1s, 15% 2s, and 15% 3s or higher.

No single pattern of Item effects could cause this overdispersion; strong Item effects could push subject scores toward the midpoint, but not lead to more 0s. The Item effects here are not very strong; including them gives a predicted distribution of 34% 0s, 40% 1s, 20% 2s, and 6% 3s or higher.

Chance would cause subject scores to vary even if there were no underlying difference in subjects' tendencies. However, the models in this chapter employ explicit Subject effects to capture residual between-subject differences, which have always risen above the level of chance. Here, the Subject effect is estimated to have standard deviation 1.479. Including it widens the predicted score distribution to 49% 0s, 24% 1s, 13% 2s, and 14% 3s or higher—quite close to the observed distribution.

3.5.13. INTERACTION BETWEEN PARENTAL EFFECTS AND SUBJECTS' GENDER. Since both parents have independent but interacting effects on a subject's response, it seemed worthwhile to investigate whether children's gender affects the relative influence of the two parents. Recall also that in NY11, which was 67% male, only a Father effect was detected, while in other subcommunities ranging from 42% to 57% male, the Mother effect appeared to be stronger.

Although mothers are generally the primary caretakers, it is plausible that sons identify more with their fathers and absorb more linguistic influence from them, although some previous work has suggested that young children of both genders hew closely to their mothers' speech when acquiring their dialects (Foulkes, Docherty, and Watt 1999; Smith, Durham, and Fortune 2007).

To investigate this issue, separate models were fit for males' and females' data, comparing the effects of distinct parents between the 408 male and 424 female subjects with merged Origin and Current Peers.[11]

Table 3.19 displays regression coefficients and mean scores for the four combinations of known-merged and known-distinct parents. These subjects all have merged peers, so merged parents were the baseline to test the effects of distinct parents against.

Subjects were more distinct when the same-sex parent was distinct; males showed a fairly small effect for distinct Father (+0.611), and females a moderate one for distinct Mother (+0.978). Having two distinct parents made the effect greater for both males (+1.232) and females (+1.382). But when just the opposite-sex parent was distinct, this had no effect on males (+0.025) and in fact had a large negative one on females (−2.210).

In this data, sons are more influenced by their fathers. Whether the mother is merged or distinct, the status of the father has a noticeable effect on male subjects. But the status of the mother is only relevant if the father is distinct; if a boy's father and peers are merged, having a distinct mother has no apparent impact.

In a parallel result, daughters are substantially influenced by their mothers regardless of their fathers' status. When mothers are distinct, the father's influence is small, but in the expected direction. However, when mothers are merged, the father's influence appears to reverse. The 16 girls with merged mothers and peers but distinct fathers have a mean score of only 0.19 out of 7, the lowest score of any subgroup we have examined.

It is plausible that girls in this situation might react against their fathers. More than their peers with a fully merged background (mean 1.07), they might recognize the distinction on the survey and be confident that they do not talk that way or do not want to. This would imply a negative evaluation of the low back distinction.[12]

While remaining somewhat skeptical of the result in this one cell, we can conclude that when parents differ from peers, parents' influence is clearly visible in children's responses. And when mothers and fathers differ from each other, we can see that both boys and girls are more influenced toward their same-sex parent than their opposite-sex parent.

TABLE 3.19
Excerpt of Parental Effects for 832 Subjects with Merged Peers

Group	Males			Females		
	Coeff.	*Mean*	*N*	*Coeff.*	*Mean*	*N*
Both parents distinct	+1.232	1.87	30	+1.382	2.39	38
Only mother distinct	+0.025	0.94	17	+0.978	1.94	16
Only father distinct	+0.611	1.31	13	−2.210	0.19	16
Both parents merged	0.000	0.89	71	0.000	1.07	83

3.5.14. EFFECTS OF AGE AND TIME ON ACQUIRING THE LOW BACK MERGER.
Payne (1980, 175) found that "age of arrival [in King of Prussia] had the
strongest effect on the success of acquisition" of Philadelphia phonetic variables, along with years since arrival.[13] On the other hand, acquisition of a
phonological variable, short a, "does not appear to be influenced by the age
at which the child moved" (Payne 1976, 210).

While few survey subjects had moved from a merged to a distinct
community, their results support Payne's contention that acquisition of a
distinction from peers is difficult (see §3.1). For example, the mainly distinct Seekonk twelfth grade (mean score 5.28) had three subjects who had
moved from merged communities, and the highest score among them was
only 2.

We will now examine how age of arrival and years since arrival affect
acquisition of the merger among the larger group of subjects with distinct
Origin and merged Current Peers. The data was restricted to the 33 subjects with at least one known distinct parent and without a known merged
parent. If subjects encountered the merger for the first time when they
moved—24 of them to Attleboro, 6 to Brookline, and 3 to Massachusetts
State College—this would presumably maximize any effects of age of arrival
and years since arrival. And in theory, a regression analysis can tease apart
these two potential effects.

There are several reasons to expect children who move to a merged
community at an earlier age to acquire the merger better. They spend fewer
years with the old dialect and more years learning the new one. And they
were younger when they moved and so better able to make the change, following critical-period arguments.[14]

The results of a regression treating the Age Moved and the Years Since
Moving as linear predictors, performed with random effects for Subject
and Item[15]—show that Age Moved is significantly related to the response,
in the expected direction: +0.213 (p = .001).

The earliest any child moved was age 6. Compared to someone of that
age, this model estimates that a child moving at age 7 would favor the distinction slightly more, by +0.213 log-odds, and a child moving at age 16
would favor it substantially more, by +2.13 log-odds. We can conclude that
the ability to learn the merger declines with age—or else, it declines with
more exposure to the original distinct dialect; these two could hardly be
disentangled.

With Age Moved controlled, there is no significant effect of Years Since
Moving (p = .99). The number of years in the merged community seems
not to matter; only the age of arrival does. Movers must relatively quickly
learn the merger to the extent they ever will.

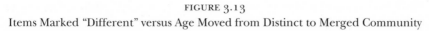

FIGURE 3.13

Items Marked "Different" versus Age Moved from Distinct to Merged Community

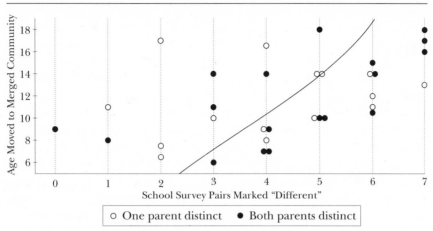

But even early-moving subjects have not acquired the merger completely. Of the 10 subjects who moved between the ages of 6 and 9, there was only one score of 0, compared with five scores of 4; the mean was 2.80. The lack of total learning is not surprising. When these subjects moved, after all, their distinct families came with them.

On average, late-moving subjects retained the distinction more; for 13 subjects who moved between 14 and 18, the mean score was 5.15. Bucking this trend, one 17-year-old girl scored a 2 only a few months after moving from Rochester, New York, to Brookline; her father's origin was unknown, however, and he could have been merged.

Figure 3.13 plots the 0–7 scores for these 33 movers against Age Moved, showing a fair amount of individual variation on either side of a trend line. Subjects with two known distinct parents—shown with solid circles—were only slightly more distinct than the others.

3.6. FACTORS AFFECTING VOWEL INVENTORY: *PALM*

In most dialects of present-day American English, the PALM and LOT classes are identical: *father* rhymes with *bother*, and *balm* and *bomb* are homophones. A phonemic difference whereby PALM has greater length, as in Moulton (1990), is no longer supported by data collected from young speakers.

As a result, in most areas where LOT and THOUGHT are merged, all three word classes are now united as PALM = LOT = THOUGHT (3-M). This three-way merger has occurred in western Pennsylvania and adjacent areas (Kurath and McDavid 1961, 7), in Canada (Boberg 2006), and wherever THOUGHT falls in with an already-merged PALM = LOT, as in the West, and increasingly in the Midland and South (Labov, Ash, and Boberg 2006, §9.1).

In Eastern New England, PALM has typically remained distinct from the combined LOT = THOUGHT (ENE). But in New York, Seekonk, and South Attleboro, we expect PALM and LOT to be merged, whether a subject has a more traditional two-phoneme low vowel system, PALM = LOT ≠ THOUGHT (MAIN), or an innovative one-phoneme system, PALM = LOT = THOUGHT (3-M).

Although anyone so close to the boundary is familiar with the dialect on the other side, we do not expect younger Seekonk speakers to be able to replicate the ENE pattern by separating the LOT words from PALM = LOT, merging them with THOUGHT, and leaving PALM by itself.

At least some Brookline and Massachusetts State College subjects are expected to retain a distinct PALM. But we do not expect in-movers to the area to acquire it. On the contrary, in-movers with the MAIN system may threaten the ENE system, such that the 3-M system arises. And the same thing could be happening in Attleboro, except that near the dialect boundary, migration is not even necessary for dialect contact.

The data on PALM come from three questions. The first was a minimal pair asking about *la* versus *law*. The answer "same" suggests the 3-M system, as both ENE and MAIN would usually pronounce this pair differently. However, the singing term *la* does not behave as an ordinary English word, so the answer "different" does not rule out the three-way merger.

Subjects also answered two questions on whether PALM ~ LOT word pairs rhymed. The pair *father ~ bother* was used in all communities. *Osama ~ comma* was used in Attleboro and New York, but was abandoned when subjects said they were unfamiliar with the name *Osama* (the name *Obama* had unfortunately not yet become familiar). In the other communities, the pair *salami ~ Tommy* was used instead. The concept of rhyme is thought to be familiar even to the youngest children surveyed. Nevertheless, a higher error rate was expected than for the LOT ~ THOUGHT minimal pairs.

3.6.1. THE STATUS OF *PALM* WHERE *LOT* AND *THOUGHT* ARE HISTORICALLY DISTINCT. In New York, 93% of 110 subjects[16] said *father ~ bother* rhymed; 89% rhymed *Osama ~ comma*. This establishes the PALM ~ LOT merger, which should make *la ~ law* just like a LOT ~ THOUGHT pair.

But while the LOT ~ THOUGHT pairs were marked "different" 68% of the time, *la ~ law* was 93% "different." Even among the six subjects with clear evidence of three-way merger—marking all 7 LOT ~ THOUGHT pairs "same" and saying both PALM ~ LOT pairs rhymed—four marked *la ~ law* "different." *La*, we must conclude, does not always behave like a member of the PALM class.

Like in NY11, in SK12 the PALM ~ LOT pairs were overwhelmingly said to rhyme: 91% for *father ~ bother*, 90% for *salami ~ Tommy*. And again, almost all the 109 subjects (95%) marked *la ~ law* "different." While *la ~ law* was marked "different" more than LOT ~ THOUGHT (75%), the two variables were correlated, as expected: the point-biserial correlation coefficient r_{pb} = +0.35 in NY11, +0.25 in SK12.

The younger Seekonk subjects (27 in SK8, 70 in SK4) marked fewer LOT ~ THOUGHT pairs "different": 52% in SK8, 37% in SK4. They were also less "different" on *la ~ law*: 78% in SK8, 71% in SK4. And the two variables were more correlated: +0.44 in SK8, +0.45 in SK4. Again, there was an asymmetry: of the 120 Seekonk subjects who were mainly distinct on LOT ~ THOUGHT (with a score of 4 of 7 or higher), 97.5% marked *la ~ law* "different"; but of the 20 subjects who scored a fully merged 0 on LOT ~ THOUGHT, only 50% marked *la ~ law* "same."

This data can be accounted for by saying that roughly half of New York and Seekonk subjects mark *la ~ law* "different" regardless of their low vowel system for ordinary words. For the rest, *la ~ law* reflects the merged or distinct status of PALM = LOT versus THOUGHT, just like *cot ~ caught*. The split in the treatment of *la ~ law* is constant across the Seekonk age levels.

What is not constant is how subjects responded to the rhyming questions. Younger Seekonk subjects were more likely to say *father ~ bother* and *salami ~ Tommy* did not rhyme. The 10% rate of "nonrhyming" in SK12 becomes 15% in SK8, and 26% in SK4.

We want to know if the increased nonrhyming reflects the development of an actual PALM ~ LOT distinction, or just a decrease in the ability to identify and judge rhymes. We know the LOT ~ THOUGHT merger is affecting Seekonk; could younger subjects be adopting ENE's PALM ~ LOT distinction as well?

It is unlikely that they are, as there is no significant correlation between LOT ~ THOUGHT scores and PALM ~ LOT nonrhyming. In the small SK8 data set, r = −0.14 (n.s.). In SK4, r = +0.003. We conclude that the increased nonrhyming by younger Seekonk subjects is unrelated to the progress of linguistic change. Younger children are simply worse at judging rhymes than minimal pairs.

3.6.2. THE STATUS OF *PALM* WHERE *LOT* AND *THOUGHT* ARE MAINLY MERGED.

3.6.2.1. *Massachusetts State College.* Recall from section 3.5.2 that 29 of the Massachusetts State College students had origins in Eastern New England; 15 of them scored a fully merged 0 of 7 on LOT ~ THOUGHT, the rest between 1 and 4. Ten of the 15 (67%) who scored 0 marked *la ~ law* "different" and said *father ~ bother* and *salami ~ Tommy* "don't rhyme." This is the full ENE pattern—PALM ≠ LOT = THOUGHT. None had a clear 3-M system— PALM = LOT = THOUGHT—with *la ~ law* "same" and both PALM ~ LOT items rhyming.

Of the 14 who scored higher than 0, seven (50%) had the ENE combination of *la ~ law* "different" and PALM ~ LOT nonrhyming. The difference in proportion is not statistically significant, but it may mean that subjects who have trouble accessing their linguistic competence on the LOT ~ THOUGHT items also struggle with the rhyming questions.

Five of the 29 "native" subjects said that both PALM ~ LOT pairs rhymed. No information gathered on the survey, such as parental backgrounds, predicts who had this minority response. It may reflect change toward the 3-M system, but not necessarily. The correlation between the two PALM ~ LOT items, *father ~ bother* and *salami ~ Tommy*, is not as high as might be expected ($\phi = 0.49$), suggesting that chance plays a role in how the rhyming items are answered.

3.6.2.2. *Brookline, Massachusetts.* In the 225-subject BR12 data set, there was a 77% rate of PALM ~ LOT rhyming (MS15 had a 37% rate overall). *La ~ law* was only 61% "different" in BR12, the lowest rate observed so far (cf. 91% in MS15). Together, this might suggest a considerable amount of three-way merger in Brookline. However, only 16% of subjects rhymed both PALM ~ LOT pairs, marked *la ~ law* "same," and scored 0 out of 7 on LOT ~ THOUGHT, thus indicating a sure 3-M system.

But this is more than the 4% of BR12 subjects who showed the full local ENE pattern (cf. 29% of MS15). Indeed, almost as many (3%) had a full MAIN pattern, scoring 7 of 7 "different" on LOT ~ THOUGHT, marking *la ~ law* "different" and rhyming PALM ~ LOT.

Only 23% of BR12 subjects, then, could be unambiguously classified as either 3-M, ENE, or MAIN based on the survey (many more would probably have shown one of these patterns more clearly in speech production). In each of these three groups, most subjects had never lived anywhere other than Brookline. We can thus examine whether their parents' origins help explain their systems.

All four Brookline natives with the full MAIN system have both parents from those dialect areas or the South. This makes sense: most BR12 peers do not have the MAIN system, so any subjects having it must have learned it from their families.

Of the seven natives with the local ENE system, most have at least one local parent. However, one young man has both parents from Long Island (MAIN). He must have acquired not only the LOT ~ THOUGHT merger, but also the PALM ~ LOT contrast, from ENE peers.

But such an acquisition, while possible, is not easy. Of six in-movers to Brookline from the MAIN area, none consistently contrasted PALM ~ LOT. Of the 138 Brookline natives, there were 22 with both parents from the Mid-Atlantic or Inland North. Only one had acquired the ENE system, two had retained the full MAIN systems of their parents, and 13 were intermediate in one way or another. The other six subjects were fully 3-M.

This three-way-merged pattern is probably the natural result of a collision between MAIN parental input and ENE peer input. Leaving phonetic details aside, both of these dialects have two low vowel categories. The learning task is to transfer the LOT word class from being merged with PALM, to being merged with THOUGHT; this would involve a difficult unmerging. It makes sense that a "compromise" three-way merger usually arises instead, especially as children continue to speak with their MAIN families even after they acquire ENE peers.

Though children with MAIN parents may be the originators of the 3-M pattern, if enough children in a community like Brookline become three-way merged, this pattern will tend to spread to the children of local parents with the ENE system.

Just 14 of the 138 native Brookline subjects had both parents from eastern Massachusetts.[17] Three of them had the full ENE pattern, like their parents probably do; one had the full 3-M pattern. As usual, most were intermediate in some way, on the survey if not in "real life."

The BR12 natives were in their last year of high school, but their dialects must have largely been formed in one of the town's eight elementary schools, which students attend from kindergarten to eighth grade. Differences between the alumni of these schools give us further reason to believe that the 3-M pattern originates with children with MAIN/ENE contact in their backgrounds and spreads from them to other children.

Of those who came to Brookline High from Driscoll, Lawrence, and Runkle schools, 54% had at least one parent from the MAIN area; 19% had both parents from there. For Baker, Heath, and Lincoln schools, only 30% had one MAIN parent; 10% had two. It is perhaps no surprise by now that the Brookline natives with one or both MAIN parents marked more

LOT ~ THOUGHT items "different" (1.60 vs. 1.13) and were more likely to say the PALM ~ LOT items rhymed (85% vs. 76%). But we are also interested in the influence of these children on their peers who have no MAIN family background.

First, we note a mild difference for LOT ~ THOUGHT; the 30 such subjects from the low-MAIN-influence schools scored 1.03, while the 18 from the high-MAIN schools scored 1.33. This difference is in the expected direction if the MAIN-background children are influencing the others, but is not significant by the Mann-Whitney test ($p = .37$).

For PALM ~ LOT, the difference is more clear. Of the 30 subjects from low-MAIN schools, whose mainly ENE systems we hypothesize would be more intact, six rhymed neither *father ~ bother* nor *salami ~ Tommy*, and 10 others said one item did not rhyme. By contrast, all 18 high-MAIN-influence subjects rhymed at least one item, and 14 rhymed both. The 89% rhyming rate of these peers is as high as the group with MAIN family backgrounds themselves, while the low-MAIN group's 63% rate is significantly lower, by the Mann-Whitney test ($p = .02$).

The effect of dialect contact is symmetrical: a child with the MAIN pattern tends to lose his LOT ~ THOUGHT distinction upon contact with the ENE pattern, and a child with ENE tends to lose her PALM ~ LOT distinction on contact with MAIN. Both can emerge with the 3-M pattern.

Note that the differences between K–8 schools are still visible in twelfth grade, and this is not because Brookline High School students simply retain their peer groups from elementary school. As chapter 5 will further demonstrate, vowel inventories are more malleable in elementary school than they are in high school. Children may exhibit linguistic patterns years before they make overt social use of them in preadolescence (Eckert 2008) and adolescence (Eckert 1989).

3.6.2.3. *Attleboro, Massachusetts.* Comments made in Attleboro about the difficulty of the rhyming item *Osama ~ comma* led to its being changed to *Tommy ~ salami* in most other communities. And, as table 3.20 shows, the performance of this item was definitely unacceptable, especially among younger subjects. There should be a positive correlation between the two PALM ~ LOT pairs, as there is in MS15 and to a lesser extent BR12, but *Osama ~ comma* is at best uncorrelated with *father ~ bother* in Attleboro. And contrary to the natural direction of change, it rhymes less as we go from AB12 to AB8 to AB4. In AB4, it seems to have been answered almost randomly, unless subjects actually had the "history quiz" tendency to mark it differently from *father ~ bother*.

TABLE 3.20
"Rhyming" Percentages and Correlations among PALM ~ LOT Items

Community	Percentage "Rhyme"		φ Correlation	N
	father ~ bother	salami ~ Tommy		
MS15	40%	34%	+0.52	35
BR12	78%	76%	+0.18	225
	father ~ bother	Osama ~ comma		
AB12	68%	72%	+0.0005	278
AB8	78%	66%	−0.08	385
AB4	72%	46%	−0.15	317

We will ignore *Osama ~ comma* and assess the status of PALM using *father ~ bother* and *la ~ law*. Unlike the decreased rhyming of *Osama ~ comma*, which would contravene Garde's Principle if it were real, the observed change in *la ~ law*—marked "same" by 22% of AB12, 35% of AB8, and 48% of AB4—may reflect substantial progress of the three-way merger. Recall section 3.6.1's estimate that roughly half of subjects with the PALM ~ LOT merger will still mark *la ~ law* "different."

Attleboro lies on the dialect boundary, but the total subject pool includes those who moved there from different communities on either side of the boundary line. Even among native subjects, many have parents from well inside the ENE or MAIN dialect area.

And then there is South Attleboro, where adults exhibit the MAIN pattern, but children are now almost as merged on LOT ~ THOUGHT as their peers in the rest of the city (see §3.5.4). Table 3.21 shows the number of native South Attleboro subjects showing one of the major low vowel patterns, against the backdrop of most subjects' being intermediate.[18]

Some twelfth graders from South Attleboro have either the formerly local MAIN pattern (usually accompanied by MAIN parents), the "interloper" ENE pattern (usually with ENE parents), or the "compromise" 3-M pattern. The eighth grade shows an increase in 3-M at the expense of the

TABLE 3.21
Low Vowel Systems of South Attleboro Natives

Grade	ENE	3-M	MAIN	Intermediate	N
ABS12	8%	7%	5%	80%	61
ABS8	2%	15%	2%	82%	55
ABS4	6%	28%	0%	81%	32

other two patterns. The fourth-grade cohort has no examples of MAIN, two of ENE (with parents from there), and a still higher rate of 3-M (with parents from all areas).

On the other side of the historical dialect boundary, table 3.22 shows that there is also progress toward a three-way-merged system in "regular Attleboro." Presumably because the peer group is more thoroughly merged on LOT ~ THOUGHT, the MAIN pattern is virtually absent, even though there are many subjects here with parents from the MAIN region. The complete ENE system is present at a low level, among subjects with ENE parentage.

But the most common complete system is becoming 3-M. And, as in Brookline and South Attleboro, this pattern is not limited to subjects who have experienced obvious conflict in their low vowel history, between parents and peers, or with their mother and father from different places. Several of the 3-M subjects have parents from Attleboro.

It does not seem likely that the apparent-time increase in the three-way merger is a form of age-grading (Labov 1994, 83–84). There is no reason to think that fourth graders have not yet acquired all the vowel contrasts of their dialects. But is it possible that we are looking at error on the survey, rather than a real increase in PALM ~ LOT merging?

Simply circling "same" or "rhyme" for each item, down the left-hand column (see figure 3.1), would have resulted in a 3-M response; but any such surveys were eliminated by *barn ~ born.* And we saw how the youngest Attleboro subjects dealt with *Osama ~ comma;* they answered it close to randomly. But the other PALM ~ LOT rhyming item was different.

For *father ~ bother,* 68% of AB12 said they rhymed, which increased to 78% for AB8. The fact that it drops back to 72% for AB4 probably reflects some of the confusion that younger subjects have shown with the rhyming items. So rather than being the cause of the 3-M patterns, young subjects' errors on *father ~ bother,* if not in other places, have probably led to an understatement of the amount of three-way merger in the community.

As chapter 4 will demonstrate, the native South Attleboro system was once MAIN, while that of "regular Attleboro" was ENE. The school survey suggests that for fourth and eighth graders, if not as completely for twelfth

TABLE 3.22
Low Vowel Systems of "Regular Attleboro" Natives

Grade	ENE	3-M	MAIN	Intermediate	N
AB12	9%	7%	0%	84%	123
AB8	6%	18.5%	0.5%	75%	201
AB4	3%	17%	0%	80%	104

graders, LOT and THOUGHT have largely merged in South Attleboro. Meanwhile, PALM and LOT are doing the same in the rest of the city.

A plausible trigger for such mergers is schoolchildren coming together from diverse family dialect backgrounds. Of native South Attleboro subjects, 30% had at least one parent from ENE, while 24% of "regular Attleboro" natives had at least one parent from MAIN. The figure for Attleboro is fairly constant, while the proportion of ENE parents in South Attleboro seems to be decreasing. These issues will be pursued further in chapter 5.

3.7. CONCLUSIONS FROM THE SCHOOL SURVEY

The school survey was an unsophisticated questionnaire that simply asked how a dozen pairs of words sounded. There was a large amount of variation in the responses. But administering the survey to a large number of subjects yielded quantitative results regarding the factors influencing low vowel inventories. Mixed-model logistic regression distinguished between by-subject variation, by-item variation, and between-subject variation.

Subject variation was substantial everywhere, meaning that subjects' scores for the seven LOT ~ THOUGHT pairs could never be predicted with great accuracy, let alone their responses to individual items. Some subject variation would correspond regularly to factors that were not asked about on the survey, while some would reflect more idiosyncratic sources of error.

Among the seven items asking, from a phonological point of view, "Do you distinguish LOT and THOUGHT?" there was no single pattern favoring and disfavoring the merger. For example, *collar ~ caller* was most often marked "different" only where the merger was the norm, while *Moll ~ mall* was most often marked "same" where the distinction was predominant. It was not clear what production patterns went along with the many intermediate responses.

The most ubiquitous between-subject effect was that of Origin. Subjects who had moved to a community from a different dialect area were always different from the natives. However, their responses were also usually distinguishable from what they would have been if they had never moved.

The age at which a subject moved from a LOT ~ THOUGHT-distinguishing dialect area to a merged one had a small effect; those who moved at a younger age ended up more merged, on average. How long ago they had moved was statistically unimportant to their response. The conclusion is that people learn a merger relatively quickly after being exposed to it.

The origins of subjects' mothers and fathers were also significant predictors of their response. This was the case even for high school students who had lived in one place all their lives. If their initial parental input—supplemented by ongoing parental and other family relationships—was different from their peer group's, there was almost always a significant effect on their survey responses. For fourth-grade students, parental effects proved weaker, possibly as a consequence of overall worse performance on the survey, but certainly an area for future investigation.

The influence of peers does not override subjects' earliest-acquired vowel systems. In merged communities, children with distinct parents do acquire the merger, but not as fully as those with merged parents. Some children do acquire it completely, others hardly at all.

So among native Brookline twelfth graders, the most common LOT ~ THOUGHT score was 0 of 7 "different," regardless of parental origin. But while only 6% (of 17) with merged parents scored above the midpoint, 23% (of 22) with distinct parents did so, including two 7s.

For native Attleboro twelfth graders, only 8% (of 40) with merged parents scored above the midpoint, the highest being a 5. But 46% (of 13) with distinct parents scored 5, 6, or 7.

The factors promoting merger—a merged mother, father, or peers—interact negatively; their effects are not fully cumulative. Having merged parents restricts the apparent effect of peers, and vice versa. This follows from two points: a distinction is harder to learn than a merger, and learning a merger has an endpoint, after which a speaker is fully merged. Any merging influence reduces the effective influence that can subsequently occur in the same direction.

As a consequence of the greater difficulty of learning the distinction, we see larger parental effects among native Seekonk twelfth graders. Of the 37 with distinct parents, 62% marked 7 of 7 "different"; only 8% scored below the midpoint. But for six subjects each with a single merged parent, the score distribution was 2×1, 2×2, 1×4, 1×7.

The data on PALM was of inferior quantity and quality—relying on rhyming pairs (pace Labov 1994, 354)—but it also reflected multiple influences, partial accommodation, and the greater ease of merging over unmerging.

Gender played a small role when the LOT ~ THOUGHT merger was in progress in Seekonk; females favored it. Perhaps more interestingly, gender interacted with the parental effects when peers were merged. Boys were more influenced toward their fathers, girls more toward their mothers—unless girls actually distanced themselves from their fathers.

Administered across three grade levels, the survey in Seekonk documented the rapid advancement of the LOT ~ THOUGHT merger. In South Attleboro, the same change had largely already happened, and it could be incipient in New York as well. In all these cases, the change would be from the MAIN (PALM = LOT ≠ THOUGHT) to the 3-M (PALM = LOT = THOUGHT) low vowel system. This latter system, with only one nonfront low monophthong, was also observed to be on the rise in the former ENE (PALM ≠ LOT = THOUGHT) territory of "regular Attleboro" and Brookline.

The survey data shows there are no absolute rules regarding the acquisition (or nonacquisition) of mergers. Even qualified statements such as the following may be too strong:

A person seven or under will almost certainly acquire a new dialect perfectly, and a person 14 or over almost certainly will not. In between those ages, people will vary. [Chambers 1992, 689]

Chambers is referring to children who move, but the survey shows that even children who have never moved give different responses based on where their parents grew up.

The relationship between subjects' survey judgments and their speech productions is not yet fully understood. But if the perceptual survey data reflects one facet of linguistic competence, then we must acknowledge that competence is affected regularly and sensitively by both recent and distant influences in people's lives.

And a complete phonological theory may need to allow for multiple, coexisting representations. Some people are best understood as simply merged or distinct with respect to a vowel contrast, while others may need to be recognized as being both merged and distinct.

4. THE GEOGRAPHIC STUDY

THE GEOGRAPHIC STUDY was inspired by observations reviewed in chapter 2: the dialects spoken in Boston, Massachusetts, and Providence, Rhode Island, differ notably, despite the cities' being less than 50 miles apart (see figure 4.1). The territory in between the two state capitals has not been extensively studied since the 1930s, and the results reported in that era proved inaccurate.

This chapter explores the low vowels of this intermediate area. Although there are no physical obstacles to communication or migration in this part of New England, a sharp dialect boundary was still found, especially for speakers born early in the twentieth century. By then, an original three-vowel system (3-D) had been largely succeeded by two different two-vowel systems (MAIN and ENE). This two-vowel phase shows the clearest geographical boundary, a phenomenon that emerged centuries after its seeds were planted in the original patterns of settlement. Recently, both of the two-vowel systems are tending to collapse into a system with a single low vowel (3-M).

For most of the twentieth century, though, Boston speakers have shown an ENE pattern, where PALM, in low central-to-front position, is distinct from a low back, variably rounded, sometimes ingliding LOT = THOUGHT. Meanwhile, Providence speakers show the MAIN pattern where a low central PALM = LOT is clearly distinct from a raised back THOUGHT.[1]

Both dialects have reduced the original inventory from three vowels to two, but by merging the word classes in different ways. The vowels' phonetic realizations (see table 4.1) are also staggered, so that tokens from any class could be misidentified by speakers of the other dialect, or at least perceived as foreign.

MAIN listeners report hearing ENE's [a] in PALM as very fronted, but have no other category to put it in. But they tend to hear ENE's [ɒ] in LOT as [ɔ] (their own THOUGHT) and the same [ɒ] in THOUGHT as [ɑ] (their own PALM = LOT) (Moulton 1990, 129). ENE listeners report analogous misunderstandings.

Other speakers are more accurate. An 82-year-old man from Millville, Massachusetts, said, "I'm gonna tell you where the boundaries are. The boundaries are between Millville and Uxbridge! ... In Uxbridge, J-o-h-n, they'll say J[ɒ]n. Down here, it's J[ɑ]n. Just in seven miles." This man clearly believed that a sharp linguistic boundary existed between adjacent towns.

TABLE 4.1

The Low Vowel Systems of Providence (MAIN) and Boston (ENE)

Example word	*father*	*bother*	*daughter*
Word class	PALM	LOT	THOUGHT
Providence	[ɑ]		[ɔ]
Boston	[a]	[ɒ]	

If, instead, a transition zone existed between fully distinct and fully merged areas, any combination of the following could occur in that zone:

1. the distinction is maintained irregularly (merger by transfer/lexical diffusion);
2. the distinction is maintained regularly in some phonological contexts, but not others;
3. the phonetic distance between the vowels decreases gradually across the zone;
4. the boundaries for production and perception are both sharp, but do not match;
5. individuals employ the distinction in some speech styles but not in others;
6. individuals are fully distinct or merged, but there is variation between them (by age, class, gender, and/or other factors).

Section 2.5 argued that the LOT ~ THOUGHT merger did not begin in Boston and spread wave-like or hierarchically to the smaller communities of Eastern New England.[2] Given its wide distribution in American English, the PALM ~ LOT merger is even less likely to have originated in Providence.

If the two mergers were spreading like waves toward each other, there might be an area in between that neither had reached, an area of three-way distinction. On the other hand, if the waves had already met and crossed, there would be an intermediate zone where the three-way-merged system prevailed.

This chapter will show that neither type of transition zone now exists. The ENE two-vowel system ends where the MAIN two-vowel system begins. And the boundary between them is close to an early settlement boundary. This, along with the historical data presented in chapter 2, points to internal change as the cause of both areas' mergers.

Indeed, the geographic diffusion of change may occur less frequently than is often assumed (see Andersen 1988). When a change spreads across a dialect boundary to an area which would probably not have undergone it otherwise, a diffusion account is certainly motivated. But if a town was settled at the same time, and by similar people, as a nearby city—or even by people from that city—their dialects' persistent similarity can derive from parallel reactions to the same inherited structural pressures, rather than parallel inundation by the same waves of external influence.[3]

This chapter analyzes speech from interviews conducted in 2005 with some 200 senior citizens and young adults in a 40-community study area. Section 4.2 gives the results of an impressionistic analysis of the interviews. Section 4.3 discusses further interviews in communities found to have undergone change. Section 4.4 presents acoustic analyses of selected speakers exemplifying the principal systems. Section 4.5 deals with the possible interaction between low vowel change and the reintroduction of postvocalic /r/; and section 4.6 is a general discussion of results and conclusions.

4.1. RESULTS OF AUDITORY ANALYSIS

In an area spanning the linguistic boundary, 40 cities and towns were investigated: 29 in Massachusetts and 11 in Rhode Island. This study area, including small towns, suburbs, and medium-sized cities, is shaded on figure 4.1, and shown with community names and abbreviations on figure 4.2 (the abbreviations also appear on table 2.1).

In each place, data was collected from at least one senior citizen and two young adults who had lived there since an early age. The seniors were contacted with the help of local senior centers, and interviewed there or at

FIGURE 4.1
Southern New England: Key Cities and Study Area

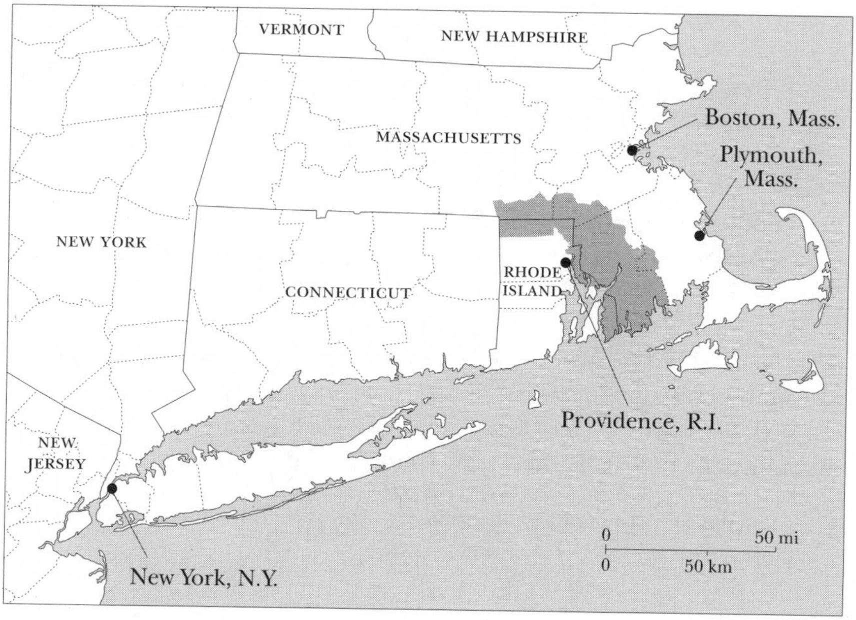

FIGURE 4.2

The Study Area: 40 Communities
(29 in Massachusetts, 11 in Rhode Island)

their homes. The young adults were almost all interviewed at their work-places. Most were found in retail and service establishments; others were municipal employees.

The final sample consisted of 67 seniors aged from 58 to 97 (most in their 70s and 80s) and 113 young adults aged from 15 to 33. Along with providing spontaneous speech, interviewees read ten cards, with sentence pairs containing over 100 low vowel tokens. Each reading card had a mini-mal pair to be repeated and judged "same" or "different." For example:

After the fourth operation on his heart, Don started walking farther and jog-ging more. He's a lot calmer now.

> Donna named her daughter Dawn to honor her father's aunt, whose death she
> was mourning.

This "covert" side of the card yielded tokens of *Don* and *Dawn* without
undue attention being called to those two words. The "overt" side was more
like a traditional minimal pair:

> **Don** started walking farther
> named her daughter **Dawn**

For this side of the card, after the repetition, speakers were asked, "Do
those two names sound the same or different to you?"

Each card also had other low vowel words (e.g., *heart*); some of these
could be paired with words on other cards (e.g., *hot*). Altogether some 30
tokens of PALM, 50 of LOT, and 30 of THOUGHT were elicited this way.

The overt minimal pairs were: *Don ~ Dawn, cot ~ caught, knotty ~ naughty*,
and *collar ~ caller* for LOT ~ THOUGHT; *balm ~ bomb* and *lager ~ logger* for
PALM ~ LOT; *ah ~ aw, Pa's ~ pause*, and *Ra ~ raw* for PALM ~ THOUGHT.[4]

From auditory impressions of these pairs and of spontaneous speech,
each speaker was classified as either 3-D (three low vowels: PALM ≠ LOT ≠
THOUGHT), ENE (two vowels: PALM ≠ LOT = THOUGHT), MAIN (two vowels: PALM = LOT ≠ THOUGHT), 3-M (one vowel: PALM = LOT = THOUGHT), or
unclear.

Despite a bias toward labeling a speaker "unclear" if there was any
doubt, there were relatively few such cases. Minimal-pair perceptions are
not dealt with here; however, they usually agreed well with productions.

4.1.1. SENIOR CITIZENS. For the 67 seniors, figure 4.3 shows a sharp picture:
58 of them (87%) exhibit one of the two-vowel systems; six (9%) retain the
three-vowel system; and three (4%) have unclear patterns.

4.1.1.1. *Two-Vowel Systems*. The 26 right-pointing triangles in figure 4.3,
each standing for a MAIN speaker, are found in all but one of the Rhode
Island communities and extend into Massachusetts in two areas. The 32
left-pointing triangles show the extent of the ENE system.

The location of the MAIN-ENE boundary reflects the settlement history outlined in section 2.1. Most of Massachusetts (formerly Massachusetts Bay and Plymouth colonies) merged LOT and THOUGHT; Rhode Island
merged PALM and LOT.

Perhaps through maritime contacts, the mixed-settlement towns on the
east shore of Narragansett Bay came to resemble Rhode Island settlements
more than the Plymouth Colony towns they sprang from politically. If this

FIGURE 4.3
Low Vowel Systems of 67 Senior Citizens

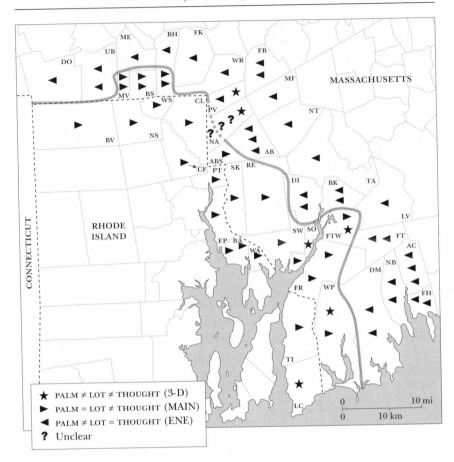

★ PALM ≠ LOT ≠ THOUGHT (3-D)
▶ PALM = LOT ≠ THOUGHT (MAIN)
◀ PALM ≠ LOT = THOUGHT (ENE)
? Unclear

happened to Fall River, which grew into an industrial city, then Fall River could have brought its own influence to bear on towns nearby.

A similar fate befell the Massachusetts towns just north across the state line from Woonsocket, Rhode Island. Their seventeenth-century Massachusetts settlement history would predict ENE systems, but MAIN patterns are found instead. This may be due to contact between those towns (Blackstone, Millville, South Bellingham) and the city of Woonsocket, which became a major industrial center in the early nineteenth century, and/or to the out-migration from that city that later turned those towns into suburbs of it.

In three places, the boundary cuts through a city or town. Seniors from the north part of Bellingham, central Attleboro, and East Freetown were all ENE. But in South Bellingham, South Attleboro, and Assonet (the western part of Freetown), MAIN patterns were found. The MAIN sections of these municipalities still have distinct identities, and even more so when these seniors were growing up. Students from South Bellingham attended high school in Woonsocket; some from Assonet went to high school in Fall River.

South Attleboro is geographically and economically close to Pawtucket, Rhode Island, but one high school has served the whole of Attleboro since the nineteenth century. The boundary within Attleboro implies that contact at high-school age does not suffice to level a vowel system difference (chapter 3 reached this conclusion as well, though it also found this particular difference within Attleboro to have collapsed).

4.1.1.2. *Other Systems.* Six seniors gave evidence of the 3-D pattern, as found in many earlier records. While their LOT was sometimes shorter, in terms of quality it overlapped considerably with PALM and THOUGHT. Two of the six were older male "Yankees" (of English descent), from relatively remote places: Assonet, Massachusetts (age 90), and Little Compton, Rhode Island (age 88). The other 3-D seniors were from less remote places, and two even had immigrant parents, which would be expected to disfavor such a conservative pattern.

Three seniors had unclear systems, and all were from North Attleborough, Massachusetts. The unique status of this town is mysterious, especially as it separated from Attleboro only in 1887. Perhaps its location on the main road between Providence and Boston led to more contact from both directions, keeping its dialect intermediate, with LOT ~ THOUGHT judged "probably distinct" and PALM ~ LOT "possibly distinct."

None of the senior citizens had a system with only one low vowel phoneme. The three-way merger (3-M) was found only among the young adult speakers.

4.1.2. YOUNG ADULTS. The more complex pattern of 113 young adults is shown in figure 4.4. Eighty-seven speakers (77%) are either MAIN or ENE, and the boundary between those patterns has changed little, despite there being substantial interaction across that boundary for most of its length.

No young adults retained the 3-D system, but 6 (5%) were clearly 3-M. Twenty speakers' systems (18%) were intermediate or could not be determined from the data collected. Table 4.2 summarizes the low vowel systems of the 180 seniors and young adults.

In the communities where the seniors had MAIN systems, 48 of 62 young adults (77%) did too. Five were ENE, one was 3-M, and eight were unclear. In the old ENE territory, 32 of 47 (68%) retained that system. One was MAIN, four were 3-M, and ten were unclear. And in formerly unclear

FIGURE 4.4
Low Vowel Systems of 113 Young Adults

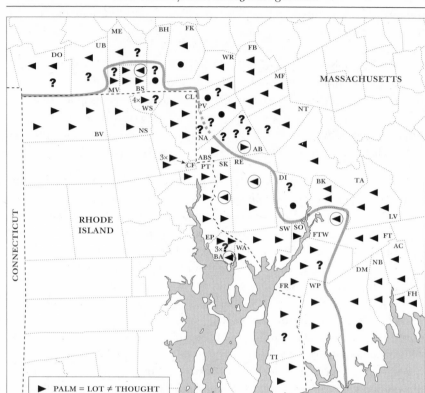

TABLE 4.2
Low Vowel Systems of the 180 Geographic Study Speakers

	3-D	MAIN	ENE	3-M	Unclear	Total
Senior citizens	6	26	32	0	3	67
Young adults	0	49	38	6	20	113

North Attleborough, one young adult was ENE, one was 3-M, and two were unclear.

Of these young adults, some differed from the seniors in their community due to parental influence; other cases suggest community change or individual idiosyncrasy. For example, while there were only three young adults whose parents both grew up on the other side of the dialect boundary from themselves, all three patterned with their ENE parents, not their MAIN peers. And of those with one parent from each side of the boundary, 33% (3 of 9) were 3-M, compared to only 3% (3 of 100) of the rest (Fisher's Exact Test, p = .007).

Among the seniors, there were three whose parents did not match their peers, and at least four whose parents did not match each other; but in all those cases the subject acquired the peers' two-vowel system. This suggests that the ENE and MAIN systems were more robust then, and that a different dynamic is now at work whereby unclear and 3-M patterns replace them. Note that 86% of the 76 young adults aged 20 and older had a clear ENE or MAIN pattern, but only 59% of the 37 teenagers did (Fisher's Exact Test, p = .004).

The interviews of young adults in South Bellingham (3-M, unclear) and Assonet (ENE) suggested those places were no longer true MAIN sub-areas (Barrington, R.I., was another such case). To find out if and when these changes occurred, more interviews were conducted in the formerly split municipalities.

4.2. MORE EVIDENCE FROM THREE FORMERLY "MAIN" COMMUNITIES

While one gauge of a vowel system's robustness in a community is how readily it is acquired by children who inherited other systems from their parents or earlier peers, the best way to date a change is by looking at speakers whose parents have the old local pattern.

Seniors of this type in two Massachusetts sub-communities, South Bellingham (ages 70 and 58) and Assonet (age 85), showed clear MAIN patterns, while young adults there were different: unclear in South Bellingham (age 18) and ENE in Assonet (age 20). The latter represents a more unexpected change, as it involves an unmerger as well as a merger.

In South Attleboro, a 26-year-old woman and a 62-year-old man were both MAIN, but the man's son, an 18-year-old from chapter 5's family study (and with a MAIN mother), was 3-M, as were many younger children.

Using a revised set of methods for eliciting tokens of the vowels of interest, including "semantic differential" questions like "What's the difference between a spa and a salon?" a further investigation was carried out in these three places. The goal was to see when, and how quickly, low vowel patterns changed there.

In South Attleboro, two 20-year-olds still exhibited a clear MAIN system. One had two MAIN parents, from Seekonk and Pawtucket. The other moved from Panama at age 9 and is a good barometer of the peer group pattern since she had no English exposure from parents.

The difference between these 20-year-olds and the 18-year-old points to a fairly sudden change. To extrapolate, children born in 1985 or before to MAIN (or foreign) parents acquired the MAIN low vowel system characteristic of adjacent Rhode Island: PALM = LOT ≠ THOUGHT. Those born in 1987 or later learned a three-way-merged (3-M) system, where PALM = LOT = THOUGHT.[5] The reasons for this merger will be discussed starting in section 4.5.

In South Bellingham, a 46-year-old and a 41-year-old, both with local parents, displayed the same clear MAIN pattern as the seniors previously noted. The son of the 41-year-old was 20, and both noted a feeling of isolation from the rest of their town and a closer connection with Woonsocket, Rhode Island (MAIN).[6] However, the son showed a 3-M system in spontaneous speech, along with inconsistent behavior on minimal pairs. A 15-year-old with MAIN parents (New York and Rhode Island) was clearly 3-M.

We can conclude that South Bellinghamites born up to 1965 have a MAIN system, assuming their parents do too. Sometime after that, but no later than 1985, PALM = LOT and THOUGHT merged, resulting in the 3-M pattern.

It is tempting to link this merger to a demographic shift. Since the 1950s, Bellingham's population expanded, with many people arriving from Greater Boston. Ties between South Bellingham and North Bellingham strengthened, while those with Woonsocket diminished.

In Assonet, the original study found a 90-year-old man with a 3-D system, while his 85-year-old wife was MAIN. However, a 20-year-old man had an ENE system, despite MAIN parents. Was this an idiosyncrasy, or a surprising community change, involving the unmerging of PALM and LOT and the merging of LOT and THOUGHT?

The follow-up study found three women, aged 74, 53, and 50, with the MAIN pattern. The 74-year-old, like the older subjects, had gone to grade school locally, but the other two were exposed to ENE influence throughout their schooling. Before 1950, Assonet children attended local schools through 8th grade; if they went to high school, it was in Fall River (MAIN). Since 1950, they have gone to elementary school together with an equal number from East Freetown (ENE). And since 1959, they have gone to middle and high school with children from the town of Lakeville (ENE).

A 31-year-old woman seemed to have an ENE system in spontaneous speech, but on minimal pairs she was MAIN, like her parents (from Somerset and Fall River). Her 28-year-old brother had a clear ENE pattern in both styles. This means the 20-year-old was no exception; Assonet changed from MAIN to ENE. However, this shift to ENE was apparently short-lived: three young women born around 1988, all with local or MAIN parents, were fairly clear examples of the 3-M pattern (which was also found in the youngest South Attleboro and South Bellingham subjects).

To recap, Assonet speakers born between 1920 and 1955 acquired the MAIN pattern. This includes the first students to attend school with ENE children. After a gap in our data, those born between 1975 and 1985 showed the ENE pattern, even if they had MAIN parents. This implies that they reversed their parents' merger of PALM ~ LOT and acquired their peers' merger of LOT ~ THOUGHT.

The conditions for such a presumably rare event may well have been in place. These children attended an elementary school where just as many (from East Freetown) had the ENE system. And in middle and high school, they would have met even more ENE children (from Lakeville). Also, substantial direct immigration from the Boston area began to affect Assonet during this period.

Each of these three formerly MAIN subcommunities has, over the decades, turned away from a declining, adjacent MAIN city to the south: Pawtucket for South Attleboro, Woonsocket for South Bellingham, and Fall River for Assonet. And in all three—though only quite recently in Assonet—there has been significant immigration from the Greater Boston area.

The level of commuting to the city of Boston, some 40 miles away, has actually been steady in South Attleboro (from 4.2% of workers in 1990 to 3.9% in 2000) and South Bellingham (5.3% to 5.2%). But it has increased, starting from a lower level, in Freetown (2.1% to 3.6%); data at the subcommunity level (Assonet) was not available (Census Bureau 1994, 2004).

Over the same period, there has been a decline in commuting to the adjacent MAIN cities: from South Attleboro to Pawtucket (from 7.2% of workers in 1990 to 5.0% in 2000), South Bellingham to Woonsocket (9.9% to 3.6%), and Freetown to Fall River (14.5% to 12.2%). More people in South Bellingham now commute all the way to Boston than work in the city next door; the same is almost true in South Attleboro.

In Freetown, a much higher proportion, though a declining one, continues to commute to Fall River. Economic ties are stronger there, despite the "disintegration" of Fall River alluded to by several Assonet subjects. Regardless of such adult connections, young people in Assonet have moved away from Fall River and MAIN, linguistically.

Chapter 5 will deal with young people merging PALM = LOT and THOUGHT in other formerly MAIN communities. In the old ENE area, too, the PALM ≠ LOT = THOUGHT distinction seems to be weakening, with the same outcome: 3-M.

TABLE 4.3
Decreasing Stability of the ENE System:
Behavior of PALM ~ LOT = THOUGHT versus Age

	Ages 24–33	Ages 20–23	Ages 15–19
PALM ≠ LOT = THOUGHT (ENE)	15	9	8
PALM ≟ LOT = THOUGHT (unclear)	1	5	4
PALM = LOT = THOUGHT (3-M)	0	1	3

Section 4.1.2 noted that teenagers were less likely than older young adults to preserve the MAIN and ENE systems. Within the historically ENE area, table 4.3 divides the 46 young adults with a clear LOT ~ THOUGHT merger, according to the status of PALM. We see that the younger subjects have more 3-M systems and more unclear ones (whether due to missing data or actual close or inconsistent minimal-pair productions).

In the historically MAIN area, apart from the above three subcommunities, the geographic study does not show the PALM = LOT ≠ THOUGHT distinction to be as endangered as the PALM ≠ LOT = THOUGHT contrast is in the ENE area. But chapter 5 shows that change was imminent in some of those towns as well.

When the changes in South Attleboro, South Bellingham, and Assonet are seen as part of that larger context, it becomes less attractive to explain their timing by referring to local demographic events.

4.3. ACOUSTIC ANALYSIS OF PRINCIPAL LOW VOWEL SYSTEMS

Instead of a comprehensive acoustic analysis of all the geographic study subjects, four seniors and three young adults were analyzed, illustrating the most common low vowel systems. Most were from the "focus area," the central part of the study area. Two were from South Attleboro (MAIN), two from North Attleborough (ENE and 3-M), and one from Norton (ENE). A speaker from Plainville was possibly 3-D; one from Somerset, outside the focus area, was more clearly 3-D. These seven speakers, whose parents came from the same side of the dialect boundary as they did (or else from abroad), are compared in table 4.4.

The acoustic analyses confirm the basic systems, while also revealing complexities not detectable by ear. These include differences between "overt" (minimal pair) and "covert" (sentence-embedded) reading pronunciations, as well as the possibility of regular small distinctions between two word classes that completely overlap in phonetic space.

TABLE 4.4

Summary of Background and Linguistic Behavior Based on Auditory Impressions
of Seven "Typical" Speakers to Be Analyzed Acoustically

Speaker	Community	Age	Sex	Mother from	Father from
ABS62M	S. Attleboro, Mass.	62	M	Pawtucket, R.I.	Pawtucket, R.I.
NT86F	Norton, Mass.	86	F	Norton	Milton, Mass.
PV81M	Plainville, Mass.	81	M	Poland	Poland
SO85F	Somerset, Mass.	85	F	Fall River, Mass.	Swansea, Mass.
ABS26F	S. Attleboro, Mass.	26	F	Pawtucket, R.I.	Portugal
NA30M	N. Attleborough, Mass.	30	M	Plainville	N. Attleborough
NA19F	N. Attleborough, Mass.	19	F	N. Attleborough	N. Attleborough

Speaker	r-ful	saw[ɹ]a	Broad a	LOT ~ THOUGHT	PALM ~ LOT	PALM ~ THOUGHT	System
ABS62M	some	—	Y	D	S	D?	MAIN
NT86F	no	Y	Y	S[a]	D	D	ENE
PV81M	no	Y	N	D?	D?	D	3-D?
SO85F	no	N	Y	D[a]	D	D	3-D
ABS26F	some	Y	N	D	S	D	MAIN
NA30M	no	Y	N	S?	D	D	ENE
NA19F	some	N	N	S	S	S?	3-M

a. Only *Don ~ Dawn* behaved deviantly.

4.3.1. PROCEDURES FOR ACOUSTIC ANALYSIS. Speakers' low vowels were analyzed in Praat using methods adapted from Labov, Ash, and Boberg (2006, chap. 5). For each stressed vowel of interest, a single measurement point was chosen by a combination of several criteria. Ideally, the perceived nucleus would coincide with: (1) an F_1 maximum or steady state; (2) an F_2 minimum (or maximum) or steady state; (3) an F_3 minimum, maximum, or steady state; and/or (4) an intensity maximum.

Bearing in mind these criteria in descending order of importance, the earliest qualifying point was selected (assuming it sounded and looked free of the influence of surrounding consonants). Many of the low vowels in the study area are ingliding toward similar central targets. So if we have ENE [kɔɐt] (*cot, caught*) versus [kæɐt] (*cart*), the later in the vowels we measure, the more obscured the phonemic difference will be.

Following Baranowski (2007), five formants were estimated by linear predictive coding (LPC). Occasionally, when a false formant appeared at the nucleus, four formants were used instead. For men, their maximum was set to 5000 Hz; for women and children, 5500 Hz.

Most often, the F1 and F2 tracks were strong and reasonably steady, and selection of a measurement point was not difficult. But it was noted that the consonants surrounding the measured vowel had a profound influence on the position and shape of the formant tracks.

Phonetic environment affects vowel quality as perceived by the ear, but its influence on formant measurements is even greater. This ensures that diverse tokens of any word class plotted based on acoustic measurements will always form a cloud rather than a tight cluster.

Many factors (e.g., pitch and stress) affect formant values, especially the phonological context the vowel is in. But not all allophonic effects are predictable coarticulations; some are part of "dialect competence." For example, American English dialects differ in the effects of the following environment on short *a*. Such effects should be attended to, not factored out.

4.3.1.1. *The Acoustic Analysis of Ruth Herold.* The difficulties associated with determining phonemic low vowel systems by acoustic analysis are well illustrated by reviewing Herold (1990, 60–91). Herold's auditory impressions told her that the oldest speakers in Tamaqua, Pennsylvania, had MAIN patterns, while those under 70 years of age were 3-M, pointing to fairly sudden community change. Herold (1990, 60–73) measured tokens of PALM = LOT and THOUGHT from the spontaneous speech of ten speakers. Herold eliminated all tokens before /l/, which have particularly low F2. Since THOUGHT is more common before /l/, not excluding such tokens could produce a spurious distinction.

For the three speakers identified by ear as distinct, there was no problem; unpaired *t*-tests reported highly significant differences in both F1 and F2. But several of those judged by ear as completely merged also showed significant differences in one or both formants (74).

In a multivariate analysis performed so that "the effects of phonetic conditioning were factored out" (78), although one speaker's differences became less significant, two others' were unchanged; for two speakers, accounting for environment made the acoustic word class distinction—again, unsupported by auditory impressions—appear more significant.

A multivariate approach can make such "false positives" less likely. Because THOUGHT almost never occurs before /p/ in a word, the high F2 observed for LOT before /p/ would skew LOT's overall mean in a simple *t*-test, suggesting a distinction; a multivariate regression could avoid this trap.

Herold (1990, 80–82) notes another case where many monosyllabic THOUGHT words followed by /l/ were used (*all, ball, call,* each several times), but the only examples of LOT plus /l/ were *collie* and *volleyball*. Here, if a regression factored out consonantal environment but ignored the potential effect of syllabic structure, it could lead to a false report of a word class distinction.

Herold resolves the issue by siding with her auditory judgments over these acoustic/statistical results. For the acoustic analysis in this study, deliberately paired tokens were measured, so that the paired *t*-test is an appropriate and effective statistical method.

4.3.1.2. *Phonemic Analysis by Paired Acoustic Measurements.* The measurement of some vowels from spontaneous speech is important, if only to ensure that they are being pronounced the same as in more formal methods, but using paired tokens from read sentences and minimal pairs makes it easier to assess phonemic differences.

From the ten cards read by each speaker were extracted 21 minimal pairs (and other multiples) involving PALM, LOT, and THOUGHT, given in table 4.5. The measured vowels for each speaker were plotted using an R routine that also calculated the mean F1 and F2 distances between any two word classes and their statistical significance according to paired *t*-tests.

A minor advantage of this method is that it eliminates the assumption that the vowel measurements are normally distributed, allowing its use without necessarily having vowels in a full range of phonetic environments. The differences between pairs are now assumed to have a normal distribution, a reasonable assumption if the vowels are merged—the mean difference would be zero—and not unreasonable if the vowels are distinct.

The major advantage of the paired method is that phonetic conditioning is directly factored out, as long as minimal or near-minimal pairs are used. Comparing *cot* only with *caught*, *collar* only with *caller*, and so forth, leads to a better evaluation of mergers and distinctions, although not all pairs were perfectly matched prosodically (*a narrow cot* vs. *caught the ball*) or contextually (*heart* vs. *hot* might be a problem for rhotic dialects; even though most of the speakers selected were nonrhotic, the postvocalic /r/ could still have an effect: see Labov, Yaeger, and Steiner 1972, 229–34).

Another advantage is that since the same words are analyzed for each speaker, between-speaker comparisons can be made more precisely. Data from multiple speakers can also cast light on the behavior of words. If *caught* were centralized versus *cot* in several people's speech, we might consider it a result of the different prosody of the carrier sentences, or a word-level difference, rather than a sign of merger, as we might in a single individual. Having a predetermined set of words also eliminates any unconscious bias that may affect the analyst as he or she chooses which tokens to measure.

TABLE 4.5

Principal Paired Words from Geographic Study Reading Cards

	PALM	LOT	THOUGHT
LOT ~ THOUGHT		collar	caller
		cot	caught
		Don	Dawn
		John	Shawn
		knotty	naughty
		Molly	mall
		sod	sawed
		stocking	stalks
PALM ~ LOT	balm	bomb	
	calmer	comma	
	card	cod	
	darkness	doctors	
	harder	hotter	
	heart	hot	
	lager	logger	
PALM ~ THOUGHT	ah		aw
	Pa's		pause
	Ra		raw
Multiple	aunt	on	gone
	Bach, bark	bock	balk
	ah's, r's	Oz	aw's

NOTE: Words set in bold were repeated as "overt" minimum pairs; others were read only in a "covert" sentential context.

A disadvantage to the method is that it cannot easily be applied to spontaneous speech, which we are fundamentally most interested in. But compared to an unpaired *t*-test, the paired *t*-test reduces the chance of a phonetic imbalance leading to a spurious distinction. And it increases the chance that a small, systematic word class distinction will be detected.

If there is a consistent difference between minimal pairs, but one that is small compared to the phonetic range of each word class—that is, the two vowel clouds overlap substantially—an unpaired *t*-test would probably not detect a significant difference, but a paired test might.[7]

It may be unusual for two phonemes to overlap so thoroughly. Even situations of near-merger, where small formant differences are preserved, are not always characterized by extreme overlap. In Tillingham, Essex (England), some speakers have /ai/ and /oi/ as close as 100 Hz in F1 and little more in F2, but with hardly any overlap between classes (Labov 1994,

382). The word classes of MEAT and MATE in vernacular Belfast English do overlap, even while MEAT-words are transferring into a third category of MEET (Labov 1994, 384–87; data from Harris 1985). And the case of New York City *source ~ sauce* (Labov, Yaeger, and Steiner 1972, 229–34) shows considerable, stable acoustic overlap, not merger, even with a fully vocalized /r/ in source.

Aside from near-mergers—a relatively stable, if rare, property of speech communities—two circumstances in an individual's life could result in closely approximated vowels.

If a speaker learned a vowel distinction as a child but has since abandoned it because of relocation or communal change, an acoustically small vestige of it might remain. This could either be amplified or further suppressed when greater attention is paid to speech.[8]

Or consider a speaker who was originally merged, but recently has been in contact with the distinction. Distinctions are rarely acquired in full, even by young learners (chap. 3), but microdistinctions between word classes could develop through subconscious accommodation. Exactly what is predicted to be learned is different under traditional and word-based phonological theories.

Nycz (2005) showed that a New York City speaker produced a smaller low back distinction while performing a task with a merged partner. Nycz (2010) further explores the accommodation between merged and distinct speakers that occurs in both directions—experimentally and in real time—and its theoretical implications.

4.3.2. ACOUSTIC ANALYSIS OF SENIOR CITIZENS. Four senior citizens were analyzed; three from the focus area (AB, NT, PV) and one from further south (SO); see figure 4.5.

ABS62M, a 62-year-old man from South Attleboro, is a good example of the MAIN system, PALM = LOT ≠ THOUGHT. NT86F, an 86-year-old woman from Norton, exemplifies the ENE system, PALM ≠ LOT = THOUGHT. However, ABS62M and NT86F were not selected because they were particularly good examples. Most of the senior citizens had low vowels similar to one of these two subjects.

PV81M, an 81-year-old man from Plainville, had more unusual low vowels. He has, or perhaps had, a three-way distinction (3-D), PALM ≠ LOT ≠ THOUGHT. But acoustic analysis does not straightforwardly confirm this. SO85F, an 85-year-old woman from Somerset, 15 miles southeast, exemplified the 3-D pattern more convincingly.

FIGURE 4.5

The Focus Area: Four Seniors and Three Young Adults Acoustically Analyzed

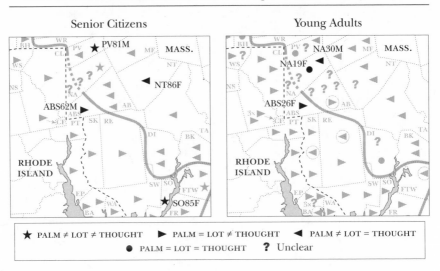

4.3.2.1. *A Typical MAIN System.* Plots of ABS62M's paired tokens of PALM, LOT, and THOUGHT are shown in figure 4.6, which highlights the relationship of LOT and THOUGHT, and in figure 4.7, which focuses on PALM ~ LOT.

Figure 4.6 shows THOUGHT much higher and backer than LOT. While THOUGHT is tightly clustered, we see phonetic conditioning for LOT; tokens of the same word are usually close together.

The solid lines connect the 4 overt pairs—*Don ~ Dawn, cot ~ caught, knotty ~ naughty, collar ~ caller*—which were all judged "different" by both speaker and analyst. The mean difference, subtracting THOUGHT from LOT, is 269 Hz for F1, 430 Hz for F2. This will be reported giving the speaker, style, and number of pairs:

$$\Delta \text{LOT} - \text{THOUGHT (ABS62M, O, 4)} = +269, +430.$$

The dashed lines connect the 6 covert pairs, which are the same words as above read in sentential context, plus *sod ~ sawed* and *stocking ~ stalks*. Note that the mean difference is slightly smaller for the covert pairs, for both formants:

$$\Delta \text{LOT} - \text{THOUGHT (ABS62M, C, 6)} = +240, +407.$$

Performing a paired *t*-test on the ten pairs gives an unsurprising result. The *p*-value is 1×10^{-6} for F1 and 1×10^{-7} for F2. These word classes are clearly not merged. A 95% confidence interval for the difference in means can be incorporated into the shorthand thus:

FIGURE 4.6
ABS62M: Paired Tokens of LOT ~ THOUGHT

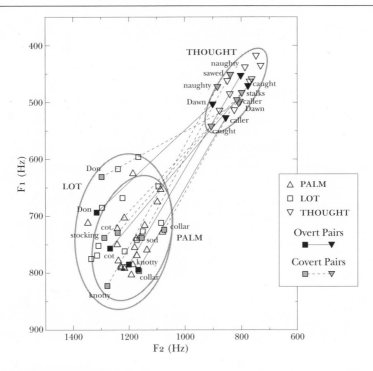

Δ LOT − THOUGHT (ABS62M, CO, 10) = +252 ±49 ($p = 1 \times 10^{-6}$), +417 ±64 ($p = 1 \times 10^{-7}$)

For ABS62M, the true LOT ~ THOUGHT difference almost certainly falls within these ranges.

The zoomed-in view of figure 4.7 allows a better comparison of the PALM and LOT classes, which overlap almost completely. The ellipses enclose 90% of the tokens of each class.

Only one overt pair, *balm ~ bomb*, differs moderately (+58, −152). The difference is not like in ENE, where PALM is fronter than LOT. Here *balm* is somewhat backer than *bomb*, but the tokens sounded very similar and were judged "same" by both speaker and analyst.

The six covert pairs were also judged "same," and the paired *t*-tests yield the following:

Δ PALM − LOT (AB62M, C, 6) = −51 ±41 ($p = .02$), −20 ±60 ($p = .43$)

The F1 result is significant: for 5 of 6 pairs, PALM is consistently slightly higher than LOT.

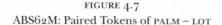

FIGURE 4.7
ABS62M: Paired Tokens of PALM ~ LOT

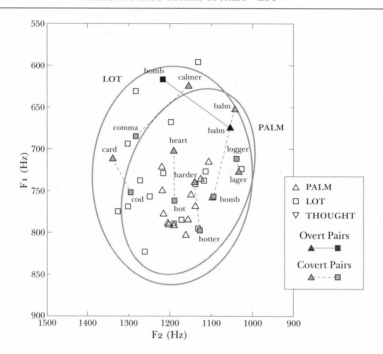

Three of these pairs involve PALM followed by /r/, and seeing as this speaker variably pronounced postvocalic /r/, the phonetic influence of that consonant could be at work. But significantly, there is no following /r/ in *balm* and *calmer*, which are still higher than their pairs, *bomb* and *comma*.

The PALM and LOT word classes, as a whole, occupy the same phonetic space. They also sounded identical to both speaker and listener, so ABS62M will be categorized as MAIN, or PALM = LOT ≠ THOUGHT. However, the possibility that PALM may nevertheless be somewhat raised with respect to LOT is worth bearing in mind when analyzing the vowels of other MAIN speakers.

4.3.2.2. *A Typical ENE System.* NT86F's LOT and THOUGHT are displayed in figure 4.8. Figure 4.9 shows how PALM is related to the other two classes. The clouds for LOT and THOUGHT overlap almost completely; the *t*-test for covert pairs suggests merger:

$$\Delta \text{LOT} - \text{THOUGHT (NT86F, C, 7)} = -20 \pm 58 \ (p = .43), +39 \pm 117 \ (p = .45)$$

The difference between word classes is small, but more importantly, it is very variable. For both F1 and F2, four pairs differed in one direction while

FIGURE 4.8
NT86F: Paired Tokens of LOT ~ THOUGHT

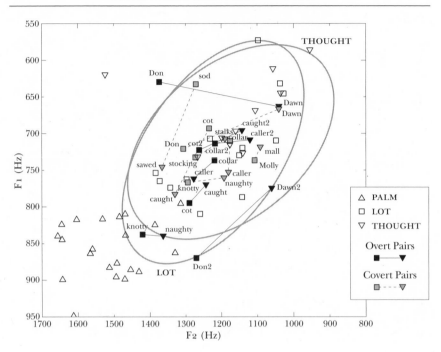

three went the other way. With so much variation, mean differences of −20 or +39 Hz could easily arise by chance. A result like this is a strong indication of merger, but not a foolproof one. The confidence intervals for each formant include zero (hence the result is "nonsignificant"), but they also are consistent with there being an underlying difference in any direction.

In responding to the overt pairs, NT86F said most of the key words twice. This highlighted an interesting discrepancy between *Don ~ Dawn*, which she pronounced differently each time (including the covert context), and the other three LOT ~ THOUGHT pairs, which she pronounced alike, in her judgment and mine. We cannot be sure if *Don ~ Dawn* is a lexical or phonological exception. Of all the pairs, it was the most likely to behave idiosyncratically—in both directions. This could happen if people tend to pronounce personal names in a way that is influenced by acquaintances who bear those names. As long as *Don ~ Dawn* is omitted, the overt pairs do not show a significant difference:

ΔLOT − THOUGHT (NT86F, O, 5) = +6±27 (*p* = .56), +53±85 (*p* = .16)

In going from covert to overt pairs, NT86F moved in the direction of the typical (positive) distinction. Four of five overt pairs show THOUGHT

FIGURE 4.9

NT86F: Paired Tokens of PALM ~ LOT and PALM ~ THOUGHT

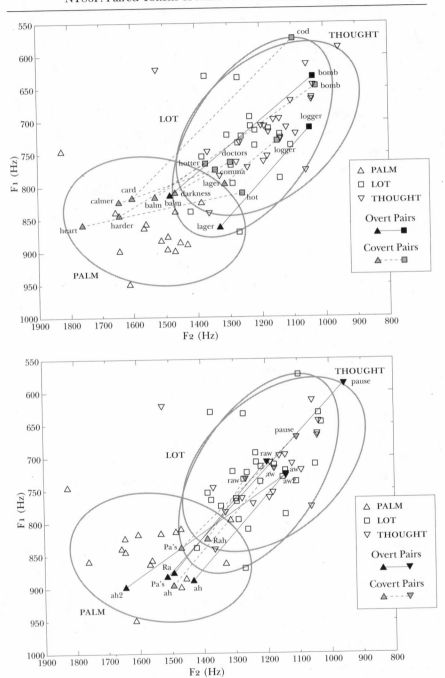

backer than LOT, by 46 to 120 Hz. This is reminiscent of how ABS62M pronounced most PALM words slightly higher than the corresponding LOT words, within a context of complete overlap. For NT86F, LOT and THOUGHT completely overlap, but on a "microscopic" phonetic level, the two may not be identical. In terms of gross production and perception, however, the LOT and THOUGHT word classes are merged for NT86F, except for *Don ~ Dawn* (and perhaps for other words not investigated).

Figure 4.9 shows that the PALM class is distinct from the merged LOT = THOUGHT class. The difference is not extreme, and there is a small amount of overlap. But it is phonetically dissimilar tokens that overlap; potentially contrasting ones show a clear difference.

The top panel of figure 4.9 displays PALM ~ LOT pairs, judged "different" by speaker and analyst. There is a distinction in both formants for the covert pairs. There are only two overt pairs, resulting in nonsignificant *p*-values, but the differences are as large or larger:

$$\Delta\text{PALM} - \text{LOT (NT86F, C, 7)} = +101 \pm 71 \ (p = .02), +346 \pm 144 \ (p = .001)$$
$$\Delta\text{PALM} - \text{LOT (NT86F, O, 2)} = +168 \pm 184 \ (p = .06), +366 \pm 1061 \ (p = .15)$$

The only overlap between these word classes involves PALM tokens that are far back for PALM—*lager* and *balm*—and tokens of LOT that are low and front for LOT—*hot, hotter, comma*. Each of these words is far apart from its pair, as *logger* and *bomb* are among the furthest back in the LOT class, and *heart, harder*, and *calmer* are some of the frontest PALM words.

The bottom panel of figure 4.9 shows PALM ~ THOUGHT pairs, which were impressionistically judged "different." The picture is similar, which makes sense if LOT and THOUGHT are merged:

$$\Delta\text{PALM} - \text{THOUGHT (NT86F, C, 3)} = +148 \pm 118 \ (p = .03), +267 \pm 321 \ (p = .07)$$
$$\Delta\text{PALM} - \text{THOUGHT (NT86F, O, 4)} = +201 \pm 102 \ (p = .01), +411 \pm 223 \ (p = .01)$$

These pairs were already distinct (covert), but moved apart under conscious focus (overt). With PALM ≠ LOT = THOUGHT, NT86F has the ENE low vowel system. Her almost total nonrhoticity and use of broad *a*—twice in *half*—completes her Eastern New England sound, though variable nonrhoticity and some broad *a* were also found in the MAIN speaker ABS62M.

4.3.2.3. *A Possible 3-D Pattern.* PV81M was one of six speakers who seemed to have a three-way low vowel distinction (3-D). The auditory impression was that PALM was sometimes quite fronted (like ENE), that LOT spanned a wide range—sometimes front and unrounded (like MAIN), sometimes back and rounded (like ENE)—and that THOUGHT was sometimes very high and back (like MAIN).

These speakers explicitly judged LOT ~ THOUGHT "different" in minimal pairs, yet reported PALM ~ LOT to be "different" too. If *balm* has a different vowel from *bomb*, and *Don* is different from *Dawn* too, the system has to
be three-way distinct, unless we are willing to say the LOT class has divided
between PALM and THOUGHT (as it seemed phonetically).

Figure 4.10 highlights PV81M's LOT and THOUGHT. Of the covert pairs,
some sounded and measured very close: for example, *collar ~ caller* (+43,
+52). Others were far apart; *stocking ~ stalks* (+191, +323), for example.
Together, the seven covert pairs support a distinction:

$$\Delta \text{LOT} - \text{THOUGHT (PV81M, C, 7)} = +96 \pm 53 \ (p = .005), +138 \pm 93 \ (p = .02)$$

The overt pairs were more consistently different, all four over 100 Hz apart
in F1 and F2:

$$\Delta \text{LOT} - \text{THOUGHT (PV81M, O, 4)} = +141 \pm 57 \ (p = .004), +204 \pm 96 \ (p = .007)$$

Only the closest, *collar ~ caller* (+105, +122), was judged "same" by the
informant (and "close" by the analyst). We see that PV81M's LOT ~ THOUGHT
distinction is roughly 50 Hz larger (in both formants) when greater atten-

FIGURE 4.10

PV81M: Paired Tokens of LOT ~ THOUGHT

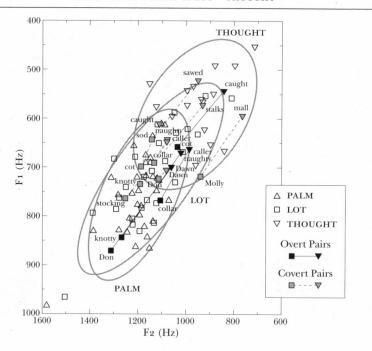

tion is paid to it, a greater shift than ABS62M made. Also note that even ABS62M's closest pairs were further apart than PV81M's most distinct pairs.

Things become more complicated with PALM. Based on his covert PALM ~ LOT pairs, shown in figure 4.11 (top), one would think PV81M had merged the two classes. Each of the seven pairs is close together. Other than *card* being 104 Hz front of *cod*, none of the formant differences exceeds 41 Hz, and the differences go in all directions. The paired *t*-test indicates merger:

$$\Delta \text{PALM} - \text{LOT (PV81M, C, 7)} = +9 \pm 21 \ (p = .31), +17 \pm 42 \ (p = .37)$$

Acoustically, the PALM ~ LOT difference is inconsistent, and much smaller than the contextual effects separating, for example, *lager* and *logger* from *calmer* and *comma*. But PV81M's covert PALM and LOT did not sound as close together as the F_1/F_2 measurements suggest, nor did many examples observed in his spontaneous speech. Some of PV81M's LOT tokens sounded noticeably rounded—unlike those of MAIN speakers—while his PALM tokens never did. Table 4.6 contrasts the nonsignificant measured formant differences with the auditory impressions gained after repeated listening.

Considering the small formant differences, it is likely that the perceptual difference between the pairs derives from other acoustic properties, including rounding, a property noted in most of the LOT words here, although it is difficult to measure (Johnson 2000) and even to accurately hear (Ladefoged 1960). Recall that ABS62M showed a 50-Hz F_1 difference between most PALM and LOT pairs; however, those pairs sounded identical, even on repeated listening. For PV81M, while the formant values were even closer, a subtle difference was audible in some cases.

When PV81M repeated some of the PALM ~ LOT pairs in the "overt" condition, the difference increased dramatically, as seen in figure 4.11 (bottom). For two examples of *balm ~ bomb* and *lager ~ logger*, LOT is now higher and/or backer than PALM, not just rounder.

Even the closest of these four pairs, *balm2 ~ bomb2*, is still fairly far apart in F2 (+5, +153); the most different one, *lager2 ~ logger2*, is very distinct in F_1 and F_2 (+220, +376). Because of this variation, the combined result is not quite statistically significant:

$$\Delta \text{PALM} \sim \text{LOT (PV81M, O, 4)} = +122 \pm 141 \ (p = .07), +195 \pm 193 \ (p = .05)$$

The greater distinctions made by PV81M in the overt contexts may involve a conscious effort to distinguish the pairs, but this is probably only

FIGURE 4.11
PV81M: Paired Tokens of PALM ~ LOT

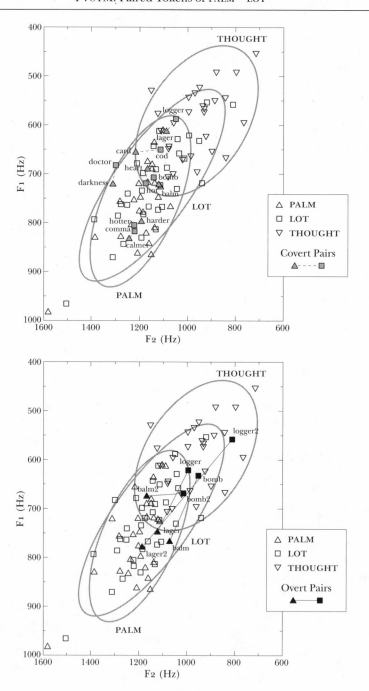

TABLE 4.6

PV81M: Acoustic Differences and Auditory Impressions
of Covert PALM ~ LOT Pairs

PALM-LOT Pair	*ΔF1*	*ΔF2*	*Impression (live)*	*Impression (repeated)*
balm ~ bomb	15	−21	??	same
card ~ cod	6	104		quite different
calmer ~ comma	16	22		different
darkness ~ doctor	39	10		different
heart ~ hot	−29	−8		same
harder ~ hotter	−7	−31		different?
lager ~ logger	25	41	different	same?

possible because he possesses an underlying knowledge of the difference between the three word classes. ABS62M and NT86F did separate their merged vowels slightly in the overt context, but never judged them distinct, as PV81M did.

Especially in the overt PALM ~ LOT context, PV81M's LOT entered the acoustic territory of THOUGHT. But in the overt LOT ~ THOUGHT context, for example, some LOT's were very PALM-like.

Figure 4.12 summarizes the overt and covert tokens of the three word classes, with means and whiskers (which extend to ±1 standard deviation from the mean for each formant). The thicker, bolder symbols represent the overt minimal pair context.

The pattern from the covert pairs is PALM = LOT ≠ THOUGHT (MAIN); tokens from spontaneous speech (not shown) look similar. But under overt focus, the mean of LOT moves into the middle, suggesting PALM ≠ LOT ≠ THOUGHT (3-D). As the token clouds and whiskers show, LOT now extends across a wide, overlapping area, rather than having its own intermediate quality.

One possibility is that the PALM ~ LOT distinction is not natural, or not native, to PV81M's phonology, but that he consciously imitates it, being familiar with the ENE system from his summers in Maine or from contacts much closer by.

I would argue instead that PALM and LOT are underlyingly distinct for PV81M. However, he does not typically distinguish them with significant F1/F2 differences, but with other cues, such as rounding. He seems to partially suppress the distinction in less self-conscious contexts; this may be due to contact with MAIN speakers—for example, his wife from Rhode Island. When attention is called to the distinction, he recalls and reproduces it accurately.

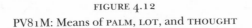

FIGURE 4.12
PV81M: Means of PALM, LOT, and THOUGHT

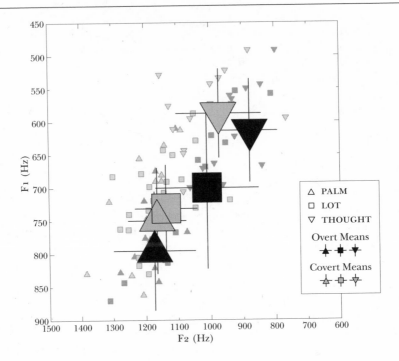

Other seniors exhibited the 3-D pattern more clearly than PV81M, yet the phonetic impression of their vowels was similar to his. This makes it more likely that he is 3-D as well.

4.3.2.4. *A Probable 3-D Pattern.* SO85F produced a clearer 3-D pattern, although her low vowel behavior—especially regarding LOT—was still not entirely straightforward. For LOT ~ THOUGHT pairs (figure 4.13), SO85F made a sizable distinction when the pairs were covert, especially in F2. She showed an even larger difference in both formants when the pairs were overt:

ΔLOT – THOUGHT (SO85F, C, 8) = +85 ±75 (p = .03), +295 ±164 (p = .004)
ΔLOT – THOUGHT (SO85F, O, 7) = +140 ±73 (p = .004), +389 ±146 (p = .0007)

The pair *Don ~ Dawn* again behaved exceptionally; it sounded "close" to both speaker and analyst. Acoustically, it was only close (+38, –61) on one occasion (the speaker repeated many pairs). All the other pairs were judged "different"; indeed, some measured extremely far apart.

FIGURE 4.13
SO85F: Paired Tokens of LOT ~ THOUGHT

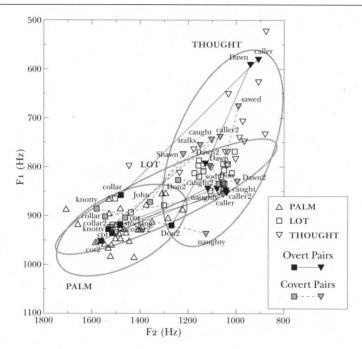

Unlike PV81M, SO85F distinguished the PALM ~ LOT pairs (figure 4.14, top) in the covert reading context as well as under overt focus as minimal pairs. Some were judged "close" by the speaker, but they were all "different" to the analyst. The nonsignificant *p*-values in the overt case are simply a result of there being only two pairs (both were quite distinct):

ΔPALM – LOT (SO85F, C, 7) = +59 ±50 (*p* = .03), +161 ±120 (*p* = .02)
ΔPALM – LOT (SO85F, O, 2) = +68 ±426 (*p* = .29), +282 ±635 (*p* = .11)

So PALM ≠ LOT, and LOT ≠ THOUGHT, but with LOT represented by a different set of words in each case. Consistent with a 3-D pattern, when SO85F's PALM and THOUGHT are compared directly (fig. 4.14, bottom), the difference is greater than either her PALM – LOT or her LOT – THOUGHT:

ΔPALM – THOUGHT (SO85F, C, 3) = +161 ±114 (*p* = .03), +446 ±253 (*p* = .02)
ΔPALM – THOUGHT (SO85F, O, 3) = +176 ±316 (*p* = .14), +509 ±238 (*p* = .02)

However, this is not because the LOT tokens occupy a clearly intermediate position between PALM and THOUGHT. Rather, as figure 4.15 shows, SO85F

FIGURE 4.14

SO85F: Paired tokens of PALM ~ LOT and PALM ~ THOUGHT

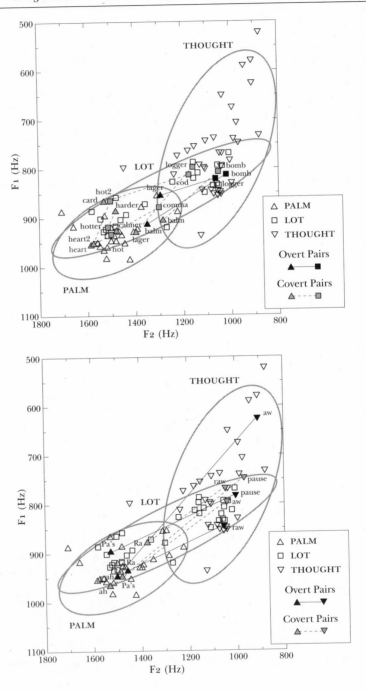

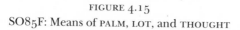

FIGURE 4.15
SO85F: Means of PALM, LOT, and THOUGHT

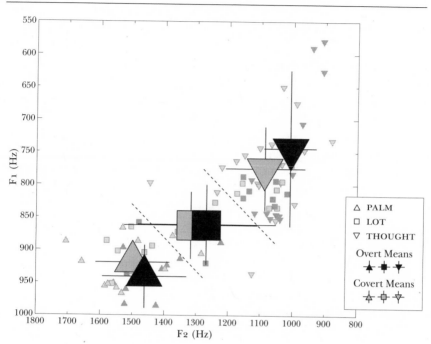

seems to have a split LOT. Both covert and overt means indicate a 3-D system, but few tokens of LOT are near its mean. About half are clustered near the mean of PALM, and half near the mean of THOUGHT. Importantly, LOT never achieves the extreme values of the frontest PALM or the highest THOUGHT. But, at least in terms of F1 and F2, LOT certainly overlaps with typical realizations of both PALM and THOUGHT.

In table 4.7, 33 tokens of LOT were sorted into columns by phonetic realization and into rows by following segment type. The tokens of LOT were divided into three groups (indicated by the diagonal dotted lines in figure 4.15). The 14 PALM-like tokens are those where $F1 + F2/2 > 1580$ (the mean of PALM was 1674 by this measure); the 15 THOUGHT-like tokens are those where $F1 + F2/2 < 1415$ (cf. 1285 for the mean of THOUGHT). Only four tokens fell between 1415 and 1585, even though the mean of LOT, 1507, was in this range.

We see that the phonetics of SO85F's LOT is fairly predictable by the nature of the following consonant. With one exception, words where LOT was followed by an underlyingly voiceless stop were realized fairly low and/ or front—more like PALM. All words where a voiced stop followed were real-

TABLE 4.7
SO85F: Realization of LOT by Following Segment

Following Segment	$F1 + F2/2$ (Hz)		
	> 1580 (≈ PALM)	1580–1415	< 1415 (≈ THOUGHT)
Voiceless Stop	cot (COOᵃ)		
	hot (CCb)		
	hotter (C)		
	knotty (CO)		
	stocking (C)		bock (O)
Voiced Stop			cod (C)
			sod (C)
			logger (CO)
Fricative	**bothers** (C)		**Oz** (OOOᵃ)
Nasal		comma (C)	bomb (CO)
		John (C)	con (CCᵇ)
		Don (COᵇ)	**Don** (COᵇ)
Lateral	collar (COCOᵇ)		**doll** (C)

NOTE: Bold tokens are close to paired word.
a. SO85F repeated this minimal pair in judging it.
b. SO85F read the card containing this word twice.

ized rather high and/or back—more like THOUGHT. Most prenasal tokens were like THOUGHT, while the small prelateral group was split, with four examples of a front vowel before intervocalic /l/ in *collar* and a far-back token before final /l/ in *doll*.

This phonetic conditioning causes some LOT words (bolded in table 4.7) to end up close to their paired words, while others end up very different. For example, *hot* is very close to the PALM word *heart* (−22, −83), and *sod* is quite close to the THOUGHT word *sawed* (+160, +83). But because of the same phonetic effects, *cot* is PALM-like and very far from *caught* (+161, +359), while *cod* is THOUGHT-like and far from *card* (−54, −356).

However, even the PALM-like LOTS are not identical to the actual PALMS, and the THOUGHT-like LOTS are different from the real THOUGHTS. The token clouds overlap substantially, but when appropriate pairs could be compared, differences were audible if not acoustically demonstrable.

To describe the low vowel system of SO85F, we could say that there is a three-way distinction, and that one of the categories, LOT, has a wide range which overlaps considerably with the other categories, PALM and THOUGHT. This would predict the minimal pair contrasts that we (mostly) find, but it would not explain the bimodal distribution of LOT in phonetic space.

Another view is that SO85F has only two low vowels, PALM and THOUGHT. Instead of LOT having merged with one or the other of them, as in most dialects nearby, perhaps it has split between them, on mainly phonetic grounds. This would explain the phonetic dispersion of the LOT group, but it would not predict contrasts to be maintained between PALM-like LOT words and PALM or between THOUGHT-like LOT words and THOUGHT. Yet there is some acoustic evidence for the first type of contrast (*hot ~ heart*), and convincing evidence for the second (*sod ~ sawed*).

Or we could imagine a distinct LOT class which alternates between the phonetic positions of PALM and THOUGHT. Herold (1990, 186–200) discusses this possibility regarding the Belfast data of Harris (1985), who suggests that word classes which partially overlap can remain distinct. Herold wonders if even complete phonetic overlap might not necessarily equate to merger:

word-class identity may be maintained by patterns of alternation within a phonetic continuum … and variably neutralized distinctions acquired, as long as each of the phoneme-classes involved … has a different probability of being realized with a specific phonetic value. [1990, 206–7]

But with SO85F, individual words are quite consistent in their phonetic realizations, making it unclear how they could be acquired as members of an alternating class. With more data, we might notice that individual LOT words did alternate between PALM-like and THOUGHT-like realizations. Even if not, it seems the PALM-like LOT words are not learned as tokens of PALM and the THOUGHT-like LOT words are not real THOUGHTs. Small but reliable phonetic contrasts are maintained, establishing an unusual bimodal LOT class, and with it the 3-D system.

4.3.2.5. *Summary of Senior Citizens.* Figure 4.16 displays the tokens, means, and standard deviation whiskers for the four senior citizen speakers. The figure uses one set of axes for the two male speakers and another for the females, whose axes are shifted and expanded—that is, the plot is shrunk—by 20%.

Though it is not possible to compare speakers precisely without normalizing, ABS62M clearly has the greatest distance between phonemes. His THOUGHT is high and ingliding, typical of Mid-Atlantic speech. Its nucleus is far removed from his merged, overlapping PALM = LOT.

There is less distance between NT86F's PALM and her merged LOT = THOUGHT, but the difference is still substantial. The PALM vowel is in a further front position than for any other speaker.

The 3-D speakers, PV81M and SO85F, have three vowels in roughly the same phonetic space as the others' two. The PALM is not particularly fronted,

FIGURE 4.16
Senior Systems: ABS62M (MAIN), NT86F (ENE),
PV81M (possible 3-D), and SO85F (probable 3-D)

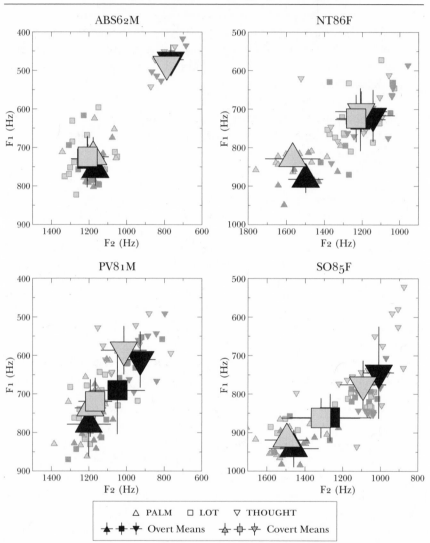

nor is THOUGHT very high. For PV81M, all word classes shift between contexts, but the most notable movement is of LOT.

In general, pairs had greater acoustic differences in the overt context. This may be unsurprising if the two word classes involved are clearly distinct. But even when they are essentially merged, as with NT86F's LOT ~ THOUGHT, they may still be treated differently on a "micro" level.

4.3.3. ACOUSTIC ANALYSIS OF YOUNG ADULTS. Many young adults in the focus area had "unclear" low vowel systems. Those selected with "traditional" two-vowel systems were still less clear-cut than their senior counterparts.

ABS26F, a 26-year-old woman from South Attleboro, was still clearly MAIN. A 30-year-old man from North Attleborough, NA30M, was judged impressionistically as clearly ENE, but acoustic analysis showed extensive overlap of PALM and LOT = THOUGHT. While his formant differences were significant, he probably represents phonetic progress toward 3-M.

NA19F, a 19-year-old woman from North Attleborough, had the three-way merger unambiguously. Her low vowels made a very different auditory impression than NA30M's, reinforced by her pronouncing and perceiving all the minimal pairs she read as "same."

4.3.3.1. *The MAIN System, Preserved.* ABS26F is 36 years younger than ABS62M and also from South Attleboro. Her MAIN low vowel system is not as extreme as ABS62M's, but it is essentially congruent.

For the overt LOT ~ THOUGHT pairs—all of which were auditorily judged "different"—she approaches ABS62M's size of distinction; her covert pairs are closer but still definitely distinct:

ΔLOT – THOUGHT (ABS26F, O, 5) = +281 ±224 (p = .03), +335 ±183 (p = .006)
ΔLOT – THOUGHT (ABS26F, C, 8) = +162 ±90 (p = .004), +278 ±56 (p = 8 × 10^{-6})

Figure 4.17 shows that AB26F's highest tokens of LOT (e.g., *sod*) acoustically overlap her lowest tokens of THOUGHT (e.g., *stalks*). However, even the closest minimal pairs, such as the two examples of *knotty ~ naughty*, differ by a comfortable margin of 100 Hz in F1 and 150 Hz in F2. ABS26F's overt instances of *Don ~ Dawn* are very widely separated, approximately 450 Hz apart in both formants; these proper names are again behaving exceptionally.

The PALM ~ LOT pairs of ABS26F (see figure 4.18) illustrate merger well. The covert pairs exhibited moderate (100–200 Hz) PALM ~ LOT differences, but without any common trend:

ΔPALM – LOT (ABS26F, C, 7) = −25 ±89 (p = .52), +22 ±93 (p = .58)
ΔPALM – LOT (ABS26F, O, 1) = +9, −43

The acoustic data support ABS26F having a MAIN system, PALM = LOT ≠ THOUGHT. As she read the cards, she reacted to her own accent, in an amused and slightly troubled way. It was especially her high back THOUGHTs that struck her, and some "correction" of THOUGHT may account for its wide phonetic range on figure 4.17 (compare ABS62M's tight cluster on figure 4.6). But her correction of THOUGHT does not go so far as to confuse it with PALM = LOT.

FIGURE 4.17

ABS26F: Paired Tokens of LOT ~ THOUGHT

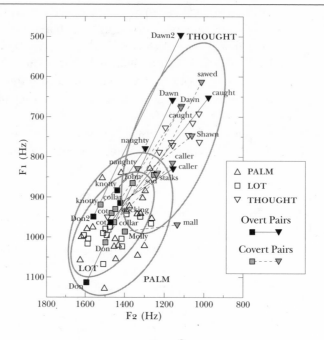

FIGURE 4.18

ABS26F: Paired Tokens of PALM ~ LOT

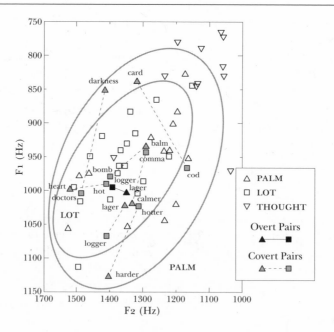

4.3.3.2. *The ENE System, Threatened?* NA30M was considered from auditory impressions to be a perfectly good example of the ENE system surviving close to the linguistic boundary. However, acoustic analysis reveals that his pattern, PALM ≠ LOT = THOUGHT, is not as robustly maintained as it was for NT86F. Figure 4.19 shows the complete overlap of the LOT and THOUGHT word classes. Neither the seven covert pairs nor the six overt pairs reflected a significant distinction (although the small shift between the two styles was in the direction of the usual distinction):

$$\Delta\text{LOT} - \text{THOUGHT (NA30M, C, 7)} = -16 \pm 24 \ (p = .15), -4 \pm 67 \ (p = .90)$$
$$\Delta\text{LOT} - \text{THOUGHT (NA30M, O, 6)} = +16 \pm 30 \ (p = .23), +23 \pm 57 \ (p = .36)$$

Of the overt pairs, only the second repetition of *cot ~ caught* (+69, +107) sounded different to the analyst. The subject also heard *collar ~ caller* and *Don ~ Dawn* as different—"the *o*, as opposed to the *a*"—but their acoustic measurements were very close.

Recall that for NT86F, whose LOT and THOUGHT were also merged, PALM was a very distinct vowel. Although there was some overlap at the extremes, the average PALM ~ LOT pair differed by more than 100 Hz in

FIGURE 4.19
NA30M: Paired Tokens of LOT ~ THOUGHT

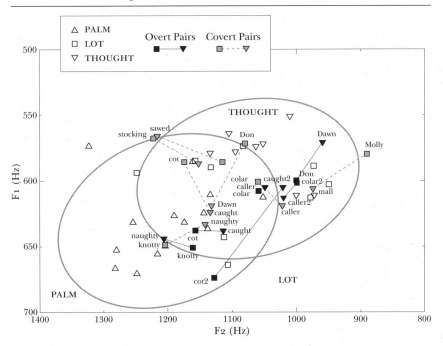

F_1 and more than 300 Hz in F_2, producing a clearly audible distinction. For NA30M, the auditory impression was of a more moderate distinction between PALM and LOT = THOUGHT, and the acoustic difference is smaller than NT86F's, with substantial overlap.

The top panel of figure 4.20 plots five PALM ~ LOT pairs, four covert and one overt (NA30M pronounced /l/ in *balm*, disqualifying that pair). There is a consistent F_2 difference of 150–200 Hz, except for one pair, *calmer ~ comma*, where it is only 61 Hz. The F_1 difference is smaller, less consistent, and not statistically significant:

Δ PALM – LOT (NA30M, C, 4) = +21 ±59 ($p = .34$), +141 ±85 ($p = .02$)
Δ PALM – LOT (NA30M, O, 1) = +8, +185

The bottom panel of figure 4.20 plots three PALM ~ THOUGHT pairs in both covert and overt conditions. We observe a regular difference in both formants, but greater in F_2:

Δ PALM – THOUGHT (NA30M, C, 3) = +67 ±33 ($p = .02$), +173 ±249 ($p = .10$)
Δ PALM – THOUGHT (NA30M, O, 3) = +70 ±108 ($p = .11$), +198 ±333 ($p = .13$)

The covert and overt pronunciation of each pair is almost identical; the differences between pairs can be considered phonetic-environment effects. The word-class differences for PALM ~ THOUGHT are slightly larger than those for PALM ~ LOT, which may also be a phonetic effect. It is likely that the morpheme-final PALM words (e.g., *ah, Pa's*) used in the comparison with THOUGHT are lower and fronter than the PALM's (e.g., *calmer*) used in the comparison with LOT.

If the PALM ~ LOT and PALM ~ THOUGHT pairs are combined in one test, we see that NA30M has only half NT86F's distance between PALM and LOT = THOUGHT, but a distinction certainly still exists:

Δ PALM, LOT – THOUGHT (NA30M, CO, 11) = +46 ±26 ($p = .003$), +169 ±55 ($p = 5 \times 10^{-5}$)

Compared with the seniors, the two young adults above have phonetically weaker distinctions in their low vowels. The MAIN distinction, with a high back THOUGHT, was dramatic for the older generation (ABS62M) and is still fairly robust (ABS26F). The ENE distinction, with a low front PALM, was robust (NT86F) and is now somewhat less healthy, but in no obvious danger (NA30M).

4.3.3.3. *"I Want to Say It Differently, but I Can't": The 3-M Pattern of NA19F.* Another North Attleborough native, eleven years younger than NA30M, had a very different low vowel system. NA19F did not have time to read

FIGURE 4.20

NA30M: Paired Tokens of PALM ~ LOT and PALM ~ THOUGHT

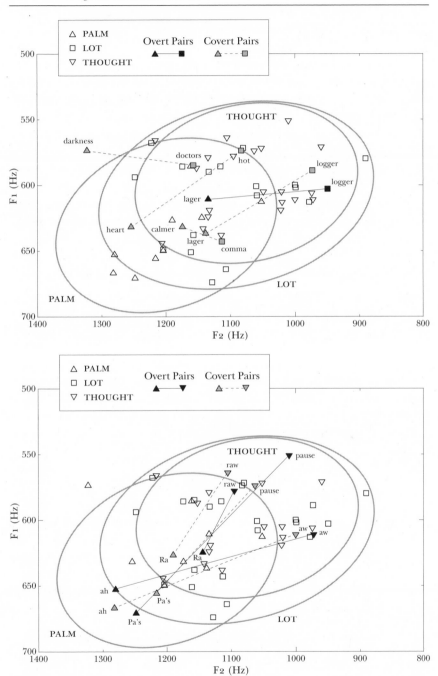

every card, but read enough pairs to suggest she distinguishes neither LOT ~ THOUGHT nor PALM ~ LOT. Supplemented by unpaired reading tokens and some from spontaneous speech, her data mostly pointed to a three-way-merged (3-M) system. Some of her tokens, including those of *ah* and *aw*, were harder to interpret.

Except for one case of *Don ~ Dawn*, the pairs were judged "same" by the analyst; all were "same" for the speaker. NA19F was aware that others distinguish LOT ~ THOUGHT. When a Rhode Island customer demonstrated the distinction, NA19F (a tanning salon employee) found it amusing and imitated it. But as she heard herself reading the cards and pronouncing the pairs virtually the same, NA19F became almost wistful about her merged status. She remarked in mock-complaint, "It's like, I want to say it differently, but I can't!"

Acoustically, the three word classes almost completely overlapped, each having a wide range. For the LOT ~ THOUGHT pairs, most differed in the usual direction of distinction, but others differed in the opposite direction (figure 4.21, top left). There was no significant overall difference in F1 or F2, even when covert and overt pairs were combined together:

ΔLOT – THOUGHT (NA19F, C, 5) = +13 ±102 (p = .75), +48 ±227 (p = .60)
ΔLOT – THOUGHT (NA19F, O, 4) = +56 ±152 (p = .33), +41 ±155 (p = .47)
ΔLOT – THOUGHT (NA19F, CO, 9) = +32 ±66 (p = .30), +44 ±110 (p = .38)

The only PALM ~ LOT pairs were *balm ~ bomb* and *lager ~ logger*. NA19F produced one covert and one overt example of each, plus another overt *balm ~ bomb*. As with LOT ~ THOUGHT, some pairs were close, while others differed by up to 200 Hz, but the differences went in either direction (fig. 4.21, top right). There was no consistent PALM ~ LOT difference:

ΔPALM – LOT (NA19F, C, 2) = −23 ±133 (p = .28), −9 ±260 (p = .75)
ΔPALM – LOT (NA19F, O, 3) = −69 ±326 (p = .46), −9 ±252 (p = .89)
ΔPALM – LOT (NA19F, CO, 5) = −50 ±120 (p = .31), −9 ±91 (p = .80)

If PALM = LOT and LOT = THOUGHT for NA19F, one would not expect a difference between PALM ~ THOUGHT pairs. But in fact, the pair *ah ~ aw* ("doctors ask you to say ah" vs. "aw, how cute!") was pronounced somewhat differently, three times over. The one covert and two overt instances of *ah ~ aw* differed in the same direction and to a similar extent (fig. 4.21, bottom left). Together they yield a significant *t*-test result:

ΔPALM – THOUGHT (NA19F, CO, 3) = +92 ±21 (p = .003), +202 ±88 (p = .01)

The bottom right panel of figure 4.21 shows the means of the paired tokens from the other three panels. Each symbol contains a smaller symbol

FIGURE 4.21

NA19F: Paired Tokens of LOT ~ THOUGHT, PALM ~ LOT, and PALM ~ THOUGHT, and Means of PALM, LOT, and THOUGHT

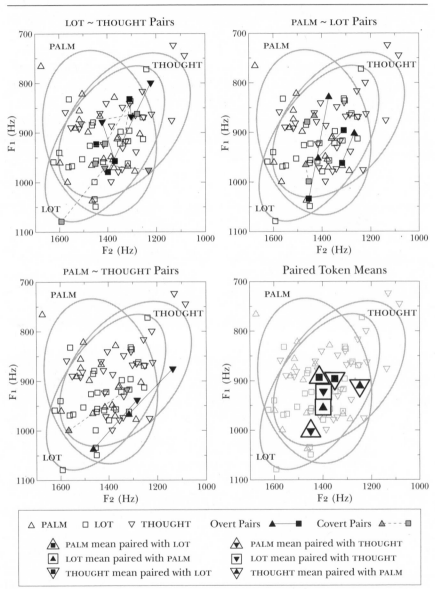

indicating the vowel class it was paired with. When each is paired with LOT, PALM and THOUGHT are close to each other (and to LOT). But when they are paired with each other (i.e., *ah ~ aw*), PALM and THOUGHT are much further apart.

One potential explanation for this discrepancy is that *ah* and *aw* are not ordinary words (see the discussion of *la* in chapter 3). And indeed, there were other young speakers who had a three-way merger in every other respect, except for *ah* and *aw* being different. However, those speakers' productions of *ah* and *aw* sounded (and were judged) different; NA19F's sounded very close and were judged the same.

To determine whether or not NA19F is three-way-merged with ordinary words, 30 low vowel tokens were measured from spontaneous speech—7 of PALM, 10 of LOT, and 13 of THOUGHT (fig. 4.22, top left). NA19F also produced 45 unpaired reading card tokens, consisting of 13 examples of PALM, 17 of LOT, and 15 of THOUGHT (after eliminating one token of *Dawn* made in imitation of a Rhode Island accent).

Like the paired tokens, the spontaneous and unpaired tokens of the low vowel classes overlap greatly. The spontaneous speech means of PALM (849, 1420), LOT (901, 1393), and THOUGHT (892, 1329) are close. The classes are not significantly different, by unpaired t-tests.

The unpaired reading tokens have similar means: 904, 1459 for PALM; 923, 1436, for LOT; and 877, 1362 for THOUGHT. This time, when THOUGHT is compared by t-test with the other two classes (or with PALM alone), the 100-Hz difference in F2 is significant ($p = .04$).

If we combine the spontaneous and unpaired reading tokens (figure 4.22, bottom left), the statistical significance of these fairly small differences increases. The combined PALM mean is 884, 1445; LOT is 915, 1420; and THOUGHT is 884, 1346. We have a 74-Hz F2 difference for LOT ~ THOUGHT ($p = .04$) and a 99-Hz F2 difference for PALM ~ THOUGHT ($p = .0.006$). Like Herold (§4.3.1.1), we seem to have found acoustic differences between word classes that impressionistically sounded merged.

If NA19F really produces small word-class distinctions, unconsciously, within a cloud of largely overlapping tokens, it might be her everyday exposure to dialects with the relevant distinctions that makes this possible. Before concluding this, however, we will see if what seem to be word-class differences are really phonetic conditioning effects in disguise.

F2 is lowered by a following /l/; before /l/, THOUGHT is simply more common than LOT. On the 1995 General Service List of 2,284 common words (Bauman and Culligan 1995), the 13 words with THOUGHT plus /l/ have a mean Brown Corpus frequency of 561. The 12 words with LOT plus /l/ have a mean frequency of 116. Also, all but one of these LOT words—and none of the THOUGHT words—have the clearer intervocalic /l/, which lowers F2 less than the darker coda /l/.

Therefore, a naive acoustic analysis of spontaneous speech can falsely show a low back distinction. The 75-word sample of unpaired reading and

FIGURE 4.22

NA19F: Means of PALM, LOT, and THOUGHT from Spontaneous Speech Tokens, Unpaired Reading Tokens, and Both Combined

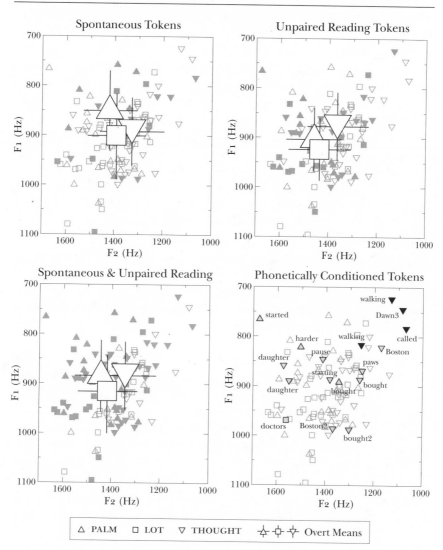

spontaneous tokens has four examples of THOUGHT plus /l/ (*ball, called, fall* × 2) and two of LOT plus /l/ (*college, doll*). Removing just these six words cuts the F2 difference between PALM and THOUGHT from 99 to 76 Hz; the *p*-value rises from .006 to .03. The LOT ~ THOUGHT difference drops from 74 to 64 Hz; the *p*-value goes from .04 to .06.

Another environment that lowers F2 is a preceding /w/. Two tokens of *walking* bear this out; they measured among the furthest back of all these tokens, although they did not sound it. With these words removed—there were no PALM or LOT words with a preceding /w/—the PALM ~ THOUGHT difference dropped to 61 Hz ($p = .08$), the LOT ~ THOUGHT difference to 49 Hz ($p = .15$).

Just by removing two of the most likely sources of bias—and only 8 words out of 75—the effect whereby THOUGHT appeared to be further back than the other word classes taken separately is reduced by one-third in size and no longer reaches the usual threshold for statistical significance.

The comparison of tokens from conversation is adequate to broadly delineate vowel classes as clearly distinct or possibly merged. But it cannot decide whether or not a speaker maintains a small, regular difference between two classes that almost completely overlap.

Measuring many tokens will not necessarily help the matter, because word classes do not appear with the same frequency in the same phonetic environments. A method where tokens are paired—or at least collected in coherent phonetic groups—seems essential.

NA19F was less consistent than some subjects (cf. PV81M in fig. 4.11, top) when pronouncing similar words from the same class or from classes believed merged. For example, her F2 in *started* was 1625 Hz; in *starting* it was 1296 Hz, a difference of 329 Hz.

NA19F also showed phonetic conditioning. For example, F2 was low in two tokens of *Boston* (1171, 1370) and three of *bought* (1262, 1304, 1383), in keeping with their labial onsets. Similar tokens with coronal onsets, *daughter* (1552, 1575) and *doctors* (1563), had much higher F2 measurements. These words are labeled on figure 4.22 (bottom right).

Neither variability on individual words nor allophonic effects lead directly to a word class difference. Yet, even after removing the tokens with following /l/ or preceding /w/, a statistically significant difference of around 50 Hz in F2 remains between the combined PALM = LOT and THOUGHT.

Even if such differences are not due to chance, they are not necessarily real phonemic (word-class) differences either. They may be statistical regularities deriving from the different frequencies of various phonetic environments within the vocabulary of each class.

Table 4.8 shows all 109 of NA19F's measured tokens, divided into four equal groups according to F2. At first glance, the table suggests a word-class difference: THOUGHT has lower F2. But the table also reveals how imbalanced some important phonetic environments are. For example, 13% of THOUGHT tokens (5/40) are before /l/, compared to 7% of LOT tokens (3/41) and 0% of PALM tokens (0/28). A preceding labial consonant—

TABLE 4.8
NA19F: Low Vowels by Word Class and F2

	1675–1470	1469–1380	1379–1310	1309–1070
PALM	ah	**ah**	ah2	
	are	balm	**balm**	balm2
	car	calmer	aunt	
	card	*calming*	*far*	
	farther	lager	lager1	lager3
	farther	**lager**	lager2	
	harder	*market*	father's	
	heart		*part*	
	smartie		*starting*	
	started			
LOT	bothers	bomb		*college*
	doctors	**bomb**	bomb2	con
	dodge	common	clock	doll
	Donna	*contact's*	*hot*	*Foxboro*
	honor	cot	logs	*lot*
	John	**cot**		Don
	not	**Don**	Don4	**Don2**
	Roxy	jogging		possibly
	Roxy2	**logger**	**logger**	sod
	shot	lot		
	(short)stop	Molly		
		mom		
		not		
		popular	popular	
THOUGHT	daughter	**caught**		caught
	daughter	bought		*bought*
	Shaw's	Shawn		*bought2*
			aw	**aw**
		lawn	dog	**aw2**
		Dawn4	Dawn	**Dawn**
			talk	**Dawn2**
	talks		*talk2*	mall
			fall	*fall*
				ball
		cost		*called*
		cost	*Boston2*	Boston
			boss	toss
		pause		paws
	off2		*off*	walking
	sawed		saw	**walking**

NOTE: Italics indicate spontaneous speech; bold, overt; all others, covert.

/b/, /p/, /m/, or /w/—accounts for 30% of THOUGHT (12/40), 22% of LOT (9/41), and 18% of PALM (5/28).

To choose an environment where F2 might be higher than average, only 10% of THOUGHT tokens (4/40) occurred before an intervocalic consonant, compared to 29% of LOT tokens (12/41) and 29% of PALM tokens (8/28).

While more data would be needed to conclusively establish correlations like these, unpaired tokens can clearly carry the baggage of the allophonic environments they occur in. Differences in these distributions can be misconstrued as word-class differences. This can be avoided with multiple regression or using paired tokens.

So, while NA19F is effectively three-way merged (3-M), a fuller analysis of her speech could show she produces very small word-class differences within one overlapping range. Such microdifferences could be called vestigial if they are retained from parental or early childhood exposure. If they have arisen from accommodation to recent interlocutors, they could be called nascent. If one of these is the case, then as with *ah ~ aw*, NA19F can "say it differently" better than she thinks.

4.3.3.4. *Summary of Young Adults.* Figure 4.23 compares the means and standard deviations of the low vowels of the young adults, ABS26F, NA30M, and NA19F. South Attleboro is only five miles from North Attleborough along Route 1, but we observe great diversity among these speakers' systems.

The females' vowels are on axes intermediate in scale between the ones used for the male and female seniors in figure 4.16. This slightly understates how much PALM = LOT and THOUGHT are closer for ABS26F than for ABS62M. Their MAIN systems are still very similar.

Comparing NA30M on figure 4.23 with NT86F on figure 4.16, we see that PALM appears to be roughly twice as close to LOT = THOUGHT for the younger speaker. This is despite a more zoomed-in scale on the younger speaker's plot. NA30M has an unusually compact vowel space, in terms of Hertz. Impressionistically and acoustically, his ENE pattern was clear, though moderate.

NA19F's low vowel pattern is quite different from either MAIN or ENE. We have called it 3-M; although, as discussed in section 4.3.3.3, all possibility of word-class differences cannot be ruled out. Comparing speakers is risky without normalization, but NA19F's merged low vowel(s) seem to occupy less space than the systems with distinctions. This matched the impression of a moderate phonetic range, without the extremes of ENE PALM or MAIN THOUGHT.

FIGURE 4.23
Young Adult Systems: ABS26F (MAIN), NA30M (ENE), and NA19F (3-M)

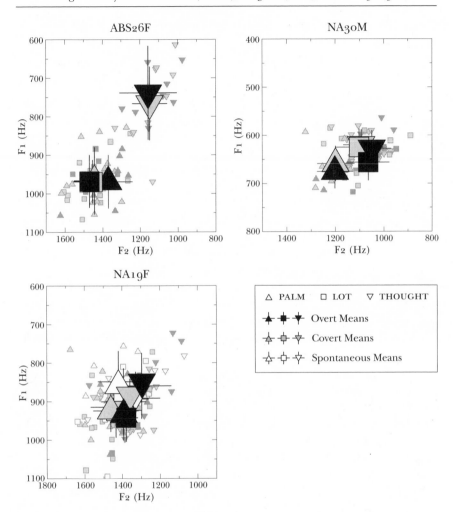

It is not known what in NA19F's background—her parents also grew up in North Attleborough—triggered this reorganization to one vowel, something observed in several other young speakers. Similarly, it was not known why a few seniors retained a three-way distinction while most had reduced their low vowels to two.

4.4. THE INTERACTION OF RHOTICITY
AND LOW VOWEL SYSTEMS

Besides her three-way-merged vowels, NA19F differed from the other speakers analyzed by usually pronouncing postvocalic /r/, especially in the reading tasks. Kurath and McDavid (1961) connect these phenomena, saying a distinction between PALM and LOT is not found in rhotic areas:

The free low vowel /a ~ ɑ/ occurs only in areas in which post-vocalic /r/ is not preserved as such, that is, in Eastern New England, Metropolitan New York [and the South] ... dialects that preserve post-vocalic /r/ lack the free /a ~ ɑ/ as a feature of their vowel system. [5, 113]

Because PALM occurs very frequently before underlying coda /r/ and LOT never does, the two vowels would nearly be in complementary distribution in a rhotic dialect. This could lead to a reanalysis where PALM merges with LOT (3-D to MAIN) or with LOT = THOUGHT (ENE to 3-M).

But does the geographic study show a correlation between rhoticity and the lack of a distinct PALM? Table 4.9 cross-tabulates speakers' low vowel patterns with a three-level rhoticity rating: "mostly r-less," "somewhat r-less," and "completely r-ful." No senior citizens were completely /r/-ful, while only one in eight young adults was mostly /r/-less.

The six speakers with a likely three-way-merged system are not noticeably skewed toward rhoticity. One, a 16-year-old from Dartmouth, Massachusetts, was even rated mostly /r/-less.[9] And 13 ENE speakers maintain a clear PALM ~ LOT distinction despite being completely /r/-ful.

This suggests that Kurath and McDavid's (1961) correlation between nonrhoticity and an independent PALM is a typological generalization

TABLE 4.9
Cross-Tabulation of 174 Low Vowel Systems by Degree of Rhoticity

| | Low Vowel System | | | | | |
	3-D	MAIN	ENE	3-M	Unclear	TOTAL[a]
Senior Citizens						
mostly r-less	5	19	18	0	0	42
somewhat r-less	1	6	14	0	0	21
Young Adults						
mostly r-less	0	7	6	1	0	14
somewhat r-less	0	31	19	3	7	60
completely r-ful	0	10	12	2	13	37

a. Four seniors and two young adults were accidentally left out of this analysis.

rather than a statement about structural incompatibility. If it is the latter, then those 13 speakers have an unstable combination, and the ENE low vowel pattern will eventually collapse if postvocalic /r/ is fully reintroduced to the area.

4.5. DISCUSSION OF THE GEOGRAPHIC STUDY: INTRODUCING THE MIGRATION HYPOTHESIS

The three original low vowels of southeastern New England underwent one round of mergers when LOT either remained rounded, lengthened, and fell in with THOUGHT (in most of eastern Massachusetts) or unrounded, lengthened, and fell in with PALM (in Rhode Island and some adjacent parts of Massachusetts). In the first area, merger was largely complete by 1900. In the second, some speakers remained three-way distinct for another few decades.

After decades where complementary two-vowel systems faced off across a sharp dialect boundary, a second round of mergers is affecting young people today. It may eventually dissolve the boundary that crystallized most prominently during the two-vowel stage.

Section 2.6 proposed that the first round of mergers had internal causes, for two reasons. First, the nineteenth-century data of chapter 2 did not show the mergers occupying less territory then, as a wave model would expect. For example, Martha's Vineyard had two ENE speakers (with the LOT ~ THOUGHT merger), while at least two of their Boston-area contemporaries were still 3-D.

Second, the early twentieth-century data in this chapter shows a sharp boundary between the ENE and MAIN two-vowel systems. There is neither a 3-M area of overlap (affected by both mergers) nor a 3-D area of "underlap" (untouched by either merger). There were 3-D seniors and 3-M young adults, but in both cases they were geographically scattered.

Moreover, the linguistic areas more or less correspond to the seventeenth-century settlement areas: most of (eastern) Massachusetts Bay and Plymouth colonies developed the ENE pattern; Rhode Island became MAIN. All three colonies were likely seeded with a phonologically identical three-vowel system. But starting with some phonetic difference(s) between them,[10] each area's communities evolved, in parallel, in opposite directions, eventually undergoing one or the other merger.

It is possible that social, migratory, and economic networks among communities helped spread the relevant changes. But since these networks tended to coalesce within the original settlement areas, it is usually impossible to tell.

The geographic study subjects lived no more than ten miles from the dialect boundary; most lived much closer. Still, very few (7%) of the senior citizens' parents had come from the other side of that boundary. Most of their parents (63%) had grown up on the same side of the line, with a substantial minority (30%) coming from foreign countries. Thirteen percent of the seniors were still living in the same city or town where they, and both of their parents, grew up.

For the young adults, an equally small proportion (8%) of their parents came from the other dialect area. The great majority of young adults' parents (78%) came from the same side of the dialect boundary as the subjects themselves. Foreign-born parents were now half as common (14%). Nineteen percent of young adults lived in the same city or town where they, and both of their parents, grew up.

The nature of this rootedness is slightly different from that found in Pennsylvania by Herold (1990, 168–69), who noted in a telephone survey that "more than 60% of the participants had two locally born parents; almost 87% had at least one locally born parent," and in the field that "almost every person I encountered was a native of the town in which we met." In this geographic study, quite a few parents had relocated some distance within the ENE or MAIN areas, just not usually across the boundary between the two.

Because interdialect migration does not appear to be increasing, it is hard to see how it could be responsible for the general weakening and sporadic collapse of the ENE and MAIN systems among the young adults—the second round of mergers.

However, nonmigratory contact between adult speakers seems even less likely to be responsible for community change, despite the probable increase in such contacts, for example, in the workplace. People from Fall River, for example, tend not to migrate across the boundary, but many of them cross it daily to reach jobs in places as close as Dartmouth or as far away as Boston.

For one thing, the vowel systems of most adults are relatively immune to change.[11] But even if adults did substantially accommodate, it would not lead to dialect change of the rapid type observed in the geographic study (and in the family study of chapter 5), unless parents abandoned a distinction quickly and thoroughly enough that their children did not acquire it. Otherwise, any merger would only occur by gradual approximation.

Parental change may have some limited effect on the initial input to children, but parents have a greater effect if they migrate to another dialect area while they have young children (or before they are born). The first dialect these children are exposed to—that of their family—will differ from the one they are exposed to from around the age of four—that of their peers.

If a single child joins a peer group with a different vowel system, we can ask to what extent the individual will adapt to the group and what factors promote or prevent this adaptation (see chap. 3). But the peer group—and the larger community—is unlikely to change unless joined by a critical mass of speakers who differ from the locals.

Migration is one of the most likely sources of child-to-child dialect contact. Except for some preschools, after-school activities, and visits with cousins, most children interviewed had little contact with children in other communities, even adjacent ones. This makes the mechanism of any contagious diffusion unclear.[12]

But, even if a general increase in interdialect migration is questionable, in the particular, formerly MAIN places where PALM = LOT and THOUGHT are merging—South Attleboro and South Bellingham (§4.2); Seekonk, Cumberland, and Warwick, Rhode Island (chap. 5)—we may propose that the merger is triggered by people migrating from the ENE side of the boundary.

Over the last few decades, as real estate prices closer to Boston have risen, people have moved further from the city and its older suburbs. And, perhaps for the first time, this migration is passing beyond the old dialect boundary, reaching places such as the ones just mentioned. This demographic argument will be considered using U.S. Census data in §5.9.2.1.

The second round of mergers also includes the merger, observed sporadically among the younger geographic study subjects, of PALM and LOT = THOUGHT in the ENE territory. The evidence of migration from MAIN to ENE—with its source not just in Rhode Island but in western Massachusetts, Connecticut, New York, New Jersey, and elsewhere—will be treated in section 5.9.2.2.

For these arguments to be most compelling, they require not only a sufficient current level of migration, but a level that has recently been on the increase. For if migration has been constant for decades, we are left with the question of why these mergers are happening now.[13]

If the second round of mergers is not caused by juvenile dialect contact as the result of migration, what else could account for it? The internal pressure that may have existed in the old 3-D days to simplify a crowded three-vowel system is not likely to apply to the ENE and MAIN systems. Some discussion of other possibilities is found in section 5.10.

Although the geographic study area was fairly large, it did not extend very far on either side of the original dialect boundary. So, a change observed in the study area could be happening over a wider area, or it could just be happening near the dialect boundary. But even in the latter case, the change would not necessarily be happening because of the proximity of speakers of the other dialect. This is because a moving boundary can be of (at least) three types: change spreads from place A to adjacent place B (contagious or relocation diffusion); change spreads from C to A, then later from C to B (hierarchical or relocation diffusion); or change develops internally in A before it develops in B (no diffusion).

We could better classify the newer round of mergers by looking at places far from the dialect boundary, ones that receive little in-migration from other dialect areas. If children are merging *cot* and *caught* not only in South Attleboro, but also in rural southwestern Rhode Island, or if they are rhyming *father* and *bother* not only in Dighton, Massachusetts, but also in small towns in Maine, then we will know these mergers are not (always) caused by migration across a dialect boundary. This might lead us to adopt a language-internal explanation, or even an account involving the mass media.

Focusing on a densely populated area along a dialect boundary, the geographic study has shown how 350-year-old phonetic patterns developed in parallel into two internally uniform phonological dialect areas. Once manifested, these remained stable for several generations despite being in close contact. This argues for the reality and autonomy of dialect areas and against the view that change primarily proceeds by diffusion.

This study had neither the time depth nor the spatial width to fully test Herzog's Principle and its prediction of merger expansion. However, it did demonstrate that dialects can be in close contact for some time without the spread of mergers.[14]

The study also revealed one case where a distinction expanded along with a merger: in Assonet, the community pattern evolved over the twentieth century from 3-D to MAIN to ENE to 3-M. The step from MAIN to ENE involved unmerging LOT from PALM and merging it with THOUGHT. This occurred several decades after Assonet children began to attend school with a large number of ENE speakers from East Freetown and Lakeville.

This chapter has looked at the phonological patterns among three low vowel word classes, PALM, LOT, and THOUGHT. If low vowel systems had no meaningful correlations with other phonological and lexical differences between dialects, then this study would have little relevance beyond the subfield of vowel mergers.

And indeed, not every linguistic (let alone cultural) phenomenon persists and simplifies in the same way these vowel systems have. Lexical innovations must spread quickly through contact, while patterns of vowel chain shift may be even more structurally predestined than mergers. However, assuming the low vowel systems found in the dialects of the geographic study area meaningfully relate to the rest of their phonologies, the principles sketched here will be seen to bear more generally on the processes underlying dialect stability and change.

5. THE FAMILY STUDY

THE FAMILY STUDY focused on merger at the level of the speech community, as opposed to the dialect (chap. 4) or individual (chap. 3). Speech communities are more socially real than dialect areas—at least, their members are more closely interconnected—and linguistically more consistent than idiolects (Weinreich, Labov, and Herzog 1968, 188). Here, a speech community is equivalent to a city or town, or division thereof.

The study area's speech communities differ from some urban ones in that many adults work outside their boundaries. But this does not affect the children growing up there. Especially for younger children, almost all peers are residents of the same city or town, whose boundaries (as is typical in New England) almost always coincide with those of the school system.

Traditional dialect geography, in Europe (Pop 1950) and New England (Kurath et al. 1939), took the town or village as the sampling unit that combined to form dialect areas. Towns in New England are no longer self-sufficient entities; many now function as suburbs. But the results of chapter 4 suggest that the town is still a valid unit of linguistic patterning.

Inspired by Herold (1990), the family study focused on the short period over which a speech community's children can stop acquiring a vowel distinction: that is, learn a merger. In Tamaqua, Pennsylvania, Herold found this period of change to be as short as ten years. In South Attleboro, Massachusetts, section 4.2 found merger overtaking the community in just two or three years.

The geographic study found substantial stability over 50–60 years; many young adults had the same patterns as senior citizens in the same community. Individuals sometimes differed, often by following parents rather than peers. But South Attleboro, South Bellingham, and Assonet, Massachusetts, showed community change between seniors and young adults.[1] The family study was conducted (in 2005–6) where this kind of change was found among younger children.

Figure 5.1 shows the family study communities, using the young adults' map as a background. The family study mostly took place within the territory of right-pointing triangles—the "Mid-Atlantic" (MAIN)—where, at least in the past, PALM = LOT ≠ THOUGHT. The term "distinction" refers to this two-vowel pattern; "merger" refers to PALM = LOT = THOUGHT (3-M).

The first family study community was Attleboro, Massachusetts, where the geographic study adults were divided between MAIN in South Attle-

FIGURE 5.1

Locations of 47 Families Interviewed

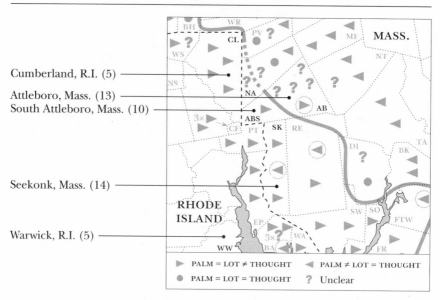

Cumberland, R.I. (5)

Attleboro, Mass. (13)
South Attleboro, Mass. (10)

Seekonk, Mass. (14)

Warwick, R.I. (5)

boro and ENE in the rest of the city. In South Attleboro, ten families were interviewed, with 18 children ranging in age from 5 to 19. In the rest of Attleboro, there were 13 families, with 26 children ranging from 3 to 18.[2]

The initial intent was to observe younger children from the two sections before they came together in high school, comparing them with high schoolers who were mixed. However, in line with section 4.2, we will see in section 5.1 that South Attleboro children did not retain their parents' distinction. In other words, community change had already occurred; it was too late in South Attleboro to observe contact between children with different low vowel systems.

The focus was shifted south and west, to towns where some children were distinct. Unlike Attleboro, these places had no geographic divide, but there was a temporal one.

Perhaps the most interesting community was Seekonk, Massachusetts, where 14 families were interviewed, including 34 children, ages 3–17. Section 5.2 shows a break between children over 10, who maintained their parents' low back distinction (MAIN), and those under 10, who were merged (3-M). Although section 5.2.3 discusses a family with a distinct 3-year-old son, this is an exception that proves the rule, since he did not have a peer group yet.[3]

The geographic study's young adults were too old to have shown this PALM = LOT ~ THOUGHT merger, but the school survey did show clear evidence of the same change between the twelfth grade (largely distinct), eighth grade (mixed), and fourth grade (more merged than distinct).

The five families interviewed in Cumberland, Rhode Island, with 13 children between 5 and 16, were similar in that, within families, older children were distinct and younger ones merged. But unlike in Seekonk, no overall age cutoff could be drawn in Cumberland; for example, there was a distinct five-year-old, but a merged eleven-year-old (in different families).[4]

The nearby ENE area where LOT and THOUGHT are merged—leaving aside that PALM is traditionally distinct there—is a potential source of this change, if it is diffusion. We can distinguish contagious diffusion ("the merger is spreading from town to town"), hierarchical diffusion ("the influence of Boston and/or its speech is growing wider and wider"), and relocation diffusion ("people from Greater Boston are moving further and further out from the city").

Non-diffusionist accounts of the change include internal/structural explanations, as well as those pointing to the influence of the mass media or of a growing national standard.

To help decide between these, an ideal test site would have been deep in the interior of the MAIN dialect area (see §5.10). The final family study community, Warwick, Rhode Island, was in fact only slightly further from the original MAIN/ENE boundary, lying to the south of Providence (Seekonk is east of Providence, Cumberland north).

Five families were interviewed in Warwick, with 12 children, ages 4 to 15. Four of the families had Rhode Island parents; the other set were from Maine and Texas, so their children presented an interesting example of the acquisition from peers of local norms, including the low back vowel distinction.

But the distinction, while stronger, was not universally maintained by the children in Warwick either. It appeared as though Warwick might be just five or ten years behind Seekonk and Cumberland in progressing toward the low back merger. Because Warwick is such a locally rooted Rhode Island community, if the merger is indeed taking hold there, it would probably indicate the recessive status of the distinction everywhere in the vicinity.

The family study communities are profiled in table 5.1. In each community, parents and children were interviewed talking about their lives and backgrounds to obtain spontaneous speech, and with formal methods to obtain a concentration of the vowels of interest.

A smaller set of reading cards was used than in the geographic study, with simpler vocabulary targeted at young children. In (South) Attle-

TABLE 5.1
Summary of Families in the Study

Community	Families	Children	Recruited via	LOT ~ THOUGHT in Adults	LOT ~ THOUGHT in Children
Attleboro	13	26	PTA	merged	merged
S. Attleboro	10	18	PTA	distinct	merged
Seekonk	14	34	survey	distinct	under 10 merged
Cumberland	5	13	network	distinct	younger merged
Warwick	5	12	PTA	distinct	incipient merger?

boro and Cumberland, five cards contrasted *cot ~ caught, Don ~ Dawn, knotty ~ naughty, tot ~ taught,* and *Otto ~ auto.* The last of these proved difficult for some children and was replaced in Seekonk and Warwick by *nod ~ gnawed* and *tock ~ talk.*

The "covert" reading of the key words embedded in sentences was judged "same" or "different" by the analyst. Both analyst and subject gave their impressions of the "overt" repetition, when the minimal pairs were presented out of context on the back of the card.

Subjects too young to read these cards were given a series of picture flashcards. Each of these had a photograph or drawing of a common object, such as a ball, a doll, pasta with sauce, and so on.

Based on auditory impressions, almost all of the adults and most of the children in the family study were easy to label as either "merged" or "distinct" with respect to the low back vowels. Of 86 parents, 75 (87%) were judged clearly merged or distinct, and 8 (9%) were judged probably merged or distinct. Only 3 parents (3%) were more profoundly unclear.

Among children, only 65 of 107 (61%) were confidently labeled merged or distinct, with 40 (37%) labeled probably merged or distinct. Only 2 (2%) seemed truly unclear.

Some "probably merged" children pronounced most LOT and THOUGHT words alike, with a low unrounded vowel, but then one or two of their THOUGHT words would be more back and raised. Other children sounded merged in their spontaneous speech, but in reading—especially in overt minimal pairs—they showed evidence of the distinction.

This difference between styles was never extreme, nor very consistent, but it does differ from the "perception leading production" reported for mergers in progress (Herold 1990, 94–99). Instead, spontaneous speech more closely matches the peer group (or incoming norm), while more conscious productions (and judgments) reflect the dialect learned from parents (or older norm).

5.1. THE FAMILIES OF ATTLEBORO
AND SOUTH ATTLEBORO, MASSACHUSETTS

The 44 children of the 23 Attleboro and South Attleboro families are shown on figure 5.2. In this figure (and subsequent ones), each vertical line represents one family, with the children arranged by age along that line. Boys are represented by squares, girls by circles.

Children with a clear low back merger have black symbols; those with a probable merger have symbols that are black with a white center. Children with a clear low back distinction have white symbols; those with a probable distinction are white with a black center. (Any more unclear cases will be colored grey, although there are no such children on figure 5.2.)

The families are divided between South Attleboro, on the right, and the rest of Attleboro, on the left. And each group is divided according to the low back vowel status of the childrens' parents.

The left side of the figure is like a control group, as Attleboro has had the low back merger for a century. There, when both parents were merged, all five children (100%) were "definitely merged." When only one parent was merged, six children (50%) were definitely merged and six probably merged. When both parents were distinct, three children (33%) were definitely merged, five probably merged, and one was judged "probably distinct."

This was Nora Lucas, age 6 (all names are pseudonyms). Her parents grew up in New York State; both had clear low back distinctions. The Lucas family had lived in eastern Connecticut, also in the MAIN area of low back

FIGURE 5.2

The Children of Attleboro and South Attleboro, Massachusetts

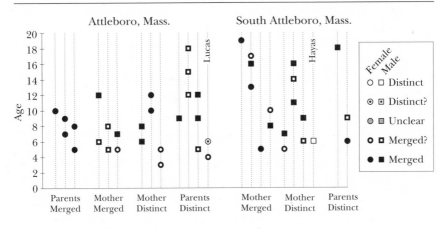

distinction, before moving to Attleboro. Nora had spent preschool and half of kindergarten in Connecticut and was in the middle of first grade in Attleboro when interviewed. Though she now exhibits a probable distinction, she is young enough that we might expect her to eventually acquire the merged pattern of her current peers.

Missy Lucas, age 4, had not attended school in Connecticut. She was in her first year of preschool in Attleboro. Judged "probably merged," she is more like the other Attleboro children than her sister. Since the sisters had the same distinct parental exposure, it is likely Nora's longer exposure to the distinction from peers that has led to her currently anomalous status.

As well as serving as a control group, the Attleboro families show a merger in progress between LOT = THOUGHT and PALM. Although LOT and THOUGHT, not PALM, were the principal focus of the formal methods, we can still identify three Attleboro families—shown at the left in figure 5.2— where the parents had the ENE pattern: a merger of LOT ~ THOUGHT and a distinct PALM.

Their 5 children all had the LOT ~ THOUGHT merger. For a 10-year-old and a (unrelated) 7-year-old, PALM was possibly distinct. For the 7-year-old's 9-year-old sister, PALM was possibly merged with LOT = THOUGHT (3-M); the same was true for sisters, ages 8 and 5, in another family. Even for the possible 3-M speakers, some tokens of LOT = THOUGHT retained a lightly rounded, back quality not shared by PALM, suggesting an underlying distinction may still exist.

Recall that NT86F, the ENE senior citizen analyzed acoustically (§4.3.2.2), had a wide phonetic distinction between PALM and LOT = THOUGHT, averaging over 300 Hz in F2. For NA30M, the ENE young adult (§4.3.3.2), F2 was some 150 Hz greater in PALM than in LOT = THOUGHT.

Judging by ear, the younger children in Attleboro are continuing this merger by approximation between the word classes PALM and LOT = THOUGHT, a progression also visible on the school survey (§3.6.2.3). If the classes are not now merged, they are so close that many tokens would be needed for an accurate analysis.

Moving to the right side of figure 5.2, recall from section 4.2 that South Attleboro adults 20 and older have the low back distinction (MAIN). But there has been rapid and dramatic change; of the 18 children, 11 were definitely merged (3-M) and six probably were. The merger was found even in the children whose parents were both distinct (just two families here, this is the most common South Attleboro family type and the most important for tracking the appearance of merger).

The exception to merger was Caleb Hayas, age 6. Caleb's mother was from Rhode Island and had a strong distinction. His father had come from

South America in his 20s, and his nonnative low vowels did not follow any clear pattern. Caleb's spontaneous speech was "definitely distinct"; in identifying the flashcards he was "probably distinct."

Two other children interviewed in Caleb Hayas's first-grade class were "definitely merged" and "probably merged," making it unlikely that Caleb Hayas has a distinct peer group. Rather, Caleb may still be dominated by the linguistic influence of his mother, despite being old enough to have peers. While no information was gathered on his integration with peers at school, Caleb, an only child, appeared somewhat socially awkward and/or immature. His parents also spoke of him having had a delay in learning to speak. He may be a late bloomer as far as adopting the linguistic patterns of his peers.

5.2. THE FAMILIES OF SEEKONK, MASSACHUSETTS

The 34 children from the 14 families interviewed in Seekonk are shown on figure 5.3. The five families on the left each had one parent with the low back merger (or in one case, an unclear pattern). The nine families on the right each had two clearly distinct parents (many from Seekonk themselves, most others from Rhode Island).

In the five families with a merged parent, all 12 children are either definitely or probably merged. This suggests that these children's peer groups do not maintain the low back distinction uniformly or strongly enough to reverse parental influence (§5.5 will show that this can happen).

In the nine families with distinct parents, the children pattern by age. Of the 11 children in fifth grade or higher (aged 10 or older), eight are definitely distinct and two probably distinct, with just one definitely merged.[5] The six fourth graders are evenly split, with three definitely merged, two probably distinct, and one definitely distinct. And of the six children in third grade or lower (aged 9 or younger), three are definitely merged and two probably merged, with only one 3-year-old probably distinct (see §5.2.2.4).

The young children of Seekonk, a group of whom enter (pre)school and form peer groups every year, adopted the merger around 2000, when the current fourth grade was in preschool.[6] Figure 5.3 shows neither boys nor girls in the lead in adopting the merger. Of known factors, age alone predicts vowel system (within the group of nine families with distinct parents). This is especially noteworthy for those families with children both above and below the crucial age.

FIGURE 5.3
The Children of Seekonk, Massachusetts

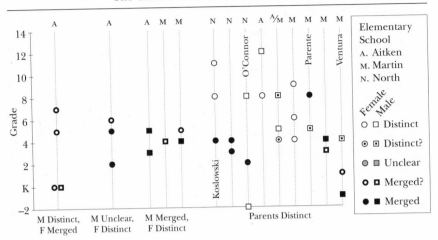

Three families show that ongoing linguistic change can separate siblings: Koslowski, O'Connor, and Ventura. For the Koslowskis, the break is between their distinct eighth-grade daughter, April, and their merged fourth-grade daughter, Sharon. For the O'Connors, eighth-grade son Daniel is distinct, and 2nd-grade daughter Alison is merged. Less clearly, for the Venturas, fourth-grade son Jacob is probably distinct, and 1st-grade daughter Jessica is probably merged.

The younger, merged siblings illustrate how children's peers can overthrow the patterns they learned from their parents and from their older siblings, their "first peer group" (Payne 1976, 268). But the fact that siblings can radically differ in their low vowel systems should not imply that they never influence each other. Apart from Sharon Koslowski and Jacob Ventura, the Seekonk fourth graders do pattern with their siblings. The two with younger siblings are merged, like those siblings. And the two with older siblings are, like those siblings, distinct.

5.2.1. THE KOSLOWSKI FAMILY. Tom (PT42M) and Lonnie (PT43F) Koslowski have robust low back distinctions. Their older daughters, Amber (SK16F) and April (SK13F), have distinctions that are much less extreme. Their youngest daughter, Sharon (SK09F), has a total merger of PALM = LOT and THOUGHT.

5.2.1.1. *Tom and Lonnie Koslowski.* Like many adults in Seekonk, Massachusetts, Tom Koslowski (a driver) and Lonnie Koslowski (a travel agent) grew up in adjacent Pawtucket, Rhode Island. And like the geographic study subjects from that city, they both maintain a robust distinction between

PALM = LOT and THOUGHT. As seen in figures 5.4 and 5.5, the token clouds for the two categories are small and well separated.

Paired *t*-tests (see §4.3.1.2) give low *p*-values for Tom, indicating a sure distinction:

ΔLOT – THOUGHT (PT42M, C, 6) = +199 ±65 (p = .0006), +374 ±151 (p = .002)
ΔLOT – THOUGHT (PT42M, O, 6) = +188 ±20 (p = 3 × 10^{-6}), +336 ±90 (p = .0002)

The average difference in F1 is almost 200 Hz, and in F2 it is around 350 Hz. The difference between styles is small and does not show the usual trend, whereby overt pairs are further apart. All pairs were judged "different" by the analyst, as well as by Tom himself.

Lonnie's pairs also sounded different to analyst and subject, and measured far apart:

ΔLOT – THOUGHT (PT43F, C, 6) = +285 ±53 (p = 4 × 10^{-5}) +430 ±194 (p = .003)
ΔLOT – THOUGHT (PT43F, O, 6) = +350 ±141 (p = .002), +490 ±78 (p = 2 × 10^{-5})

This distinction, of 300 Hz in F1 and 450 Hz in F2, is even larger in raw acoustic terms than that of ABS62M (§4.3.2.1). Lonnie's overt pairs are slightly further apart than her covert pairs, with one exception. The overt repetition of *naughty* sounded "corrected," and indeed it measured closer to the LOT tokens than to the other examples of THOUGHT.

5.2.1.2. *Amber and April Koslowski.* Amber Koslowski (SK16F) had always lived in Seekonk and was an eleventh grader at Seekonk High School when interviewed. Her low back vowels sounded distinct, but close. Acoustic measurement (figure 5.6) shows some overlap between LOT and THOUGHT, but within each pair, the THOUGHT word is usually fronter and lower than the corresponding LOT word:

ΔLOT – THOUGHT (SK16F, C, 6) = +110 ±114 (p = .06), +66 ±123 (p = .23)
ΔLOT – THOUGHT (SK16F, O, 6) = +147 ±139 (p = .05), +216 ±154 (p = .02)

Only one covert pair was robustly distinct: *Don ~ Dawn* (+310, +303), exceptional again. Two other covert pairs had a 100+ Hz difference in F1, and two more had a 50+ Hz difference in F1. The sixth covert pair, *tot ~ taught*, was pronounced more or less identically: −11, +35.

Of the overt pairs, though, only one was truly close: again *tot ~ taught* (+58, +41—so still in the "right direction"). The next-closest overt pair, *tock ~ talk*, was nearly 100 Hz apart in F1 and F2. The other four overt pairs had a 100+ Hz difference in one or both formants.

Because of the covert-pair results, we might doubt the pervasiveness of Amber's distinction. However, in her spontaneous speech she exhibited the

FIGURE 5.4
Tom Koslowski (father): LOT ~ THOUGHT Pairs

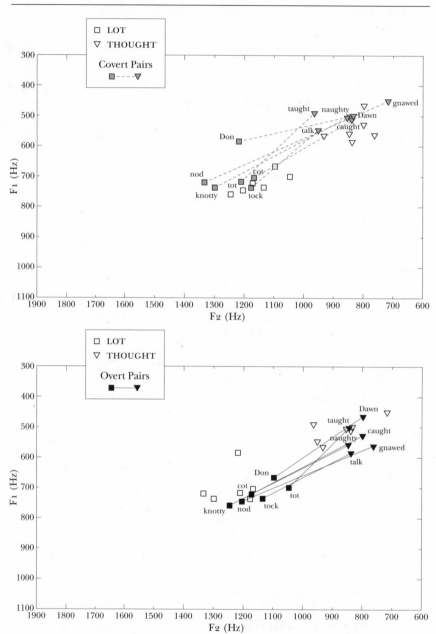

FIGURE 5.5
Lonnie Koslowski (mother): LOT ~ THOUGHT Pairs

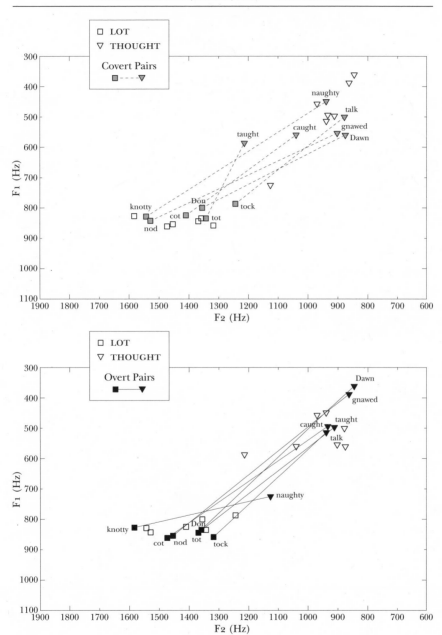

FIGURE 5.6
Amber Koslowski (oldest sister): LOT ~ THOUGHT Pairs

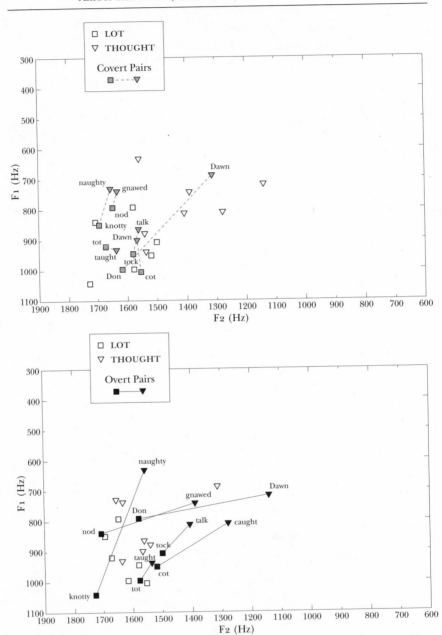

same close-but-distinct behavior. She also showed no hesitation in judging all the minimal pairs to be different.

Note also that if we boost the sample size by combining covert and overt tokens, we obtain a *t*-test result indicative of a modestly sized, but significant, distinction in both F_1 and F_2:

ΔLOT – THOUGHT (SK16F, CO, 12) = +128 ±74 (p = .003), +141 ±95 (p = .008)

April Koslowski (SK13F) had also always lived in Seekonk. When interviewed, she was in eighth grade at Seekonk Middle School, where she had marked 6 of 7 LOT ~ THOUGHT pairs "different" on the school survey. Unlike her parents, but like her older sister, April did not produce large phonetic differences between LOT and THOUGHT words. However, she gave the impression of a clear distinction and identified every pair as different.

In figure 5.7, her tokens of LOT and THOUGHT form two adjacent clouds, which only overlap slightly. Her overt token of *nod* does appear in the middle of the cloud of THOUGHT tokens, but its pair, *gnawed,* is also an outlier, measuring higher than all other tokens of THOUGHT.

The paired *t*-tests support a moderate distinction. For covert pairs, it is larger in F_2 (unlike Amber's). For the overt pairs, it is consistent, though not large, in both formants:

ΔLOT – THOUGHT (SK13F, C, 6) = +107 ±137 (p = .10), +212 ±137 (p = .01)
ΔLOT – THOUGHT (SK13F, O, 6) = +168 ±47 (p = .0003), +138 ±64 (p = .003)

The closest pair April produced was the covert *cot ~ caught*: +40, +83. Amber had produced four pairs that were closer than that (measuring along the F_1/F_2 diagonal).

The Koslowski teenagers have a much closer acoustic distinction than their parents. This does not directly imply change in Seekonk, since their parents are from Pawtucket. But section 5.2.2 will show that the O'Connor parents, from Seekonk, also have a wide distinction.

Amber and April Koslowski's distinctions are functional, audible, and phonologically intact. But phonetically, they are narrow—especially Amber's. And while a distinction this close might be able to maintain itself over time, it would not be too surprising if it were to collapse.

5.2.1.3. *Sharon Koslowski.* For Sharon Koslowski (SK09F), this collapse has occurred. Sharon was a fourth grader at North Elementary, who marked 6 of 7 pairs "same" on the school survey. She declared all the reading card pairs "same." And they sounded the same, except the covert *nod ~ gnawed.*

Figure 5.8 plots Sharon's low back vowels. Their combined phonetic area is very similar to that of her older sisters. There are considerable acous-

FIGURE 5.7
April Koslowski (middle sister): LOT ~ THOUGHT Pairs

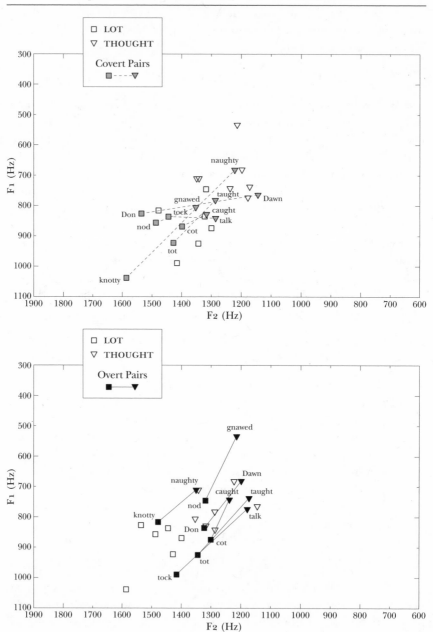

FIGURE 5.8
Sharon Koslowski (youngest sister): LOT ~ THOUGHT Pairs

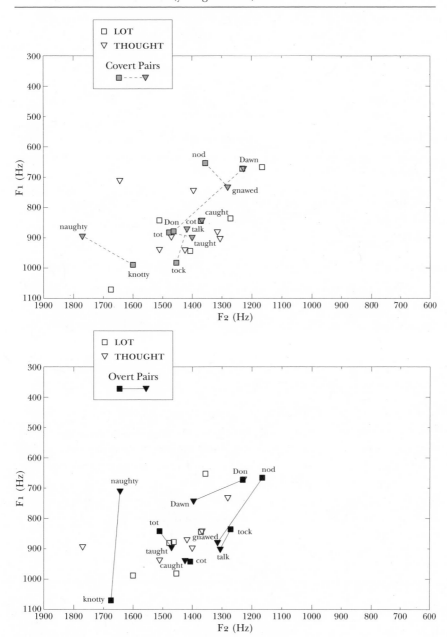

TABLE 5.2

The Koslowski Family: Summary of Reading Card Productions

Speaker		Covert Pairs (F1, F2)	
	Mean LOT	Mean THOUGHT	Δ LOT − THOUGHT
Tom, 42	699, 1234	500, 860	+199, +374
Lonnie, 43	820, 1405	535, 975	+285, +430
Amber, 16	919, 1627	809, 1561	+110, +66
April, 13	891, 1480	784, 1268	+107, +212
Sharon, 9	871, 1454	817, 1411	+54, +43
Speaker		Overt Pairs (F1, F2)	
	Mean LOT	Mean THOUGHT	Δ LOT − THOUGHT
Tom, 42	720, 1150	532, 815	+188, +336
Lonnie, 43	846, 1426	496, 936	+350, +490
Amber, 16	922, 1601	775, 1385	+147, +216
April, 13	864, 1363	696, 1225	+168, +138
Sharon, 9	838, 1377	844, 1426	−6, −49

tic differences between most pairs. But there is no regularity to the direction of these differences. For example, the overt token of *knotty* is 361 Hz higher in F1 than *naughty*; but the overt *nod* is 212 Hz lower in F1 than *gnawed*. The paired *t*-tests return nonsignificant results in all respects:

Δ LOT − THOUGHT (SK09F, C, 6) = +54 ±109 (*p* = .26), +43 ±138 (*p* = .46)
Δ LOT − THOUGHT (SK09F, O, 6) = −6 ±203 (*p* = .95), −49 ±92 (*p* = .23)

When Sharon was asked if she could say the words differently, she produced an accurate imitation of a distinct pattern. She knows which words belong in which class, perhaps dating from their initial acquisition from her distinct family. But she normally ignores or suppresses this knowledge. This makes her an excellent example of merger by expansion. The merger has literally taken place within a generation: only four years separate April and Sharon (neither of whom was very interested in the linguistic difference revealed between them).

Table 5.2 summarizes the Koslowskis' performances on the reading card LOT ~ THOUGHT pairs. Highlighted figures represent significant differences (*p* < .05) on the paired *t*-test.

5.2.2. THE O'CONNOR FAMILY. Jeff (SK37M) and Rochelle (SK37F) O'Connor were clearly distinct. Their children are Daniel (SK14M), with the distinction, Alison (SK08F), with a full merger, and Casey (SK03M), of pre-preschool age. Casey may grow up to be merged, but he currently exhibits the distinction, reflecting the predominant influence of parents on children his age.

5.2.2.1. Jeff and Rochelle O'Connor. While Tom and Lonnie Koslowski moved from Pawtucket to Seekonk in adulthood, Jeff and Rochelle O'Connor grew up Seekonk and attended Seekonk High School. Jeff is a correctional officer, while Rochelle stays home taking care of Casey and an infant. Their robust low back distinctions (figs. 5.9 and 5.10) are similar to those of the Koslowski parents.

Jeff's tokens of LOT and THOUGHT form tight clouds that are well separated. He judged all six pairs to be "different," and the paired *t*-tests confirm a definite low back distinction:

$$\Delta \text{LOT} - \text{THOUGHT (SK37M, C, 6)} = +129 \pm 60 \ (p = .003), +385 \pm 79 \ (p = 6 \times 10^{-5})$$
$$\Delta \text{LOT} - \text{THOUGHT (SK37M, O, 6)} = +154 \pm 97 \ (p = .01), +392 \pm 83 \ (p = 7 \times 10^{-5})$$

There is only a very small, non-significant increase in separation for Jeff's overt pairs.

Rochelle O'Connor produced an even greater distinction than her husband, just as Lonnie Koslowski had. Rochelle also judged all six pairs different. While Rochelle O'Connor's THOUGHT was not as high and back (in absolute acoustic terms) as Lonnie Koslowski's, her LOT was fronter and lower, so the overall size of the distinction was comparable:

$$\Delta \text{LOT} - \text{THOUGHT (SK37F, C, 5)} = +337 \pm 190 \ (p = .008), +495 \pm 211 \ (p = .003)$$
$$\Delta \text{LOT} - \text{THOUGHT (SK37F, O, 6)} = +308 \pm 116 \ (p = .001), +435 \pm 94 \ (p = 8 \times 10^{-5})$$

Rochelle is slightly less distinct on the overt pairs, suggesting some correction (an extreme distinction can be stigmatized). But even her closest pair, the overt *tock ~ talk*, was far apart (+167, +381); her covert *nod ~ gnawed* differed immensely (+571, +761).

Although their older children would show approximation of the low vowels and their younger children merger, the Koslowski and O'Connor parents show no sign of either.

5.2.2.2. Daniel Peterson. Daniel Peterson (SK14M) is the oldest child of Rochelle O'Connor by her first husband, who was from Wisconsin and Florida, hence probably distinct and, phonologically at least, like the parents Daniel has lived with since age 4. An eighth grader at Seekonk Middle School, Daniel marked all seven LOT ~ THOUGHT items "different" on the school survey.

In the interview, he produced a much narrower distinction than his parents, but still a clear and consistent one (fig. 5.11). He judged all six

FIGURE 5.9
Jeff O'Connor (father): LOT ~ THOUGHT Pairs

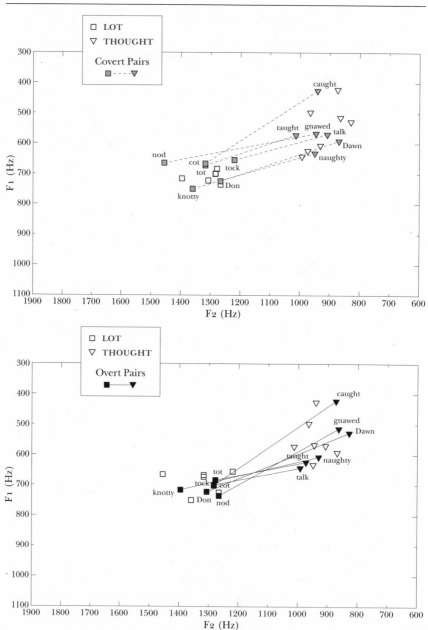

FIGURE 5.10
Rochelle O'Connor (mother): LOT ~ THOUGHT Pairs

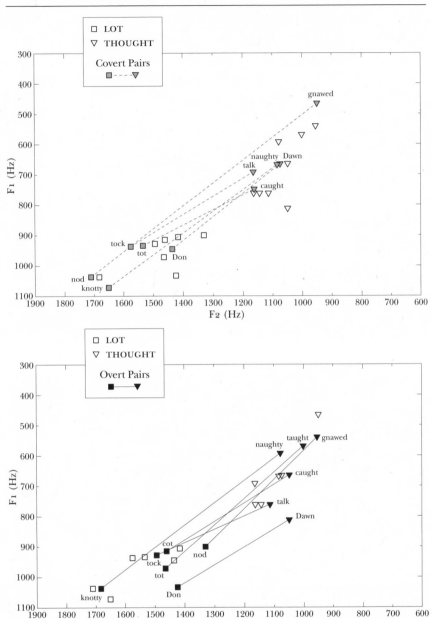

FIGURE 5.11
Daniel Peterson (oldest brother): LOT ~ THOUGHT Pairs

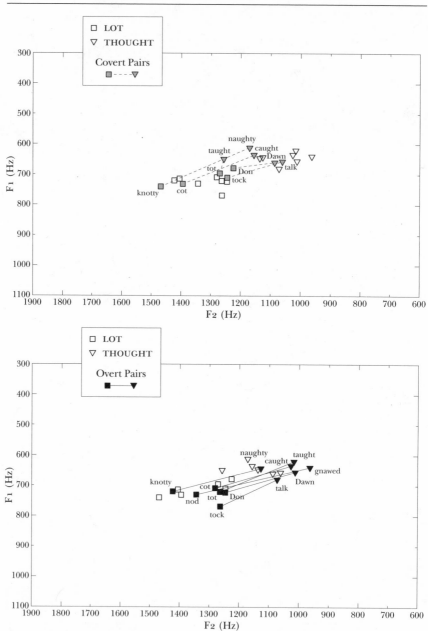

pairs "different." Only one pair measured close: the covert *tot ~ taught* (+47, +13). Paired *t*-tests are significant, rejecting the hypothesis of merger. They also show the overt pairs further apart than the covert ones:

ΔLOT – THOUGHT (SK14M, C, 5) = +68 ±54 (*p* = .03), +175 ±135 (*p* = .03)
ΔLOT – THOUGHT (SK14M, O, 6) = +83 ±13 (*p* = 2 × 10⁻⁵), +267 ±68 (*p* = .0002)

Daniel's LOT is in the same absolute position as his stepfather's. Daniel's THOUGHT is higher and backer than LOT, in the same direction as his stepfather's, but only half as far apart.

There has been much phonetic approximation in Seekonk between Jeff and Rochelle's generation and Daniel's. But Daniel's low vowels are still consistently distinct in perception and production; they are not acoustically close either in reading or spontaneous speech.

Daniel differs from April Koslowski, his classmate, in being higher and backer—more like their parents' generation—in both LOT and THOUGHT. Daniel's distinction is also less in F1 and more in F2 than April's. But the overall size of their moderate distinctions is similar.

5.2.2.3. *Alison O'Connor.* Daniel's half-sister Alison O'Connor (SK08F), a second grader at North Elementary when interviewed, produced vowels similar to Sharon Koslowski's: merged in low-central position.

Alison was given both the picture flashcards and the reading cards. She read well, but hesitated on some of the key words in context (covert pairs). When this happened—or when Alison said *catched* for *caught* on a picture card—her mother would model the word, and Alison would repeat it. Her repetitions of her mother's pronunciation were quite faithful, including a high back THOUGHT. But when Alison then produced the same words on her own (overt pairs), this phonetic quality disappeared; the pairs sounded more or less the same. Alison did not express strong opinions regarding whether pairs were same or different.

Excluding those words repeated after her mother, Alison O'Connor's vowels (fig. 5.12) resemble Sharon Koslowski's, in their random appearance. The furthest-apart pairs differ in the opposite direction from a MAIN pattern: covert *knotty* is 303 Hz higher than *naughty*, overt *Don* is 587 Hz higher than *Dawn* (while these pairs do sound "backwards," the auditory effect is not that extreme). The nonsignificant *t*-tests indicate merger:

ΔLOT – THOUGHT (SK08F, C, 3) = −116 ±452 (*p* = .39), +28 ±588 (*p* = .86)
ΔLOT – THOUGHT (SK08F, O, 5) = −114 ±337 (*p* = .40), −9 ±208 (*p* = .91)

Sharon Koslowski, age 9, could imitate the low back distinction on request; Alison O'Connor, age 8, produced it when repeating her mother's

FIGURE 5.12
Alison O'Connor (middle sister): LOT ~ THOUGHT Pairs

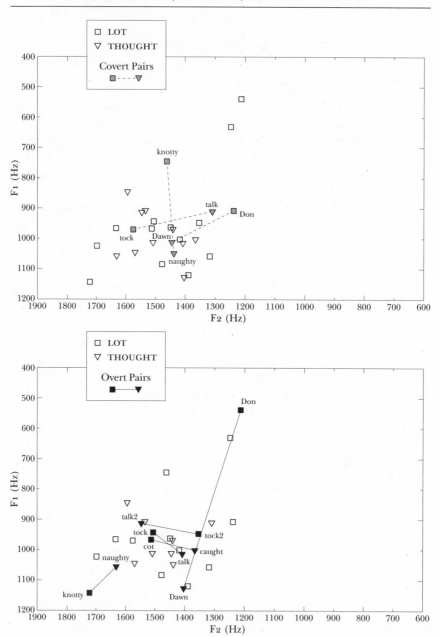

words. In more natural speech, both exemplified merger by expansion, in contrast to the distinction shown by their parents and teenage siblings.

5.2.2.4. *Casey O'Connor.* Three-year-old Casey O'Connor (SK03M) was taken care of by his mother at home; he did not yet attend any preschool and had no significant contact with other children his age. He was given the picture cards to identify, and some of the resulting tokens, along with some from spontaneous speech (bolded), are plotted in figure 5.13.

Other than *Bob2*, which is very high, *box*, which is fairly high, and *all*, which is fairly low, the LOT and THOUGHT clouds are widely separated. Without minimal pairs, a paired *t*-test cannot be run, but an unpaired *t*-test indicates a significant distinction in F1 and F2.

The mean value of F1 is 1273 Hz for all 12 LOT tokens and 818 Hz for all 15 THOUGHT tokens, a difference of 455 Hz, with a *p*-value of 9×10^{-8}. For F2, the mean is 1793 Hz for LOT and 1319 Hz for THOUGHT, a difference of 474 Hz, with a *p*-value of 2×10^{-7}. (If unpaired *t*-tests are run on Rochelle O'Connor's data, the *p*-values are in the same 10^{-7}–10^{-8} range.)

Casey's distinction sounded wide; indeed, it is the widest measured in raw acoustic terms, though his small vocal tract is partly responsible for the large frequency range. By the age of 3, Casey has acquired the distinction of his parents (and brother), dispelling any potential suggestion that 8-year-old Alison (or 9-year-old Sharon Koslowski) is simply too young to have mastered the low vowel distinction.

Assuming the conversion of successive grades of Seekonk children to the merger is permanent, we will expect Casey O'Connor to abandon his distinction when he acquires peers in preschool and kindergarten, like his sister Alison presumably did before him.

This conversion will probably happen quickly, judging by the Ventura family. The Ventura parents are clearly distinct, their 10-year-old son probably distinct, and their 7-year-old daughter probably merged; all this is expected given their ages. But their 4-year-old son Eddie was definitely merged, even though he was still home with his mother (like Casey O'Connor). Eddie hardly had a full peer group, but he did have a few "little friends." Not much peer contact with the merger seems to have been necessary for Eddie to adopt it. Having a merged older sister may have helped.

5.2.3. SUMMARY OF SEEKONK FAMILIES. Table 5.3 summarizes the vowel measurements for the O'Connor family. Children of distinct parents in Seekonk show change, with older children distinct (though not as much as their parents), fourth graders divided, and younger schoolchildren merged.

FIGURE 5.13

Casey O'Connor (youngest brother): Tokens of LOT and THOUGHT

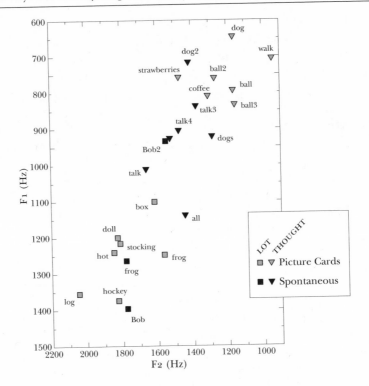

TABLE 5.3

The O'Connor Family: Summary of Reading Card Productions

Speaker	Covert Pairs (F1, F2)		
	Mean LOT	Mean THOUGHT	Δ LOT − THOUGHT
Jeff, 37	689, 1323	560, 938	+129, +385
Rochelle, 37	985, 1582	648, 1087	+337, +495
Daniel, 14	711, 1322	643, 1147	+68, +175
Alison, 8	874, 1425	990, 1397	−116, +28
Casey,[a] 3	1273, 1793	818, 1319	+455, +474
Speaker	Overt Pairs (F1, F2)		
	Mean LOT	Mean THOUGHT	Δ LOT − THOUGHT
Jeff, 37	710, 1303	556, 911	+154, +392
Rochelle, 37	964, 1476	656, 1041	+308, +435
Daniel, 14	729, 1304	646, 1037	+83, +267
Alison, 8	909, 1462	1023, 1471	−114, −9

a. For Casey, data are from picture cards and spontaneous speech.

Previously, Seekonk children "agreed to disagree" with respect to the low back vowels. Most now in fifth grade or higher have maintained the system they inherited from their parents. Those who had the merger kept it, and almost all those who had the distinction kept it.

More recently in Seekonk, inherited distinctions have not survived the formation of the peer group and the transition to school. Half the fourth graders, and everyone younger (while still old enough to have peers), has lost the distinction and learned the merger from their peers. Adjacent South Attleboro underwent the same change about ten years earlier.

In both places the change appears to have occurred in just a few years. Revisiting the school survey reveals some more variation on either side of the critical age range. In general, the school survey and family study concur as to the dynamics of the recent mergers.

5.3. THE FAMILY STUDY AND THE SCHOOL SURVEY: SEEKONK AND SOUTH ATTLEBORO

Extrapolating from the family study, we would expect the Seekonk twelfth graders and eighth graders to maintain inherited distinctions, but for the fourth and fifth graders to be partially merged. The school survey does reflect this change, though more gradually and with earlier evidence of merger. The differences between methods are hard to interpret: while many children behaved inconsistently between pairs on the survey, not many clearly did so in the interviews.

Figure 5.14 gives the distribution of school survey responses for those Seekonk natives with definitely distinct parents who were not also interviewed in the family study. For the 37 twelfth graders—at 17 or 18, well above the age where any merger was observed in the families—92% marked more pairs "different" than "same" (62% marked all 7 pairs "different"). The most merged responses, obtained from only 3% of students, still had 2 of 7 pairs marked "different."

For the eighth grade, the family study had found four distinct children and one with the merger. On the school survey, the five students ranged from fully distinct to fully merged, with two (40%) marking more pairs "different" than "same." This suggests more merger in perception (school survey) than production (family study), but the numbers are too small for significance.

For the fourth and fifth grade, the family study had found a roughly even split: five children distinct, three merged. On the school survey, the 13 students spanned the range, but only 15% marked more pairs "differ-

FIGURE 5.14
Seekonk School Survey: Number of Subjects versus Items Marked "Different"

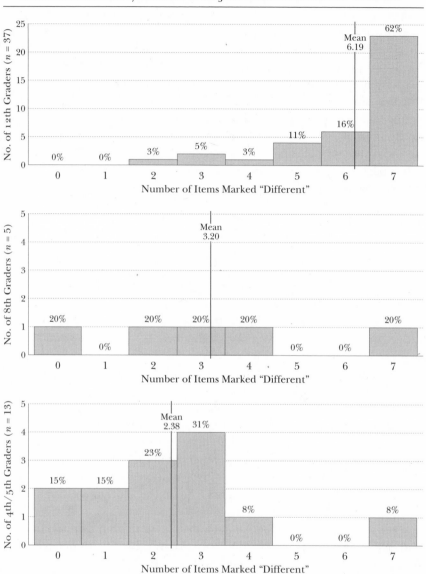

ent" than "same." The difference could be due to sampling error (p = .o6, Fisher's Exact Test), but more likely, we see perception leading production here. (When we compare the same children on both tasks, as in §3.4.2, we see production can lead perception, as well as vice versa.)

The children of definitely distinct parents are losing ground linguistically, but this group is not steadily declining as a proportion of Seekonk natives. They comprise 67% of the 55 twelfth grade natives, 47% of the 15 eighth graders, and 64% of the 25 fourth/fifth graders. (Unlike above, these figures include children also interviewed in the family study.)

And the proportion of natives with one or both parents with a definite merger—the pattern now being adopted by the rest—is neither large nor growing. It went from 11% (twelfth grade) to 13% (eighth grade) to 12% (fourth/fifth grade). But we have yet to consider other elements of the population, such as in-movers (nonnatives) from distinct and merged areas.

We turn to South Attleboro, where the geographic and family studies indicated a rapid merger some ten years before the one in Seekonk. Several South Attleboro natives 20 and older—with distinct parents—were distinct, while an 18-year-old, a 9-year-old, and a 6-year-old were merged. The oldest subject with the merger entered preschool around 1990.

But the school survey reached more subjects, and it shows that not all South Attleboro teenagers with an inherited distinction have lost it. Based on this data (fig. 5.15), the lag between merger in South Attleboro and merger in Seekonk looks more like five years than ten.

The native South Attleboro twelfth graders form a fairly flat distribution with one response at each extreme. Most students were intermediate; five of ten (50%) marked more pairs "different" than "same." This result is similar to the Seekonk eighth grade.

The South Attleboro eighth graders' distribution is more merged; only three of the 11 (27%) marked more pairs "different" than "same." The most distinct response was one score of 6 "different." The result resembles the Seekonk fourth/fifth grades.

None of the five South Attleboro fourth graders marked more pairs "different" than "same." Their distribution spans the merged half of the spectrum.

Despite high response rates from Attleboro schools, the above distinct-parent totals are small. In part, this is because some students wrote "Attleboro" under parental origin, when they probably meant South Attleboro. "Attleboro" parents had to be coded as "unknown."

But even if we call all "Attleboro" parents distinct, the proportion of South Attleboro natives with distinct parents is still much smaller than in Seekonk, where close to two-thirds have families that preserve the distinction. In South Attleboro, the inflated figure would be only 36% (22/61) for twelfth grade, 33% (19/58) for eighth grade, and 38% (12/32) for fourth grade.

FIGURE 5.15

South Attleboro School Survey: Number of Subjects vs. Items Marked "Different"

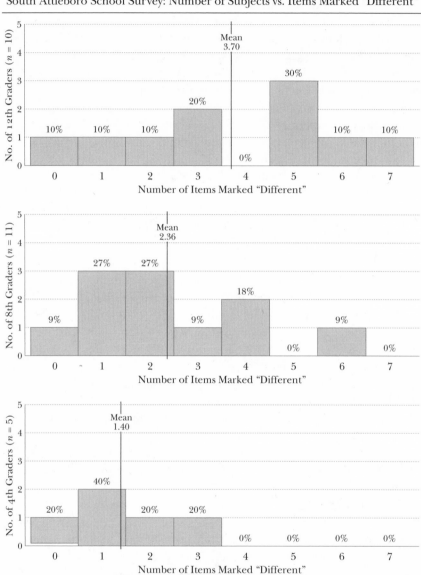

And the proportion of South Attleboro natives with a merged parent is much higher than Seekonk's approximate 12% level: 39% (twelfth grade), 26% (eighth grade), and 19% (fourth grade). Given this, perhaps it is not surprising that the merger affected South Attleboro first.

This reasoning (see §5.8 and subsequent) suggests that changing community demographics trigger merger, as more children with merged family backgrounds enter the mix combining to form each peer group as it begins school. Under this account, merger does not spread from place to place in a direct sense, nor is it passed down from older to younger children.

Rather, merger by expansion would be the "natural" result of certain combinations of demographic and linguistic circumstances. Just as Herold (1990) found the low back merger wherever a large number of European immigrants had settled in northeast Pennsylvania, it may be that whenever a certain percentage of Eastern New England families move to adjacent towns in the Mid-Atlantic territory, the low back distinction will be lost there.[7]

5.4. THE FAMILIES OF CUMBERLAND, RHODE ISLAND

Cumberland, Rhode Island (2005 est. pop. 34,000), lies directly west of South Attleboro. The southern corner of the town abuts Pawtucket; the northwestern end touches Woonsocket.

Northeast Cumberland is less densely populated and more affluent. One family there was referred by a South Attleboro mother, whose children had gone to the same preschool, For Pete's Sake, as one of theirs. Four more families were recommended by the first one.

The five Cumberland families were a homogeneous group. They all lived in the same part of town, and 12 of their 13 children attend (or attended) the K–5 Community School. All ten parents had the distinction, being either from Rhode Island or another MAIN state.

Their children's low back vowels did not pattern neatly by age, however. Unlike in Seekonk, there was no one age above which Cumberland children were distinct and below it merged. But figure 5.16 does show a trend toward merger, including within families.

The Champagne family had daughters in second grade and kindergarten; both were clearly distinct. In the Gill family, a boy in the same kindergarten was probably merged, while a sixth-grade girl was definitely distinct, and a third-grade boy probably distinct. The Graham family was quite like the Gills: a fifth-grade boy was probably distinct, and a third-grade girl definitely so, while a girl in preschool was probably merged. The Springer family showed the same progression, but shifted in time: a distinct twelfth-grade boy, a probably distinct seventh-grade boy, and a fourth-grade boy who was merged in production and on minimal pairs, though he judged most pairs "different." The Olafson family had a sixth-grade daughter and a

FIGURE 5.16
The Children of Cumberland

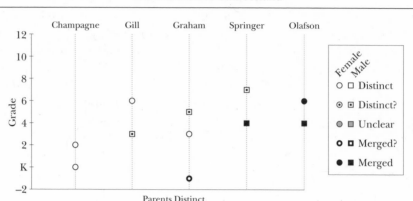

Parents Distinct

fourth-grade son, both definitely merged. The daughter attended a private girls' school in Providence, while the son had always gone to Community School in Cumberland.

Cumberland's trend toward merger is clear, but not orderly. Community School has two merged fourth graders (Springer, Olafson), but also two distinct third graders (Gill, Graham), a second grader (Champagne), and a kindergartner (Champagne). Other factors in addition to age and parental vowel systems must determine whether a child grows up merged or distinct here.

Within each age cohort at Community School, we could imagine two separate peer groups, correlated with low back vowel status as well as other personal characteristics. But this would not explain why we never see a distinct child with a merged older sibling.

The spread of this linguistic change through a school community more likely happens unconsciously, without piggybacking on a social difference. Presumably, the merger would at first be limited to a few in-movers from merged areas, or natives with merged parents. Such children would likely be outsiders to the dominant or popular network. Later, when the merger becomes the majority pattern, the only children with the distinction might be ones with unusually strong ties to older siblings or other older locals.

If the spread of merger depended on its gaining a positive social evaluation, it is unlikely that we would have seen it take over one elementary school in South Attleboro, three in Seekonk, and, probably soon, one in Cumberland, with such speed and regularity.

5.5. THE FAMILIES OF WARWICK, RHODE ISLAND

The previous sections have shown that the low back merger is affecting children in several communities where the geographic study's young adults gave no hint of merger. A final community, Warwick, Rhode Island, was expected to retain the MAIN distinction more tenaciously, because of its location and its population being in large part Rhode Island natives.

Warwick is a blue-collar suburb of 87,000 (2005 est. pop.), located five miles south of Providence, on the other side of the city from Cumberland, Seekonk, and Attleboro. According to the 2000 Census, 76% of the population of Warwick was born in Rhode Island (compared to 69% of Cumberland, around 60% of Seekonk, and around 40% of South Attleboro). Five Warwick families were recruited to participate through school principals and parent/teacher associations (one was through a personal connection). Four of the families had Rhode Island parents with the low back distinction. The Patrick family had merged parents from out of state.[8]

5.5.1. NATIVE RHODE ISLAND FAMILIES. Children of distinct parents in Warwick did retain the distinction more than in South Attleboro, Seekonk, and Cumberland. Still, there were possible signs of an incipient merger.

In the Bloomberg and Barlow families, as seen on figure 5.17, the four children—aged 8 to 14—were definitely distinct. Of the two Mahoney daughters, Celeste—age 4 and in preschool—was clearly distinct. She may be equivalent to Casey O'Connor. But Hope Mahoney—age 7 and in first grade—displayed an unclear pattern.

FIGURE 5.17
The Children of Warwick

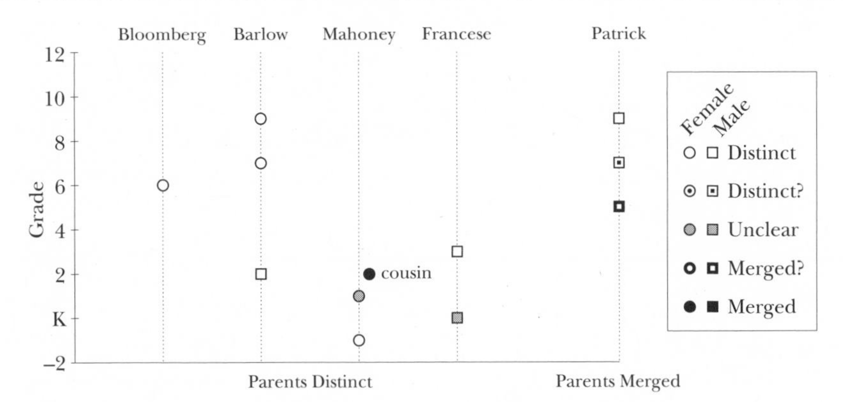

In spontaneous speech, and in naming the picture cards, Hope produced some tokens of THOUGHT high and back (like a distinct speaker) and some front and unrounded (like a merged speaker). She pronounced most reading card pairs the same (or very close) when embedded in sentences, but she clearly distinguished them when they were overt minimal pairs.

For several speakers, more informal styles yielded pronunciations associated with current peers, while more self-conscious styles reflected earlier-acquired norms. In Hope Mahoney's case, the earlier norm is her distinct parents'. The peers could be her Warwick friends or her merged cousin Robin, with whom she was playing before her interview.

Seven-year-old Robin had lived in Warwick for two years, but she originally lived in Coventry and went to day care in West Greenwich (smaller, inland Rhode Island towns). Robin was definitely merged in spontaneous speech and probably merged on the picture cards.

Hope Mahoney might have displayed a more consistently distinct pattern had she not been interviewed during a visit from Robin, with whom she spends time about twice a week. That is, Hope may be showing short-term accommodation toward the merger. But Robin's merger is itself significant, since she has always lived in central Rhode Island and her parents are distinct. Rhode Island, where the distinction was all but universal 15 years earlier, may be succumbing to merger.

The Francese family may also show a trend toward merger. Mark, a third grader, displayed a clear distinction in spontaneous speech; of the reading cards, most pairs sounded different. Greg, a first grader, did not produce much spontaneous speech. Like Hope Mahoney, he produced an unclear, mixed-sounding pattern in naming the picture cards. He could imitate his brother's distinction, but this skill—shared by Sharon Koslowski and Alison O'Connor—says little about natural production patterns.

5.5.2. THE PATRICK FAMILY. In Seekonk, children with one or both parents merged were probably or definitely merged themselves. In the Patrick family of Warwick, both parents exhibited the merger—at least at first glance—yet their three children had acquired the distinction, to varying degrees.

This shows that a distinction can be learned from peers even though the corresponding merger was learned from parents. That the distinction is more entrenched in Warwick must be related to the Patricks' greater ability in acquiring it. Besides the issue of change in progress, it is likely that children of merged parents form an even smaller minority of the school population in Warwick than in Seekonk. Merged children in Warwick would have fewer peers like themselves; this presumably promotes their learning of the distinction.

5.5.2.1. *Mike Patrick.* Mike Patrick (ME48M), a 48-year-old attorney, grew up in southern Maine, an ENE region. In keeping with this, his PALM was clearly further front than any of his LOT or THOUGHT tokens. His spontaneous LOT ~ THOUGHT sounded merged, and all but one of the reading pairs sounded the same. *Cot ~ caught* sounded different to both of us; Mike also judged *nod ~ gnawed* and *tock ~ talk* "different."

Figure 5.18 shows that Mike's tokens of LOT and THOUGHT form a single small cloud in mid-back position, a distribution highly suggestive of the low back merger. However, when we compare the word classes with paired *t*-tests, this diagnosis becomes much less certain:

ΔLOT – THOUGHT (ME48M, C, 6) = +50 ±37 (*p* = .02), +30 ±64 (*p* = .28)

ΔLOT – THOUGHT (ME48M, O, 6) = +12 ±25 (*p* = .27), +72 ±72 (*p* = .05)

ΔLOT – THOUGHT (ME48M, CO, 12) = +31 ±22 (*p* = .001), +51 ±42 (*p* = .02)

The Patricks went to college in Providence, then lived in Washington, D.C., for 12 years before returning to Rhode Island. After 30 years in the MAIN area, then, Mike Patrick appears to have learned a small, almost subliminal low back distinction (Mike's father, from Connecticut, would also have exposed him to it).

His formants differed by 20 Hz or more in the "correct" direction 9 of 12 times for F1 and 10 of 12 times for F2, which is unlikely to have occurred by chance. Mike Patrick does not have a true merger; his LOT and THOUGHT are not identical.

However, his word classes overlap almost completely in acoustic space. Mike's LOT ranged from 584 to 746 in F1, from 1020 to 1180 in F2. His THOUGHT ranged from 570 to 697 in F1, from 921 to 1180 in F2. Besides being practically coextensive, these between-pair ranges are larger than the average within-pair difference of +31, +51. It seems likely that anyone listening to these vowels—for example, Mike's children—would interpret them as merged.

Figure 5.18 helps show why Mike Patrick's distinction is likely nonfunctional. His *knotty* is lower and fronter than his *naughty*, and similarly, *Don* is lower and fronter than *Dawn*. However, the overlap is such that *naughty* is actually lower and fronter than *Don*.

Hearers can adjust for the acoustic effects of phonetic environment, so partial overlap between distinct classes is unproblematic. However, it is unlikely that a learner could acquire separate LOT and THOUGHT word classes from a pattern with near-total overlap, such as Mike's.

Mike Patrick's low vowels still look and sound ENE, in their general positions and their allophonic conditioning. But atop this ENE pattern he has superimposed a small but consistent distinction between LOT and

FIGURE 5.18
Mike Patrick (father): LOT ~ THOUGHT Pairs

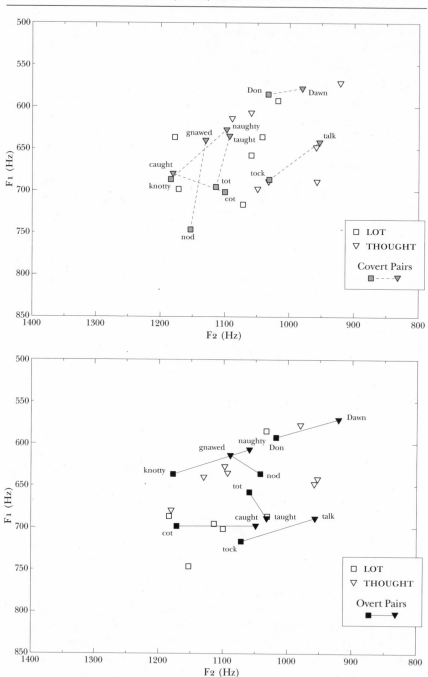

THOUGHT. How common this process is, how it operates, and what it says about phonological representations, remain interesting questions.

5.5.2.2. *Clara Patrick.* Forty-eight-year old Clara Patrick (TX48F), who worked for a nonprofit agency, had learned English upon moving to El Paso, Texas, from Mexico at age 4. She had a light Spanish accent and displayed a clear low back merger (fig. 5.19). She judged the minimal pairs to be the same, except one which she called "different" and which sounded close to the analyst.

Clara's formants differed by at least 20 Hz in the "correct" direction 6 of 12 times for F1 and 5 of 12 times for F2, a chance-level performance. One pair differed widely in the right direction—overt *tock* 589 Hz fronter than *talk*—but another was reversed—overt *knotty* 253 Hz backer than *naughty*. The impression of a phonetically wide LOT = THOUGHT class with little internal structure was reinforced when the covert and overt tokens of some words were realized quite differently. The nonsignificant paired *t*-tests diagnose merger:

ΔLOT – THOUGHT (TX48F, C, 6) = +53 ±93 (p = .21), +134 ±253 (p = .24)
ΔLOT – THOUGHT (TX48F, O, 6) = +13 ±49 (p = .53), −47 ±119 (p = .36)
ΔLOT – THOUGHT (TX48F, CO, 12) = +33 ±45 (p = .14), +44 ±129 (p = .47)

When the Patrick children were acquiring English, their father's tiny, regular LOT ~ THOUGHT distinction—assuming he even had it then—would have been lost within allophonic conditioning. Their merged mother was certainly no model for a word-class difference, either. Whatever they have of the distinction, they must have learned from their largely-distinct peers.

5.5.2.3. *Juan Patrick.* Like his brothers, 15-year-old Juan Patrick (WW15M) had gone to preschool in Providence before public school in Warwick, where he was a ninth-grade classmate of the definitely distinct oldest Barlow child. Juan's spontaneous speech was judged "very distinct." His reading card pairs sounded different, other than the common outlier, *Don ~ Dawn.*

Figure 5.20 does not show Juan's distinction to be as large acoustically as it sounded impressionistically, but the existence of a distinction is clear. The THOUGHT class forms a fairly tight cloud, with the exception of the two tokens of *naughty*, which are much lower and fronter, although they remain distinct from *knotty*. The LOT class ranges very widely, though for the most part each word is consistent between its covert and overt contexts. And although *Don* was produced close to the THOUGHT cloud, it is actually kept distinct from *Dawn.*

FIGURE 5.19
Clara Patrick (mother): LOT ~ THOUGHT Pairs

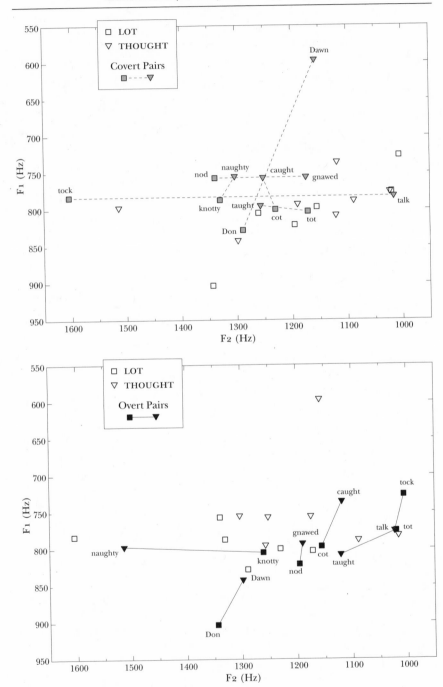

FIGURE 5.20
Juan Patrick (oldest brother): LOT ~ THOUGHT Pairs

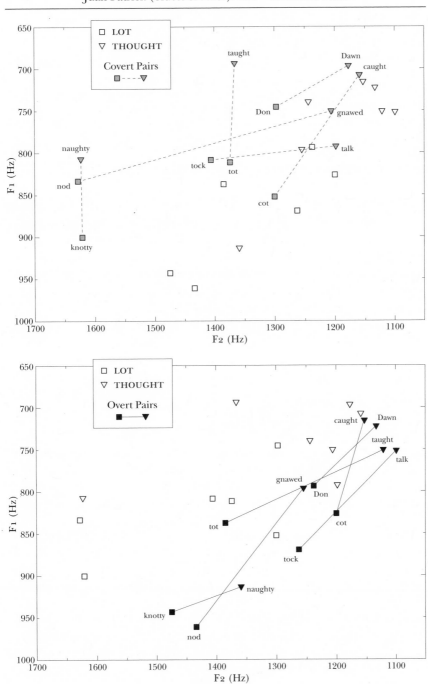

Paired *t*-tests strongly indicated the distinction for the covert pairs. For the overt pairs a more consistent difference, rather than a larger one, made the verdict even more conclusive:

$$\Delta\text{LOT} - \text{THOUGHT (WW15M, C, 6)} = +84 \pm 49 \; (p = .007), +150 \pm 164 \; (p = .07)$$
$$\Delta\text{LOT} - \text{THOUGHT (WW15M, O, 6)} = +97 \pm 48 \; (p = .004), +146 \pm 78 \; (p = .005)$$

There is no doubt that Juan Patrick has acquired the low back distinction from his peers. His productions are somewhat reminiscent of his father's, in that each word class occupies a wide, overlapping range. However, even his closest pair is a healthy 93 Hz apart in F_2.

5.5.2.4. *Roberto Patrick.* Twelve-year-old Roberto Patrick—a seventh-grade classmate of the definitely distinct middle Barlow child—presented a more complicated situation with respect to the low back vowels. In spontaneous speech, Roberto gave the impression of being distinct, though not definitely. His behavior with the reading cards gave a different impression.

While all pairs were judged "same" by the subject, *Don ~ Dawn* only sounded close in the covert context, while *nod ~ gnawed* sounded different on both repetitions. The other four pairs all showed a new pattern: different in the covert context, but as overt pairs, the same.

Acoustic measurement (fig. 5.21) shows that in the overt context, Roberto usually produces a higher, backer LOT, leading to smaller within-pair differences. But even the pairs that sounded identical to the ear mostly still show a small difference in the "right direction":

$$\Delta\text{LOT} - \text{THOUGHT (WW12M, C, 6)} = +110 \pm 69 \; (p = .009), +141 \pm 160 \; (p = .07)$$
$$\Delta\text{LOT} - \text{THOUGHT (WW12M, O, 6)} = +74 \pm 88 \; (p = .08), +105 \pm 121 \; (p = .07)$$

Several children in other communities have shown a smaller distinction in more spontaneous styles than on overt minimal pairs. That is, they naturally produced a pattern closer to that of their peers, who are likely merged, but when confronted with explicit judgments, they revealed knowledge of the original distinct pattern acquired from their parents.

On most pairs, Roberto does the opposite. He has a mainly distinct peer group, which possibly goes hand in hand with a greater distinction in more spontaneous styles. On minimal pairs—and in judgments—he reflects the merged system inherited from his parents in early childhood.

5.5.2.5. *Paco Patrick.* Eleven-year-old Paco Patrick was two years behind Roberto in school, and his low back vowels were noticeably more merged. In spontaneous speech, he sounded probably merged. The reading pairs *tot ~ taught* and *tock ~ talk* sounded the same, in both contexts. *Nod ~ gnawed*

FIGURE 5.21
Roberto Patrick (middle brother): LOT ~ THOUGHT Pairs

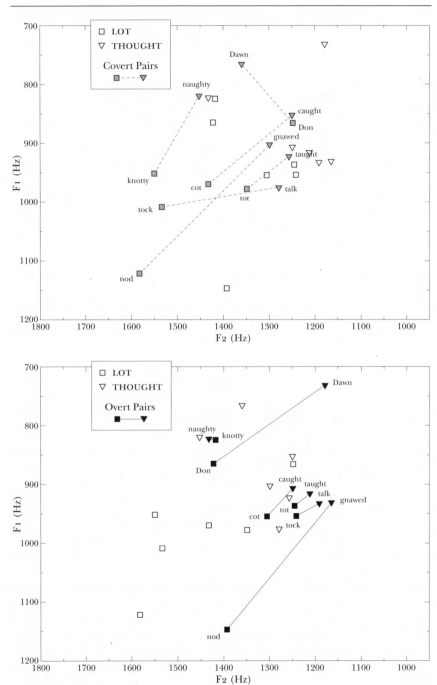

FIGURE 5.22

Paco Patrick (youngest brother): LOT ~ THOUGHT Pairs

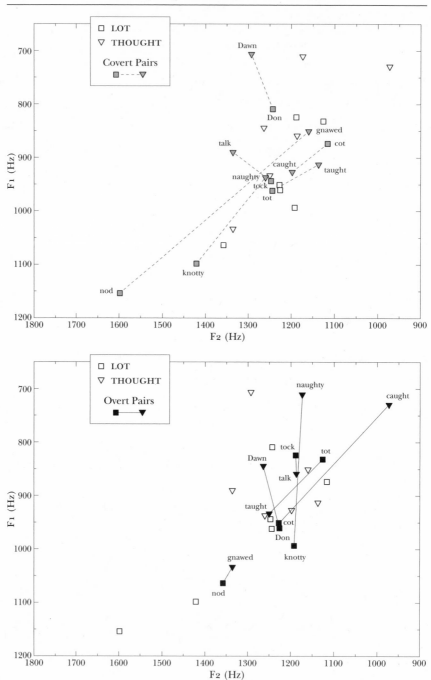

sounded further apart (covert), then closer together (overt), like Roberto's pairs had, but the other three pairs went the other way: closer in context, more different as minimal pairs.

Like his brother Roberto, Paco clearly distinguishes some pairs while others are close together or "reversed." Acoustic measurement (fig. 5.22) shows them on average to be closer together in the overt condition, where Paco declared most of them "basically the same":

$$\Delta \text{LOT} - \text{THOUGHT (WW11M, C, 6)} = +103 \pm 127 \; (p = .09), +81 \pm 214 \; (p = .38)$$
$$\Delta \text{LOT} - \text{THOUGHT (WW11M, O, 6)} = +86 \pm 157 \; (p = .22), +22 \pm 132 \; (p = .68)$$

Because of the inconsistency, none of these formant differences is statistically significant.

The oldest Patrick brother is the most distinct, the youngest the most merged. This makes sense if the distinction is learned gradually from peers: the older brothers have had longer to shift away from the parents' merged pattern. Also, if the distinction is weakening in Warwick, the younger brothers' peer groups may be less robustly distinct models.

Table 5.4 shows average formant values and LOT ~ THOUGHT differences for Mike, Clara, and Juan Patrick, based on covert and overt reading pairs. Roberto and Paco's reading card performances were less representative of their spontaneous speech, but they have nevertheless been included.

TABLE 5.4
The Patrick Family: Summary of Reading Card Productions

Speaker		Covert Pairs (F1, F2)	
	Mean LOT	Mean THOUGHT	Δ LOT – THOUGHT
Mike, 48	683, 1102	633, 1072	+50, +30
Clara, 48	793, 1328	740, 1194	+53, +134
Juan, 15	825, 1438	741, 1288	+84, +150
Roberto, 12	983, 1428	873, 1287	+110, +141
Paco, 11	973, 1312	870, 1231	+103, +81
Speaker		Overt Pairs (F1, F2)	
	Mean LOT	Mean THOUGHT	Δ LOT – THOUGHT
Mike, 48	656, 1090	644, 1018	+12, +72
Clara, 48	805, 1164	792, 1211	+13, –47
Juan, 15	872, 1333	775, 1187	+97, +146
Roberto, 12	948, 1310	874, 1205	+74, +105
Paco, 11	937, 1219	851, 1197	+86, +22

5.6. INDIVIDUAL CHANGE

Observing the children of the family study has led to the following general-izations regarding the trends and possibilities in individuals' phonological development. These have been observed regarding the low back vowels, but presumably would also apply more generally.

5.6.1. INITIAL ACQUISITION FROM PARENTS AND REORGANIZATION WITH PEERS. The youngest children interviewed—who were 3—had already acquired the low back vowel systems of their parents, merged or distinct. Children probably learn these systems along with their initial phonologies; the right methodology might reveal them at an even younger age.

As soon as children have same-age peers—as opposed to siblings—they reorganize their low back vowel systems, if necessary. When the family pattern is distinct and the peer group is merged, this can happen very quickly. Several children between the ages of 4 and 6 exhibited the merger quite clearly, despite having parents and sometimes siblings with the distinction.

The Patrick family shows the distinction can also be learned from peers, but not as quickly as the merger. Twelve-year-old Roberto Patrick still had an incomplete distinction, whereas the oldest child not to have learned a peer merger was 6-year-old Caleb Hayas.

To learn a distinction from peers seems to require quite a homoge-neously distinct peer group, just as a child needs two distinct parents to sol-idly acquire it from them.[9] In the Seekonk interviews, no child with a fam-ily-inherited merger produced the distinction in speech, probably because they had some merged peers providing continuity with the home pattern (the school survey is more equivocal; see §5.9.1.3). But in Warwick, with a higher proportion of distinct peers, the Patrick brothers did show gradual acquisition of the distinction.

Several geographic study seniors had fully acquired the pattern of where they lived, despite parents from other dialect areas. An 87-year-old man from Mendon, Massachusetts, with parents from England, had fully merged LOT and THOUGHT. A 63-year-old woman from Attleboro, with parents from New York City and Connecticut, merged LOT and THOUGHT and—unless her parental input was 3-D—also fully separated PALM and LOT.

However, people do not always learn even a merger from their peers. A 22-year-old Seekonk woman in the geographic study maintained an ENE pattern; her parents were from nearer to Boston. Section 5.2 tells us that the MAIN pattern—with its PALM ~ LOT merger—was dominant where and when she grew up.

5.6.2. CHANGE IN VOWEL SYSTEMS IN LATER LIFE: PHONOLOGICAL. After the childhood reorganization, a person's vowel inventory is very unlikely to change, regardless of exposure to other systems. Several pieces of evidence support this view.

The sharp age cutoff found in Seekonk implies that distinct children with a distinct peer group do not abandon the distinction because of contact with merged younger speakers, including their own siblings. This echoes Herold (1990), who found that older distinct speakers did not pick up their neighbors' and children's merger, even after decades of contact (see §1.1).

When they encounter merged peers, children (e.g., Eddie Ventura, §5.2.2.4) can be quick to abandon a distinction they acquired only from parents and older siblings. But they are slow (e.g., Nora Lucas, §5.1) to abandon a distinction reinforced by their own earlier peers. As children get older, their susceptibility to merger declines, approaching zero for adults.

Fourteen parents were interviewed who grew up in the MAIN area and now live in Attleboro; all were still rated "definitely distinct" on LOT ~ THOUGHT. Ten parents in South Attleboro and Seekonk grew up in ENE territory; seven were still "definitely merged," one "probably merged," one "unclear." On the whole, low vowel systems remain stable after childhood (see also §3.4.1 and §4.5).

The one father from Attleboro who was "unclear" was, in fact, married to a Rhode Islander. But the great majority of "mixed" married couples had not noticeably influenced each other's low vowels (again, see §4.5).

5.6.3. CHANGE IN VOWEL SYSTEMS IN LATER LIFE: PHONETIC. Even if vowel inventories appear stable—for originally distinct speakers, minimal pairs are still "different" and a phonetic difference is still clearly audible; for originally merged speakers, pairs are still "same" and no distinction is audible—some phonetic change might occur when speakers are exposed to a different system from the one they grew up with.

The Seekonk teenagers (§5.2.1.2, §5.2.2.2) now show much narrower LOT ~ THOUGHT distinctions than their parents do. Assuming they started out like Casey O'Connor (§5.2.2.4), the narrowing might have been caused by contact with merged peers or younger siblings. We can always imagine that a currently distinct speaker might have been more distinct originally. But it is rarely feasible to test this by comparing movers to people who never left their original dialect areas, let alone by carrying out longitudinal studies with the same speakers before and after moving.

With originally merged speakers living in distinct areas, simple acoustic measurement can reveal whether or not any separation has occurred. Even a small statistically significant difference between LOT and THOUGHT must indicate the effect of exposure to that distinction.

Mike Patrick (§5.5.2.1) showed that a long period of immersion in a distinct environment, even starting in adulthood, can result in the formation (or re-formation) of a small distinction. But this learned distinction did not resemble a native one. Mike's LOT and THOUGHT formed one acoustic group, and the differences between pairs—e.g., *knotty* and *naughty* were further front than *Don* and *Dawn*—were larger than the word-class differences within pairs. His vowels also lacked the difference in rounding that native MAIN speakers have.

Mike Patrick could hear his distinction—better than I could—in some pairs, but those he identified as "different" were no further apart in F1 or F2 than the ones he called "same." There was also no clear effect of word frequency. For example, the words *Don* and *Dawn* must be heard more often than *nod* and *gnawed*, yet a similar-sized acoustic separation had occurred for both pairs.

The mover parents identified in §5.6.2 might display a similar "microdistinction" if they were analyzed acoustically. South Attleboro and Seekonk parents who had grown up in the ENE area would be like Mike Patrick, potentially separating LOT and THOUGHT. Attleboro parents who had grown up in the MAIN area might be learning to separate PALM and LOT.

If adults slightly separate originally merged word classes, given enough exposure to a distinction, it is very likely that originally distinct vowels will move closer together, given long-term exposure to a merger (an approximation that would be undetectable without data from comparable nonmovers or a longitudinal study). In both cases, adults' malleability is less than children's. Adults may accommodate phonetically but probably never reorganize their vowel systems to an extent we would call phonological.

5.7. DIALECT CHANGE

Chapter 4's geographic study discovered that the dialect boundary separating ENE and MAIN low vowel systems did not change very much over the course of the twentieth century. In most places, senior citizens and young adults had the same phonological pattern.

However, some younger speakers in the ENE area had collapsed PALM and LOT = THOUGHT, resulting in three-way merger. On the MAIN side of the line, the merger of PALM = LOT and THOUGHT was seen in South Bellingham and Assonet, Massachusetts, and was underway in Barrington, Rhode Island, resulting in the 3-M pattern there too.

The family study found three-way-merged children in the main part of Attleboro, Massachusetts, where adults are ENE, and a more abrupt and dramatic shift in South Attleboro, where adults are MAIN: around 1990, South Attleboro children who had inherited the low back distinction began to lose it when they entered school. Around 2000, the same thing happened in Seekonk, Massachusetts. These changes did not spread to older children or to adults. There are thus 3-M children whose older siblings and parents are MAIN (but very young children still match their parents).

In nearby Cumberland, Rhode Island, the same change appears less regular. It has been in progress for some years (an 11-year-old is merged), but is not complete (a 5-year-old is distinct).

In Warwick, Rhode Island, south of Providence, the low back merger may be incipient. Two of eight children there with distinct parents had unclear patterns. If the merger is spreading to Warwick, its location makes a delay compared to the other communities understandable.

In that case, we would have an apparent slow spread of merger from South Attleboro to Seekonk and Cumberland—which border long-merged areas—to Warwick, which is not that close to any ENE community. The status of young people in Providence is important, but unknown.

The farther we find the merger from the edge of the ENE area, the less easily we can attribute the change to contact with the merged area across the line. Contagious diffusion from one community to the next might have explained the merger in South Attleboro (if not the decades of stability preceding it). However, it cannot account for it in central Rhode Island, where Robin Mahoney lived until recently. The merger is spreading faster than that model predicts.

Besides the high school students from Queens (§3.5.8), a fourth-grade class in Jersey City, New Jersey (not discussed above), gave survey responses fairly indicative of the low back merger. And the girlfriend of one geographic study young adult was fully merged despite having grown up in Manhattan with New York City parents. Based on these anecdotal observations, the low back distinction may be quite widely endangered in the Mid-Atlantic.

5.8. COMMUNITY CHANGE: DEVELOPING THE MIGRATION HYPOTHESIS

In Seekonk, our best example of community change, children with distinct parents had been entering school and maintaining their distinctions for most of a century. Then, over just a few years, a change occurred. Such children now merge PALM = LOT and THOUGHT on entering school. Demographic factors might have caused this change in the following three stages.[10]

In the first stage, there are not many merged parents in the community, so the proportion of children entering the peer group with an inherited merger is less than a certain threshold X. This small number of merged children will learn the distinction from their peers. The majority of distinct children will be mainly unaffected by the merged minority. This describes Seekonk some years ago, and Warwick today. It also describes the (merged) Canadian children who moved to England in Chambers (1992). Completely surrounded by the distinction, children will acquire it, assuming they are young enough. Chambers's data suggests the age of 10 or 11 as a cut-off, but above we have seen both exceptionally late learners and early nonlearners.

In the second stage, more merged parents have moved in. The proportion of natively merged children entering the peer group is now greater than X, but lower than another threshold, Y. Those children will encounter enough merged peers that they remain merged. But they are not numerous enough to stop natively distinct children from remaining distinct. This corresponds to the "agree to disagree" pattern of Seekonk family study children over 10. Those with a merged parent were merged, those with distinct parents were distinct.

In the third stage, the proportion of natively merged children exceeds Y. While distinct children may not be in a minority, they have enough contact with merged peers that they lose their inherited distinction. Needless to say, children with an inherited merger retain it. South Attleboro reached the third stage around 1990, Seekonk around 2000. We can also suppose that Tamaqua, Pennsylvania, did around 1920, when the children of merged foreign coal miners overwhelmed the distinction preserved among the children of native Americans. No part of southeastern New England has experienced a demographic "catastrophe" like the mining areas of northeast Pennsylvania (Herold 1990). Here, the children of foreign immigrants, while much fewer, have mostly learned the local vowel systems accurately.

The more relevant demographic shift is native English-speaking migration from the ENE area, closer to Boston, into the MAIN area. While this flow is too small to cause the kind of population growth that accompanied merger in Roswell, Georgia (B. Anderson 2005), it could have been enough to cause communities to pass through the three stages outlined above, eventually merging PALM = LOT and THOUGHT. Conversely, migration from MAIN to ENE could be leading PALM and LOT = THOUGHT to merge in the ENE territory.[11]

Indeed, many interviewees pointed out that their communities had changed in recent years, with the construction of new neighborhoods and housing subdivisions. The families occupying this new housing were often described as having moved from closer to Boston, as real-estate prices rose in suburbs closer to the city.

None of the family study children had both parents from Greater Boston, but about 10% of the young adults in the geographic study did. Most of these moves (e.g., to Foxborough or Taunton) did not take them out of the ENE dialect area. Only when parents moved across the historical boundary into MAIN territory (e.g., to Blackstone or Seekonk) could the migration potentially trigger community change in the low vowels.

If the migration hypothesis is correct, it could explain why the merger occurred when it did in the communities where it has recently been found. The location of, for example, South Attleboro is a constant; it has always been next to, and shared a high school with, Attleboro. The level of migration from Greater Boston, on the other hand, has not been constant.[12]

When the senior citizens of the geographic study were growing up, Boston was a rather far-off place. That people from Greater Boston are now settling 50 miles from the city—and sometimes still commuting to it—does reflect real-estate necessity, but also that such distances are not as daunting as before. The study area is evolving from a set of relatively self-sufficient cities and towns into a network of far-flung suburbs, where people's homes, workplaces, and leisure activities are no longer typically confined to one community.

5.9. TESTING THE MIGRATION HYPOTHESIS

5.9.1. MIGRATION DATA FROM THE SCHOOL SURVEY. The large number of responses to the demographic questions on the school survey, maximized here by including children who failed the linguistic test criteria—e.g., marking *pause ~ paws* "different"—allows us to examine demographic trends over a period of eight years. The migration hypothesis developed in section 5.8 refers to the composition of children's first peer groups as they enter school. However, in Seekonk and South Attleboro, parents have several options for preschool and kindergarten. Only starting in first grade do the children living in a certain section of town form a cohort that remains relatively stable thereafter.

This section will examine the composition of several of these cohorts of classmates since first grade, ignoring later arrivals on the assumption that they would have had little (or at least less) linguistic influence. We have no data from children who were part of the founding group but have moved away since.

For each community and current grade level, we will see how many students remaining from that original first-grade cohort had two distinct parents and how many had a merged parent. We will also note how many students had prekindergarten or kindergarten peers from distinct or merged communities.

To completely support the migration hypothesis, the data would show each Seekonk grade to have more of the distinct groups, and/or fewer of the merged groups, than the corresponding grade in South Attleboro. Ideally, there should also be a trend over time toward merger in both places. This would point toward South Attleboro having been in a similar demographic and linguistic position five to ten years ago as Seekonk is now. Table 5.5 presents the percentage of each subgroup for each cohort, also giving the mean school survey score for each.

5.9.1.1. *Migration into Seekonk.* There were 84 current twelfth graders who had been first-grade contemporaries in Seekonk. For 68% of them, both parents came from a probably or definitely distinct place, while for 18%, at least one parent was definitely merged, a figure which included parents listed as from "Attleboro," even though some of them would have been from South Attleboro and therefore distinct (only 2% had a parent from Greater Boston). Twenty percent of the cohort had distinct parents and had also gone to prekindergarten or kindergarten in Rhode Island, where they likely heard a more robust distinction. None had merged parents as well as merged kindergarten or prekindergarten exposure.

TABLE 5.5
Seekonk and South Attleboro: Proportions and Mean Survey Scores

| Grade | N | Distinct Parents (MAIN) | | | | C. Other | | Merged Parent(s) (ENE/3-M) | | | |
		A. Distinct (Pre-)K		B. Other (Pre-)K				D. Other (Pre-)K		E. Merged (Pre-)K	
SK12	84	20%	6.31	48%	6.05	14%	5.25	18%	3.73	—	—
SK8	20	15%	5.33	50%	3.56	15%	3.33	15%	2.67	5%	4.00[a]
SK4/5	48	29%	3.08	36%	2.33	12%	2.00	21%	1.00	2%	0.00[a]
ABS12	66	2%	—[b]	16%	3.45	34%	3.25	48%	1.41	—	—
ABS8	66	—	—	26%	2.43	36%	1.90	38%	0.62	—	—
ABS4	65	—	—	18%	2.11	42%	0.80	34%	1.29	6%	1.33

a. Group with one student.
b. Group with one student who marked *pause ~ paws* "different"; score not counted.

There were 20 Seekonk eighth graders who remained from their first-grade peer group: 65% had two distinct parents, while 20% had a merged parent (10% had a parent from Greater Boston). Fifteen percent had distinct parents and went to prekindergarten in Rhode Island, while 5% (one child) had a merged parent and went to prekindergarten in South Attleboro, which was mainly merged by then.

There were 48 Seekonk fourth and fifth graders remaining from their first-grade cohort: 65% had distinct parents, while 23% had a merged parent (8% had a parent from Greater Boston). Twenty-nine percent had distinct parents and had also gone to prekindergarten or kindergarten in Rhode Island, while 2% (one child) had a merged parent and had gone to preschool in merged Pittsburgh, moving to Seekonk at age 5.

The founding composition of these three Seekonk peer groups seems to have been very similar. There is only a small increase in merged parentage, from 18% (SK12) to 20% (SK8) to 23% (SK4/5). A similar calculation in section 5.3, considering only students with definitely merged parents, also showed no real increase. The percentage with a personal—kindergarten or prekindergarten—merged background is very low. And there has been no decrease over time in the proportion with parental or personal distinct backgrounds.

But over the same eight years, the cohorts' linguistic profiles shift from mainly distinct to fairly merged, with mean survey scores of 5.56 (SK12), 3.68 (SK8), and 2.22 (SK4/5). (Unlike the demographic percentages, these means exclude students who failed the *barn ~ born* or *pause ~ paws* criteria.)

5.9.1.2. *Migration into South Attleboro.* Under the migration hypothesis, we expect South Attleboro—which underwent merger earlier—to have more merged children than Seekonk's approximate 20%. We also expect an increasing trend.

Of the 66 twelfth graders who were once part of a first-grade cohort in South Attleboro, 18% had two distinct parents, a much lower level than in Seekonk. Only 2% (one child) had also gone to prekindergarten and kindergarten in Rhode Island. Forty-eight percent of the group had a merged parent (36% had one from Greater Boston). These levels of merged in-migration are more than twice as high as in any Seekonk grade, despite having excluded parents listed as from "Attleboro," since many would really have been from South Attleboro and distinct. None of these children had themselves attended prekindergarten or kindergarten in a merged community, other than Attleboro.

Of the 66 South Attleboro eighth graders, 26% had two distinct parents, and 38% had a merged parent (21% had one from Greater Boston). None in this grade said they attended prekindergarten or kindergarten outside of Attleboro.

Of the 65 South Attleboro fourth graders, 18%—all South Attleboro natives—had two distinct parents, and 40% had a merged parent (23% had one from Greater Boston). Six percent had also moved from merged communities; they had gone to kindergarten in North Attleborough, Foxborough, Brockton, and Lynn, Massachusetts.

These numbers show no clear trends over time in South Attleboro. All three cohorts have approximately 40% with a merged parent, compared with 20% in Seekonk. Much, but not all, of the difference is due to parents from Greater Boston, who are far more common in South Attleboro than in Seekonk.

The proportion of South Attleboro children with two distinct parents is only about 20%, compared to 65% in Seekonk. And while a decent number of Seekonk first graders came from kindergartens or preschools in Rhode Island, this was not true in South Attleboro. While Seekonk showed major change over the eight years, just the tail end of merger is reflected in South Attleboro's survey scores: 2.43 (ABS12), 1.55 (ABS8), 1.24 (ABS4).

5.9.1.3. *Discussion of School Survey Migration Data.* In one sense, the demographic information from the school surveys supports the migration hypothesis. It shows a substantial difference between Seekonk and South Attleboro in the composition of children's peer groups; for example, two-thirds of children in Seekonk had two distinct parents—and therefore started off life with the distinction—versus only one-fifth of children in South Attleboro. As we know, the communities differ linguistically in the same direction: children in Seekonk retained the distinction for five to ten years longer.

However, the fact that no trends were seen over time within each community is problematic in several respects. South Attleboro's high proportion of children with merged backgrounds—a majority if Attleboro parents had been included—makes the merger there very understandable. However, most children only a few years older than ABS12 were distinct, and it seems unlikely that any substantial demographic shift could have occurred so quickly.

While we may wonder why the merger did not happen sooner in South Attleboro, it may be even more puzzling that it has occurred in Seekonk, given children's continued heavily distinct backgrounds there. According to the school survey, the merger had started by SK8 and was well advanced by SK4/5. The family study found a sharper shift centered on fourth grade.

But the demographic data shows only a slight increase in the 20% or so of merged-background children. While this low level might be sufficient to trigger merger—it would be, according to the model of Yang (2009)—the virtually flat trend does not help us understand why the change happened when it did.

The mean survey scores on table 5.5 quite closely reflect students' parental and personal backgrounds, as well as their community and grade. Figure 5.23 is a graphical representation of the same data. For the survey's perception/evaluation data, the parental effect is very clear for all grades, except possibly ABS4. The patterns of scores are gradual and intermediate, though, rather than reflecting the three discrete stages of merger proposed in section 5.8 based on the production data.

5.9.2. MIGRATION AND JOURNEY-TO-WORK DATA FROM THE CENSUS

5.9.2.1. *ENE Migration into MAIN Communities: Seekonk and South Attleboro.* Census data gives an independent estimate of migration. For both 1990 and 2000 (Census Bureau 1995, 2003), we can count the people who moved to Seekonk and Attleboro in the previous five years from clearly merged areas of Massachusetts, New Hampshire, and Maine.[13]

Of Seekonk's 1990 population of 12,252, 4.8% had moved since 1985 from the above merged areas; 4.0% if we exclude Attleboro as not wholly merged. Ten years later, 3.1% of 12,674 moved from the merged areas between 1995 and 2000; excluding Attleboro, it was 2.0%. The census

FIGURE 5.23
Seekonk and South Attleboro: Proportions and Survey Scores

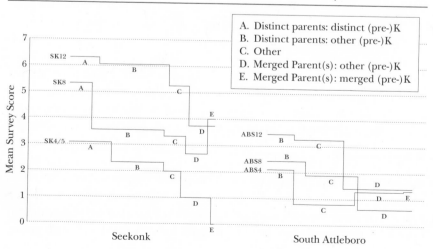

numbers are understandably lower than the school survey's because the census includes less-mobile older speakers and the survey counted students who moved any number of years ago, not just in the previous five.

In Attleboro, 10.8% of the 1990 population of 35,056 had moved from one of the merged areas above. Between 1995 and 2000, the rate was 9.4% of 39,126. Because census migration files have the city or town as the smallest unit of geography, South Attleboro's levels can only be estimated, at 6%, using the school survey's finding that merged in-migration into South Attleboro was at roughly two-thirds the citywide rate.

Though not as clearly as in section 5.9.1, we do find more merged migration into (South) Attleboro than into Seekonk, as predicted by the migration hypothesis. However, the trends over time show a decrease in merged in-migration, rather than the predicted increase.

The census numbers derive from the whole population, so they include the mobility (or lack thereof) of sectors that are not relevant for children's learning, such as senior citizens. Also, many families who moved in 1995–2000 would either not have children yet or they would be younger than those whose merger we aim to explain. Nevertheless, the downward trends—especially the one in Seekonk—are not encouraging for the migration hypothesis.

5.9.2.2. *MAIN Migration into ENE Communities: Dartmouth and Berkley.* Having inconclusively explored whether ENE migration triggered the PALM = LOT ~ THOUGHT merger on the edge of MAIN territory, we will now see if MAIN migration might be sufficient to explain the PALM ~ LOT = THOUGHT merger observed sporadically in ENE territory.

In Dartmouth, Massachusetts, most geographic study subjects were ENE, but the youngest—a 16-year-old boy—was 3-M. He had one MAIN (Fall River) and one ENE (Dartmouth) parent, which could by itself account for his three-way merger; still, it raised the question of whether natively MAIN peers are a major factor in this community.

Out of a 1990 population of 25,904, 989 (3.8%) had moved from Rhode Island, Connecticut, New York, New Jersey, or the MAIN parts of Massachusetts since 1985. Between 1995 and 2000, 2,066 of 29,296 (7.1%) did the same. Much of the increase came from Fall River, which provided a third of the migration in the first period and half in the second.

These numbers are broadly similar to those for ENE migration to MAIN communities (§5.9.2.1). So, if migration plays a role in merger there, the same may well be the case here. Dartmouth is a somewhat unusual community, with many summer homes as well as a large University of Massachusetts campus, which may contribute to the high levels.

A community where not very much cross-dialect migration was antici-
pated was rural Berkley, Massachusetts, one of the smallest towns in the
study area. However, the numbers are not inconsequential at all: between
1985 and 1990, 258 of 3,840 (6.7%) moved to Berkley from the MAIN
areas noted; between 1995 and 2000, it was 286 of 5,300 (5.4%). As in
Dartmouth, much of the migration was from nearby Fall River, and again it
was a rising proportion: half of the 1985–90 movers, three-quarters of the
1995–2000 movers.

We know from the discussion of South Attleboro and Seekonk that
overall migration rates in the mid-single digits can correspond to substantial proportions of the relevant populations of parents and children. In
general, though, much more work needs to be done to test the migration
hypothesis: dating the merger(s) in various communities, gathering appropriate demographic information, and relating the two.

Table 5.6 summarizes the census migration data. In Seekonk, MAIN
migration is higher than ENE; the reverse is true in Attleboro (though
South Attleboro is likely more balanced), while ENE predominates over
MAIN in Berkley and Dartmouth.

5.9.2.3. *Journeys to Work: Commuting between Dialect Areas.* While this study
generally takes the position that workers (16 and over) would experience
few changes to their own linguistic patterns by interacting with coworkers
in other dialect areas—and that any such changes would have little chance
of percolating down to the young children leading the vowel mergers—
it is still interesting to observe a difference between South Attleboro and
Seekonk in terms of commuting patterns (see also §4.2).

TABLE 5.6

Migration from ENE and MAIN Dialect Areas into Seekonk, Attleboro, Berkley,
and Dartmouth, Massachusetts

Community	Population[a]		Moved from ENE[b]		Moved from MAIN[c]	
	1990	*2000*	*1985–90*	*1995–2000*	*1985–90*	*1995–2000*
Seekonk	12,252	12,674	4.0%	2.0%	14.0%	10.9%
Attleboro	35,056	39,126	10.8%	9.4%	7.1%	7.0%
Berkley	3,840	5,300	23.3%	16.6%	6.7%	5.4%
Dartmouth	25,904	29,296	19.6%	14.1%	3.8%	7.1%

a. Population 5 years old and over in census year.
b. Moved from Maine, New Hampshire, eastern Massachusetts (not Attleboro, Berkley, Dartmouth, North Attleborough, or [part-]MAIN communities).
c. Moved from Connecticut, Rhode Island, New Jersey, New York, western Massachusetts,
MAIN communities in eastern Massachusetts (not Seekonk).

TABLE 5.7

Workers in Seekonk, South Attleboro, Berkley, and Dartmouth,
Massachusetts, Who Commute to ENE and MAIN Dialect Areas

Community	Workers 16 or Older		Worked in Other Mass. County (ENE)		Worked Out of Mass. (MAIN)	
	1990	2000	1985–90	1995–2000	1985–90	1995–2000
Seekonk	6,784	6,814	7.0%	10.5%	51.3%	49.0%
S. Attleboro	3,559	4,071	25.2%	27.4%	26.9%	21.3%
Berkley	2,145	3,106	33.2%	36.0%	3.7%	7.2%
Dartmouth	12,535	14,100	11.7%	12.8%	5.0%	5.7%

Here, Census Bureau (2004) tract 6311 is taken as South Attleboro, workplaces out-of-state are taken as MAIN, and workplaces in Massachusetts but outside Bristol County are taken as ENE. These leave out the majority of workers who work locally or elsewhere in Bristol County, which as we know is split between ENE and MAIN.

Seekonk stands out in table 5.7 by having much more commuting to MAIN territory than to ENE. South Attleboro is balanced between commuting in both directions, while Dartmouth and especially Berkley have more toward the ENE territory.

Between 1990 and 2000, Dartmouth and especially Berkley showed increases in commuting in both directions, which probably corresponds to them becoming more like "bedroom communities" in general. In South Attleboro and Seekonk, which touch Rhode Island, fewer people worked in that state, and more commuted toward Boston. In fact, more than the migration trends, this journey-to-work trend is in line with the linguistic changes observed.

5.10. OTHER HYPOTHESES

The migration hypothesis was intentionally stated as restrictive, almost mechanical: that after an initial period of parental dominance, children re-form their dialects exclusively on the model of their first peer groups, and if this means contact with enough natively merged children, natively distinct children will become merged (at least in production).

Demographic data from the school survey and U.S. Census finds an association between migration and merger, but in Seekonk, where the merger is well documented and dated, there does not seem to have been a contemporaneous increase in merged in-migration. This makes at least some modification to the original migration hypothesis necessary.

One plausible revision would say that while a child's first peer group is forming, he or she—and by extension the group—is susceptible to influence from older children, whether it be peers, siblings, other relatives, or less-close contacts.[14] Seekonk teenagers had fairly close distinctions; when younger children heard them, it could have contributed to merger. However, far closer distinctions (near mergers) can be transmitted from generation to generation without their loss.

Or possibly for the peer group to have a certain proportion of children with merged parents is a necessary precondition for the merger, but not sufficient to trigger it. Natively merged children could have more or less influence depending on many factors, including social class, or maybe an analogous set of categories that are more meaningful for children.

Information on class was not systematically gathered in this study, but we can speculate that the children of families from Greater Boston—especially those who live in new homes in expensive subdivisions—might have high prestige. A few such children, who "happen to" have the merger, might have more influence on their distinct peers than a larger number of merged children from closer by.[15]

The original migration hypothesis assumed that the linguistic consensus arrived at by a peer group is essentially predictable from the mix of different backgrounds of the children who come together to form the group, just as Trudgill (2004) argues for the "inevitability" of features of colonial dialects, given their input mixes.

But if social class and individual factors like popularity and personality play an important role, then merger may not be predictable at all.[16]

However, the appearance of merger roughly simultaneously in the three Seekonk elementary schools suggested that larger-scale factors, like demographics, were indeed primary. Especially because Seekonk is such a long town from north to south—eight miles separate North and Martin schools, with Aitken in the middle—it seemed unlikely that the merger was spreading between schools. A common cause was thus sought in demographics.

Another "global" external cause would be if the merger in the MAIN territory was a conscious reaction against the lower-class, urban, and/or "Rhode Island" significance of a wide phonetic distinction, or against a stigmatized raised THOUGHT vowel, in particular. In the ENE area, the stigma might apply to the distinct, fronted PALM. Now, if adolescents were leading the mergers, these attitudinal factors could very plausibly be relevant, but it seems much less likely that 4- to 6-year-olds are aware of them.

The same thing imperils a contagious diffusion account (change spreads between communities). Young children have few peers in other communities, though some do have relatives. And if adults mediated the contact, the change should show up in the adults, too, which it does not.

South Attleboro, Seekonk, South Bellingham, and Assonet, Massachusetts, have all undergone the merger, and Barrington and Cumberland, Rhode Island, have begun to merge. Pawtucket and Warwick, Rhode Island, may not be far behind. In the rest of the study area, young children were simply not interviewed, so the merger may well be underway in other historically MAIN communities.

However, following section 4.5, events outside the study area—far from the MAIN-ENE boundary—could affect the interpretation of events inside it. Suppose children are also merging PALM = LOT and THOUGHT further south and west, where in-migration from low-back merged areas is rare—for example, in rural Washington County, Rhode Island (1995–2000 migration from ENE: 1.5%; from 3-M: 1.0%) or in urban Hudson County, New Jersey (migration from ENE: 0.3%; from 3-M: 0.7%). Linking the merger to migration would be untenable there; an alternate account of its origin would be needed.

Nor could migration be responsible for the merger of PALM and LOT = THOUGHT, if it is occurring in remote parts of ENE where migration from MAIN areas is low, such as Washington County, Maine (1995–2000 migration from MAIN: 2.3%), or Coos County, New Hampshire (migration from MAIN: 1.7%). And the necessity of an alternative explanation there would cast doubt on the migration hypothesis even in places where it made superficial sense, such as along the dialect boundary.

If many three-way-merged speakers were found in places like the above, external accounts appealing to dialect contact would not work. But to classify a merger as a language-internal change—apart from being rather vague about its mechanism—is strange when it is a sudden event, rather than, say, the end-product of decades of gradual approximation.

Other external factors could be considered, including the influence of the mass media. The media is generally regarded to play a very minor role, if any, in linguistic change (Chambers 1998). But even if watching television can be ignored as a passive activity, more interactive media-based merged exposure does reach young children.

During one child's interview in Warwick, a sibling was playing an educational computer game. A song played, its lyrics appeared on the screen, and the child was supposed to find the words that rhymed. The game had apparently been programmed by merged speakers, since the child was meant to select *clock* and *chalk*, among other LOT ~ THOUGHT pairs. Such experiences could at least accelerate tendencies toward merger that derive from real personal contacts.

5.11. SUMMARY OF THE FAMILY STUDY, ETC.

Section 1.5 introduced three "levels" on which to understand merger, in southeastern New England or more generally. The dialect level was explored in the geographic study (chap. 4), the individual level with the school survey (chap. 3). The family study aimed to understand merger at the community level. Why does a community merge two vowel classes that it once distinguished? And why does such merger occur when it does, often suddenly?

Some sudden merger was observed in the geographic study and more in the family study, where 47 families with 103 children were interviewed in Attleboro, South Attleboro, and Seekonk, Massachusetts, and Cumberland and Warwick, Rhode Island.

Attleboro children (§5.1) inherited the LOT ~ THOUGHT merger, and some were now merging PALM with LOT = THOUGHT. South Attleboro adults distinguish PALM = LOT from THOUGHT, so the three-way merger among children there was an unexpected development, dating to around 1990.

In Seekonk (§5.2), children of distinct parents were divided. Those over 10 kept the MAIN distinction between PALM = LOT and THOUGHT. Younger children lost it around the year 2000. Parents and older siblings were seen to maintain the distinction even while younger siblings were merged. But a 3-year-old, too young for peers, reproduced his parents' distinction. Compared to the productions of Seekonk children in interviews, the perceptions recorded on the school survey (§5.3) showed more variability and evidence of earlier merger.

In Cumberland (§5.4), where adults are also distinct, the same trend from distinct to merged was observed within families, but it was not possible to draw a chronological line between the two groups of children, as it was in South Attleboro and Seekonk.

Warwick (§5.5) was chosen to see if children further inside the MAIN territory were resisting the merger better. On the whole, they were, but signs of incipient merger were present. One family had parents from merged areas but children who were acquiring the distinction. Acoustic analysis revealed that the father had learned something of it, too.

On the individual level (§5.6), children initially acquire their parents' systems but readily change when they form peer groups. As children age, their systems become more fixed. Teenagers and adults are probably not capable of truly changing their vowel inventories, but some phonetic changes definitely occur, even in the direction of forming new distinctions. Small shifts toward a merger may be more likely to occur, but unless speakers are tracked over time, they are less likely to be detected than small shifts toward a distinction.

On the dialect level (§5.7), three-way merger appears to be spreading from the MAIN-ENE boundary to communities further inside the MAIN area. However, the speed of the apparent spread makes contagious diffusion a questionable explanation. There is actually no clear evidence that the merger is not developing far from the historical boundary, as well as near it.

On the community level, section 5.8 developed the migration hypothesis for how a merger takes hold in a distinct place. Based on Herold's account of merger by expansion, it focuses on the proportion of a community's children with merged backgrounds: with merged parent(s) or who themselves moved from a merged area. As that proportion rises, natively distinct children should go from imparting the distinction, to just maintaining it, to suddenly losing it.

Under a radical version of the migration hypothesis, merger does not spread from place to place, nor from younger to older children, nor vice versa. Demographic changes in the peer group lead to sudden merger, and the process may be quite different from whatever usually causes incrementation (Labov 2007).[17]

In section 5.9.1, demographic data from the school survey was used to evaluate the backgrounds of children in South Attleboro and Seekonk, the two communities where sudden merger was most clear. The higher proportion of merged backgrounds and lower proportion of distinct backgrounds in South Attleboro would have been sufficient to explain the difference between the communities, had Seekonk not become merged only five to ten years later. However, because Seekonk's population did not become much more merged (or less distinct), the merger that occurred during the study period may not be attributable to migration. Also, South Attleboro's merged-migration rates seem too high and too stable to have been at Seekonk-like levels just a few years earlier. The difference between the two communities was clearly seen, but not the expected trends within each place.

Census data (§5.9.2) confirmed that there was more ENE migration into South Attleboro than Seekonk, considering their entire populations rather than just schoolchildren and their parents. However, both places showed a decrease between 1985–1990 and 1995–2000. Assuming the migration hypothesis is still tenable, the census data also showed there may be enough migration from MAIN areas to be responsible for merger in the ENE territory.

Other hypotheses (§5.10) seemed less promising, except for the idea of incorporating social factors. In the end, community merger simply may not be fully predictable. Better understanding the geography of the recent mergers might challenge any migration account, if merger were found far from the dialect boundary, where migration from the other side of it is low.

So far, the facts of change and their implications are more interesting and convincing than the hypotheses offered to explain them. Further progress might come from studying more children, in more places, in greater depth. Still, the family study has taught us much about when children's vowel systems develop and redevelop—and when they do not. It has also taken the first steps toward explaining where, when, and why communities change.

6. CONCLUSIONS
AND EXTENSIONS

This chapter will highlight the most important or surprising findings of the study and discuss questions for future research. Some points are worded more strongly than in the main text.

From chapter 1, on vowel merger:

1. When will a merger (or other linguistic change) spread across a dialect boundary, and when will it stop along the boundary, indeed becoming part of it?
2. When contact is not the reason for change, how do children implement changes in parallel throughout dialect areas?

From chapter 2, on the history of the New England low vowels:

1. All parts of New England originally had the same phonological low vowel system, where PALM, LOT, and THOUGHT represented three distinct phonemes.
2. Two settlement regions came to differ in their phonetics. In Eastern New England, LOT and THOUGHT were closer, and 250 years later, they merged. In western New England (and Rhode Island), LOT and PALM were closer; they also eventually merged. Within each region, these mergers happened by parallel internal change, not by diffusion.

From chapter 3, the school survey:

1. Children's judgments of how word pairs sound, or should sound, are sensitively affected by both recent and distant exposure to merged and/or distinct patterns.
2. Peers have the largest effect, but parents have a lasting effect as well, one that is still clearly visible in responses from 17-year-old high school seniors.
3. When parents differ, children resemble their same-sex parent more than their opposite-sex parent.
4. Most children who move to merged areas show acquisition of the merger, but they also still show the effect of having had distinct peers early in life.
5. Factors favoring merger are not additive; they interact to reduce each other's effects.
6. Children younger than high school age respond more accurately to minimal pairs ("same" or "different") than to near-minimal pairs ("rhyme" or "don't rhyme").

7. Younger children generally learn new patterns better, but there are no absolute rules for acquisition under various conditions of exposure.

8. *Cot ~ caught* and *tot ~ taught* were among the pairs most often judged "different" in distinct areas and among the most often judged "same" in merged
areas. Other pairs regularly went the other way.

9. A large sample allowed consistent, intricate patterns to emerge from crude,
noisy data.

From chapter 4, the geographic study:

1. Nearly all the senior citizens clearly had one of two systems:
PALM ≠ LOT = THOUGHT (ENE) or PALM = LOT ≠ THOUGHT (MAIN). A few
showed the older three-way distinction (3-D).

2. Surrounded by new patterns, people can retain childhood systems for many
decades.

3. A sharp geographic boundary was found between ENE and MAIN. It generally matched known settlement patterns, from a time when these systems
did not exist yet.

4. One exception to the match is where a city (Woonsocket, R.I.) likely influenced its hinterland (Blackstone, Millville, and South Bellingham, Mass.).
This influence would have begun in the nineteenth century, when both
sides were still 3-D, so the boundary could have shifted without the reversal
of any merger.

5. The twentieth-century ENE/MAIN boundary could not shift without a
merger being reversed, which was observed, temporarily, in only one place
(Assonet, Mass.) under unusual demographic conditions. Normally, any
change would result in three-way merger (3-M).

6. Most young adults were still ENE or MAIN. Some, especially teenagers, were
unclear or transitional. A few clearly had the new 3-M pattern.

From chapter 5, the family study:

1. Both South Attleboro and Seekonk underwent merger to 3-M quite suddenly. In Seekonk, it occurred 5–10 years later. It occurred around the same
time in Seekonk's three elementary schools, which are far apart.

2. In two Seekonk families, older children had a distinction like their parents'
(though phonetically closer), while a younger child had a total merger. This
shows that merger can be acquired from peers and that it does not easily
pass from younger to older children.

3. In one of these families, a three-year-old had a clear distinction, like his
parents and 14-year-old brother; his 8-year-old sister was merged.

4. In other families, children as young as 4 and 5 had a clear merger, unlike
their parents.

5. Children speak like their parents until they develop a peer group, at which point they can learn a new merger very quickly. A Warwick, Rhode Island, family showed that children can also learn a distinction from their peers, but it takes much longer.

6. After age 5 or 6, the underlying phonological vowel system is unlikely to change, although phonetic adjustment can occur. Accommodation toward merger is harder to detect: a Warwick father from Maine still distinguished PALM and LOT—but was it less than he used to? However, his 30 years in the MAIN dialect area had led to a tiny, regular LOT ~ THOUGHT distinction, albeit one which was acoustically smaller than the allophonic variation within each class.

7. Many speakers exhibited a difference, although never a dramatic one, between their productions in spontaneous speech and in reading and judging minimal pairs. Their speech was closer to that of their current peers; their more self-conscious behavior reverted toward their earlier peers' or parents' patterns.

8. The migration hypothesis sought to explain the mergers in the formerly MAIN communities of South Attleboro and Seekonk, and the difference in their timing. Herold (1990) proposed that contact with merged speakers causes others to abandon their distinctions. Perhaps a substantial number of ENE speakers arrived first in South Attleboro, then later in Seekonk. The young children of merged parents, as they formed peer groups with distinct local children, would be responsible for the others' merging.

9. Analysis of demographic data from the school survey and the U.S. Census partially supported the migration hypothesis. By all measures, South Attleboro had more ENE in-migration than Seekonk. But the predicted rising trends over time were not seen.

The low vowel mergers of southeastern New England do not necessarily behave like the same mergers in other places, let alone like other changes. Do other linguistic features show a similarly abrupt transition from parental to peer influence? And do they also show the subtle persistence of earlier patterns?

A better interpretation of the changes observed in this boundary zone would require collecting data further away from it. For example, if the PALM = LOT ~ THOUGHT distinction is breaking down in the Mid-Atlantic generally, any local explanation (like the migration hypothesis) will fall short. Also, a historical and geographic study of the earlier PALM ~ LOT merger would likely reveal enlightening parallels to the changes ongoing today.

As well as hypothesizing about externally caused change, this volume emphasized the primacy of internally caused dialect evolution. With a tip of the hat to the Calvinists of early New England, predestination is hardly too strong a word to use for the best examples of dialects evolving in parallel.

Accounts of language change that emphasize individual children's misunderstandings or errors cannot easily be reconciled with the evidence of parallel innovation, ranging from the relatively far-flung LOT ~ THOUGHT merger on nineteenth-century Martha's Vineyard to the PALM = LOT ~ THOUGHT merger happening simultaneously across twenty-first-century Seekonk.

Except perhaps on the school survey, we have seen little evidence of individual agency, or even freedom to deviate from the patterns prescribed by background and environment. Children change language—and language changes—in regular, if not yet fully predictable, ways.[1]

NOTES

CHAPTER 1

1. In this study, the word class PALM is understood to include PALM, START, and sometimes BATH, as these lexical sets are defined in Wells (1982). See section 2.1.3 for the historical evolution of these vowels.

2. The THOUGHT word class includes Wells's lexical sets THOUGHT and CLOTH, and sometimes NORTH.

3. In Boston, an example of transfer is the merger of BATH-words with the TRAP set. So [ask] could be replaced by [æsk], without intermediate stages, while [haf] and [kant] may remain unaffected.

4. In some nonmining communities in Herold's study, speakers born after 1960 were found to be merged, even though there was no heavy foreign immigration to those places. Herold proposes that recent migrants from the mining towns brought the merger with them. This study will conclude that it is the children of migrants—foreign or domestic—who are the most influential in fostering change.

5. We should distinguish between merger by expansion and the idea that merger is triggered by misunderstandings and other communicative difficulties. While the latter hypothesis is logical and appealing, Herold (1990) does not test it directly, and it is not clear if children actually experience such difficulties.

6. Even under social pressure, a clean re-separation of merged word classes is unlikely; hypercorrection often occurs. See DeCamp (1958) for an example in Old English dialect geography.

7. The confounding in some American dialects among, for example, *Mary*, *marry*, and *merry* is another conditioned merger, one that has not been reported to reverse.

8. Though not technically a merger reversal, if the Southern British English split between FOOT and STRUT is "gradually spreading northwards" (Trudgill 1986, 29), this would contravene Herzog's Principle, unless "extralinguistic factors" are involved (Herzog 1965, 211).

9. Speakers' perception of difference may block the spread of change from a perceived foreign variety, regardless of any true incompatibility. Boberg (2000) considers this in accounting for the noninfluence of Detroit speech on the adjacent Canadian city of Windsor, though ultimately relying most on a version of structural incompatibility.

10. References to "the low back merger" or "the merger of LOT and THOUGHT" should be understood to include PALM as well, unless in reference to Eastern New England. In this volume, the term "low vowel" excludes the lexical set TRAP.

11. The survey elicited the low back vowels in the surnames *Hock* and *Hawk*. Later work would show that the environment before /k/ disfavors the merger (Labov, Ash, and Boberg 2006, 65).

12. All the black informants retained the distinction. Fridland (2004) reports a similar racial difference in Memphis, Tennessee. In general, the speakers reviewed in this section were white.

13. On the other hand, the earlier mergers in Eastern New England (LOT = THOUGHT) and in Canada and Western Pennsylvania (PALM = LOT = THOUGHT) resulted in merged vowels that are noticeably rounded.

14. Merger via the loss of the THOUGHT upglide has been reported more widely in the South. Feagin (1993) found it among middle-class younger speakers in Anniston, Alabama. The merger has also been observed in Roswell, Georgia, where B. Anderson (2005) attributed it to heavy in-migration from other dialect areas. But in Griffin, Georgia, McNair (2005) found glide loss without merger among younger speakers.

15. Across Canada, the low back merger is essentially complete. Why Canadian English developed this way is beyond the scope of this study.

16. Labov, Ash, and Boberg's (2006) larger sample may be more trustworthy than the smaller selection of telephone operators. For central Pennsylvania, another set of telephone interviews conducted by Herold in 1987–88 showed solidification and eastward spread of the merger as far as the Susquehanna River (Labov 1991, 32), and yet Labov, Ash, and Boberg report the distinction in Harrisburg. The differences partly lie in the treatment of places with mixed patterns. Some studies include these in their isoglosses of merger, while Labov, Ash, and Boberg tend to exclude them.

17. The merger's definite presence in Vermont (§2.3.2) and its possible appearance in western Massachusetts may be true expansions from Eastern New England (see chap. 2). The Western Pennsylvania merger also spread to Erie, which had been a Northern city on phonological as well as lexical grounds (Evanini 2009).

18. If we use the criterion of split short-*a* (divided into two discontiguous phonetic groups, tense and lax, mainly according to the following environment) to delimit the Mid-Atlantic dialect area, it does not extend northeast much past New York City. Using the raised THOUGHT criterion, instead, the Mid-Atlantic extends into southern New England, including the area studied here.

19. "The tight bundle of isoglosses that defines the southern limit of the N[orthern] C[ities] S[hift] coincides with the North/Midland settlement line, and cuts across high concentrations of population density and high levels of communication" (Labov 2003, 15). If we accept that "when two groups are in continuous communication, linguistic convergence is expected and any degree of divergence requires an explanation" (Labov 2002), then we are led toward a structural incompatibility account (Labov 2003). However, the more nuanced perspective of Labov (2007) would not expect diffusion of the NCS, a complex structural shift.

CHAPTER 2

1. Zelinsky's Doctrine of First Effective Settlement states that "whenever an empty territory undergoes settlement, or an earlier population is dislodged by invaders, the specific characteristics of the first group able to effect a viable, self-perpetuating society are of crucial significance for the later social and cultural geography of the area, no matter how tiny the initial band of settlers.... In terms of lasting impact, activities of a few hundred, or even a few score, initial colonizers can mean much more for the cultural geography of a place than the contributions of tens of thousands of new immigrants a few generations later" (1973, 13–14). Mufwene's (1995) Founder Principle is similar.

2. In a more widely accepted view, however, the loss of /r/ in England happened only later, the earliest American settlers were therefore rhotic, and non-rhoticity arose through contact between coastal areas and the prestige variety of England (see Downes 1998).

3. Although Connecticut would undergo quite parallel low vowel developments to Rhode Island, the linguistic evolutions of the two colonies (one rhotic, one not) are assumed here to have been essentially independent.

4. Richards's (2004, 56) contention that East Anglians were the largest group aboard the *Mayflower* echoes Fischer's (1989) exaggerated claims for the pre-eminence of East Anglia in the settlement of Massachusetts Bay. "East Anglia" refers most precisely to the counties of Norfolk and Suffolk. More loosely, the term may encompass parts of Cambridgeshire, Essex, Huntingdonshire, and Lincolnshire (Banks 1930, 14; V. Anderson 1991, 232). But Fischer (1989) applies it to a much larger eastern region that would have been much more diverse linguistically.

5. The original Rehoboth settlement was in modern East Providence, not in the rural town now bearing the name Rehoboth. Usually, the most central and populous place retained the older name.

6. This classification makes sense for New England, where BATH words caucus with TRAP or with START = PALM. It breaks down in the Mid-Atlantic, where BATH can be a separate tensed/raised vowel class.

7. Wakelin (1988, 616) calls unrounded LOT "characteristically South-Western," but its appearance in Irish and Caribbean varieties (Wells 1982, 419, 576)—not to mention most American ones—may show its wider prevalence in Early Modern English. In other words, in some varieties it may have followed the path [ɔ] → [ɒ] → [ɑ] → [ɒ].

8. Due to subsequent mergers, the NORTH words will generally be omitted from discussion of the THOUGHT-class.

9. This wording may be an editorial flourish on Kurath's part. It is unlikely that the fieldworker Lowman asked subjects whether pairs of words rhymed; he was following Linguistic Atlas of New England protocol.

10. Franklin Roosevelt, though, born in Dutchess County, New York, 50 years after Barton, maintains a clear distinction between PALM and LOT.

11. The better-known Wetmore (1959) treats a few New England areas, with similar results to Chase (1935).

12. Since these northeastern areas are generally conservative, retaining older Massachusetts words and sounds (Kurath et al. 1939, 2), it is surprising that the LOT ~ THOUGHT merger is more complete there than in Eastern Massachusetts. A reviewer points out that in the later-settled areas of interior Northern New England, dialect mixture might have led to merger, but section 2.4.1 finds evidence of merger even in Biddeford and York, Maine, coastal settlements dating from the 1630s.

13. Kurath and McDavid (1961) also find 3-D systems—but with PALM further back than LOT—in the Mid-Atlantic (including New York City and Baltimore) and in the South.

14. Kurath and *LANE* headquarters were at Brown University in Providence. It is surprising that no one was familiar enough with the local dialect to prevent this editorial error, which extended to the whole area covered by Harris.

15. The main set of Hanley recordings is housed in the American Folklife Center of the Library of Congress, where it is known as the American Dialect Society Collection.

16. Some Hanley recordings are very entertaining: one elderly Rhode Islander plays the fiddle and shares his misgivings about Rachel Harris's new husband!

17. This study will judge whether vowel classes are merged or distinct using separate (univariate) *t*-tests for F1 and F2. For a multivariate statistical approach, which considers the values of multiple formants at the same time, see Nycz (2010).

18. This was the Plymouth speaker for whom Kurath and McDavid's (1961) text had described an ENE pattern (§2.2.5.1), but whose synopsis suggested 3-D (§2.2.5.2).

19. Bloch argues convincingly from *LANE* evidence that Massachusetts Bay's settlers must have been mainly /r/-less, Plymouth's mainly /r/-ful, and Rhode Island's more evenly divided. Later, Plymouth and Rhode Island became largely /r/-less under Massachusetts's influence.

20. Another hypothesis invokes contact between Eastern New England and England, as has also been done to account for its nonrhoticity and broad *a* (BATH words pronounced with the PALM vowel). Suppose that unrounded LOT was quite widespread in seventeenth-century England and that it spread to all the colonies, but then the English standard reversed course and rounded LOT again. Perhaps only Eastern New England joined in that later (eighteenth-century?) development. For this account to work, we would have to explain why LOT did not re-round in Rhode Island, even though nonrhoticity did appear there (and to some extent, broad *a*).

21. One could even propose that these two mergers were caused by the same phonological change in both areas: the lengthening of LOT. In America, LOT is a longer vowel than in England, but only because it has merged with a long class, PALM or THOUGHT. The old, short, checked LOT class is no more (unless 3-D varieties remain somewhere). Perhaps all short vowels lengthened (or length

distinctions were lost) in America, which would explain, up to a point, why the LOT class has undergone merger almost everywhere in America but almost nowhere else, except Scotland.

22. The PALM ~ LOT merger is not confined to western New England, but has affected most of the United States and Canada (Labov, Ash, and Boberg 2006). A larger study would be necessary to identify its chronology and cause(s).

23. In Taunton, a third subject gave a largely-distinct response. In New Bedford, a second speaker had an intermediate pattern. In Bellingham, a second subject was merged on the other four items, but pronounced and judged *Don ~ Dawn* "different," a pattern later found elsewhere.

24. In later work, only the distinction would be found in Westport. Pilot study informants were only asked if they were "from" the community in question. Some may have participated even though they did not grow up there from an early age.

25. The proper name pair *Don ~ Dawn* was the most likely to diverge from a subject's other responses, in both directions. There were also examples of production disagreeing with perception in both directions.

CHAPTER 3

1. This age of 13 seems to refer back to the age at interview of one child in Chambers (1992); he was actually only 11 when he moved.

2. Learning to distinguish the arbitrary LOT and THOUGHT classes may be more arduous than learning the partially predictable Philadelphia short-*a* pattern, but it is also simpler and does not involve unlearning any preexisting pattern.

3. The limited data on PALM and LOT did shed some light on the difficulty of acquisition of a distinction.

4. The second PALM ~ LOT item, originally *Osama ~ comma*, was changed because many children did not know the name *Osama*.

5. The regression models below use item effects that are constant across subjects. Actually, some subjects—e.g., nonrhotic ones, faced with *collar ~ caller ID*—are likelier to make such "mistakes" than others, but this type of interaction was not modeled.

6. In any regression with categorical predictors, a set of contrasts is used to compare the effects of the different factor levels. Here, baseline-treatment contrasts are used. For example, the baseline level for Mother is "distinct," so distinct mothers receive a coefficient of zero, while all other types of mother are evaluated in comparison to that group.

7. For information on the challenges regarding mixed model hypothesis testing, see Pinheiro and Bates (2000) and the listserv R-sig-mixed-models (https://stat.ethz.ch/mailman/listinfo/r-sig-mixed-models).

8. "Brooklynese" is a stereotype of the New York dialect, although Labov (2001, 226–27) has suggested that the accent of Brooklyn is no different from that of comparable speakers anywhere else in the metropolitan area. We now

have some evidence that Brooklyn is retaining the traditional New York City LOT ~ THOUGHT distinction more tenaciously than Queens. But remember that the NY11 students are not a good sample of the larger community (unlike those in Brookline and Attleboro). In particular, they had a disproportionately large level of foreign parentage, even by New York City standards: 74% had both parents from a foreign country.

9. This was demonstrated in section 3.5.6 for AB4. An analysis of SK4 yielded coefficients of −1.178 for a merged Mother and −0.703 for a merged Father. These coefficients are noticeably smaller than the corresponding −1.736 and −1.993 for SK12.

10. Along with a Subject effect, three separate sets of Item effects were estimated, based on the different Item patterns observed in the community analyses. The division was based on Current Peers: mainly distinct (NY11, SK12), merger in progress (SK8, SK4), and mainly merged (AB, BR, MS).

11. It was not possible to explore the effect of merged parents among the 155 subjects with distinct Origin and Current Peers, because only 9 of them definitely had a merged parent.

12. Both ENE and MAIN speakers can make fun of the other pattern. As a child in Providence, Moulton (1990, 130) found it "incredible ... that people [in Boston] could pronounce *collar* and *caller* both as /ˈkɒːlə/ where we distinguished them as /ˈkɑlə/ vs. /ˈkɔːlə/." However, the "New York" (Mid-Atlantic) realization of THOUGHT as [o̞ə] is an even more prevalent stereotype; *Saturday Night Live*'s "Coffee Talk" sketches are an example. While stigmatizing raised THOUGHT is not the same as stigmatizing the LOT ~ THOUGHT distinction itself, either attitude could favor the merger.

13. Labov (2001, 430) reanalyzed Payne's data with multiple regression, concluding that "the number of times that the speaker was mentioned by peers" was more important than age of arrival or years since arriving.

14. Section 3.4 noted that some adults can live in low-back-merged communities for decades without acquiring the merger, although mergers have elsewhere (Kerswill 1996) been shown to be learnable throughout the lifespan.

15. The movers' Item effects resemble the ones from mainly distinct Seekonk and New York. *Moll ~ mall* (−0.823) and *Otto ~ auto* (−0.717) are in the lead as these subjects learn the merger; *cot ~ caught* (+0.624) trails.

16. Due to missing data, subject totals in this section do not always exactly match previous sections.

17. Only 16% of natives had either parent from Brookline; just 2% had both. This reflects a high level of migration into Brookline, combined with an exodus of locals.

18. To be classed as MAIN, a subject had to mark all 7 LOT ~ THOUGHT pairs "different," *la ~ law* "same," and say that *father ~ bother* "rhyme." For ENE and 3-M, all 7 LOT ~ THOUGHT pairs had to be marked "same." ENE subjects marked *la ~ law* "different" and said *father ~ bother* "don't rhyme"; 3-M subjects marked *la ~ law* "same" and said *father ~ bother* "rhyme." Most responses did not fall into any of these three strict groups. As discussed in section 3.4, intermediacy on the

survey could reflect actual intermediacy in production, a mismatch between perception and production (possibly related to competing life influences), or a kind of error whereby the subject could or did not fully access his or her linguistic competence in completing the survey.

CHAPTER 4

1. The Boston stereotype *p*[aː]*k the c*[aː]*r in H*[aː]*v*[ə]*d Y*[aː]*d* focuses not just on /r/-lessness, but on PALM's front quality. Conversely, raised THOUGHT leads Providence speakers to be mistaken for New Yorkers when they travel.

2. A wave account also does not explain why the LOT ~ THOUGHT merger reached Maine and New Hampshire, but not Rhode Island, which is much closer to Boston. A gravity model (Trudgill 1974) would also predict the spread of the merger to Providence.

3. If language changes faster in larger communities—perhaps driven by the diversity or simply the quantity of interactions—we would expect purely internal developments to form geographical patterns mimicking those of a gravity model.

4. The PALM ~ LOT pairs were problematic, as *balm* is increasingly pronounced with /l/, *lager* is often in the TRAP or FACE class, and *logger* is sometimes a THOUGHT word. Two supplementary cards read *balk, bock, Bach, bark* and *r*'s, *ah*'s, *Oz, aw*'s.

5. The school survey shows that at least in perception, some South Attleboro 17- and 18-year-olds retain their parents' distinction, while many are intermediate. See sections 3.5.4 and 5.3.

6. At this time, South Bellingham public school students joined the rest of Bellingham in junior high school. Older generations went to a South Bellingham school until 8th grade, then optionally to Woonsocket for high school—they never mixed in school with children from the rest of Bellingham.

7. Even when F_1 and F_2 mostly or completely overlap, speakers might use other acoustic properties not measured in this study (such as duration, glide target, or spectral slope) to distinguish two vowel classes. The methods used here might erroneously label them merged.

8. Another result of long-term contact with a merger is the "Bill Peters effect," named for an elderly central Pennsylvanian with a wide LOT ~ THOUGHT distinction in spontaneous speech, but who produced only a very small difference when reading minimal pairs, a difference he could not hear (Labov, Yaeger, and Steiner 1972, 235–36).

9. This is one of the speakers whose 3-M pattern can be understood as a reaction to "competing" parental two-vowel systems; his mother is from Fall River (MAIN), his father from Dartmouth (ENE).

10. Chapter 2 suggested that LOT was, from an early period, closer to THOUGHT in the area that would become ENE and closer to PALM in what became MAIN.

11. Those seniors excluded from section 4.1.1, because they had not lived most of their lives in the same community, almost always retained the low vowel pattern of their early childhood homes. A 73-year-old man in Fairhaven, Massachusetts, who moved from Warwick, Rhode Island, at age 7, was pure MAIN in his spontaneous speech and on reading passages, even after 67 years in the ENE environment. (On minimal pairs, he did separate PALM ~ LOT, but did not merge LOT ~ THOUGHT.) Two other examples of adult nonaccommodation were a 76-year-old husband from Millville, Massachusetts, and his 78-year-old wife from adjacent Uxbridge, Massachusetts—55 years of marriage had had no obvious effects on their low vowel systems. Aside from one anomalous minimal-pair judgment each, UB78F had the ENE pattern, MV76M the MAIN pattern.

12. A reviewer points out that summer camps may be a major locus of dialect contact. But overnight camp, where nonlocal contact is more likely, is for children older than the youngest age seen to merge in this chapter.

13. Yang (2009) argues that a sufficient level of merged input, even if it is constant rather than increasing, will eventually lead to community-wide merger.

14. The MAIN and ENE systems had undergone complementary mergers already; only 3-M could easily emerge from their subsequent contact. But if the only difference between two systems is a single merger, then that merger may spread more readily.

CHAPTER 5

1. Barrington, Rhode Island, also showed change, perhaps due to its many transient and nonnative residents. These factors were especially salient in Barrington, where young natives also explicity disclaimed having a Rhode Island accent.

2. Most of the Attleboro and South Attleboro families were recruited to participate at parent/teacher meetings, possibly skewing the sample toward a higher socioeconomic bracket. Usually both parents were present for the interviews, but if not, the absent parent was asked to complete the school survey questionnaire.

3. In Seekonk, when parents gave permission for their children to be in the school survey, a minority indicated that they were interested in participating further. Only half of these families agreed to be interviewed. Again, this is far from a random sample, and likely skewed higher, socioeconomically, than Seekonk as a whole.

4. This is despite the fact that the Cumberland sample was more homogeneous than Seekonk's. Recruited through a chain of friends, the families lived in the same neighborhood and many of the children had gone to the same schools.

5. There was no obvious reason why 13-year-old Mara Parente was ahead of her peers and her 10-year-old brother in adopting the merger. In fact, her best friend and cousins were Rhode Islanders, hence likely distinct. But Mara was

fully merged in production and marked all LOT ~ THOUGHT pairs "same" on the survey.

6. The Seekonk families are annotated on figure 5.3 according to the K–5 elementary school their children attended: North, near Attleboro; Aitken, in central Seekonk; or Martin, in South Seekonk. But elementary school has no clear effect; the merger seemingly happened across Seekonk at the same time.

7. Phonetic approximation seems to have preceded merger by at least a few years, as seen in Amber and April Koslowski and Daniel Peterson. Of course, their approximated distinctions could have resulted from contact with their younger siblings' mergers. But if not, what caused the phonetic approximation? Contact with other merged speakers? Social factors (e.g., stigmatization of the distinction or of raised THOUGHT)? Internal factors?

8. Acoustic analysis (§5.5.2.1) revealed that the father in this family, Mike Patrick, had developed a "microdistinction" that was practically inaudible. From the point of view of linguistically influencing his children, he would have acted as merged.

9. Children with one merged parent and one distinct parent usually presented as merged. However, they were not as merged as those with two merged parents, as noted in both interview productions (§5.1) and survey perceptions (chap. 3).

10. Accounts involving contagious or hierarchical diffusion were largely dismissed in section 4.5, because it seemed clear that young children—the apparent leaders of merger—have few personal contacts outside their home communities and thus could hardly participate in these contact-driven processes. Even if they did take part, we might wonder why the mergers occurred when they did. After all, South Attleboro has always been located right next to Attleboro; why did the low back merger suddenly appear in South Attleboro in 1990, rather than in 1960 or 2020?

11. This migratory mechanism would be a type of relocation diffusion, but because children learning their first dialect are the source of change, the process also involves transmission (Labov 2007). The term transfusion may therefore be apt.

12. However, migration from near Boston to southeastern New England is not at all new. Early twentieth-century town records show quite a lot of it, and in the geographic study, several seniors had a parent who had moved from Greater Boston, although none had both parents from there. And going back much further, some communities in the northern part of the study area were first settled as offshoots of Boston-area towns (see §2.1.2).

13. While not all of these migrants will have grown up in the states they moved from—they might have moved several times—a fair number will have done so, and in any case the error should be balanced between the two target communities.

14. Many of the preschools in the study area accepted children as young as 3, and some had their own kindergartens, besides prekindergarten. Since the "grades"

are less segregated in preschools, they would seem a likely place for children of different ages to influence each other.

15. In King of Prussia, Pennsylvania, some 45% of the population was nonlocal and higher status, yet Payne (1976) found it was the migrants who (variably) accommodated, while the local dialect remained intact. About a third of Payne's out-of-state families came from merged areas. Roughly 15% of the population would thus have been merged, but no spread of merger to the locals was reported, although admittedly, Payne does not discuss the low back vowels.

16. Demographics could be irrelevant, if prestigious individuals play a major role. Perhaps the merger would not have occurred in one or both of the communities, or the chronology could have reversed, if local factors, whose nature has hardly been probed, were not as they were.

17. What looks like contagious diffusion is not necessarily contagious diffusion. As a spatial example, if we map the spread of Prohibition across the United States, we see cases where one state outlawed alcohol shortly before a neighboring one. But since the temperance movement had a long history within each state, saying Prohibition diffused from state to state would be wrong. As a temporal example, imagine a city with a rising Hispanic population, where the oldest group of Anglo children knows no Spanish, a middle group knows some Spanish, and the youngest group can converse fluently in Spanish. We would not say that younger Anglo children are incrementally building on the Spanish competence of their older siblings and friends. Rather, each cohort is independent and learns Spanish according to the amount of exposure it has to Spanish-speaking children. (The second example is analogous to the migration hypothesis.)

CHAPTER 6

1. Andersen (1988) came to my attention after this study was completed. Explaining the developments found in "open" (often central) versus "closed" (often peripheral) dialects, his article discusses many matters in similar terms to this study: "There are cases in which the geographical spread of a linguistic innovation is best understood not as diffused, but as resulting from independent, internally motivated developments in structurally similar dialects" (76), developments which "may appear to spread merely because they arise in different places at different times" (54). Andersen also deals with external change and the differences between the types carried out by adults and children. The latter occurs when "learners of a language have to infer their individual grammars from speech data manifesting heterogeneous norms of usage which are not ascribed distinct values by the community" (47). If the heterogeneity is caused by intermarriage across a boundary, Andersen expects the boundary to gradually shift. The present study concludes that with more migration, changes like mergers may also "appear to spread," though they are really caused independently in each place, by contact among children from different backgrounds.

REFERENCES

Allen, Harold B. 1976. *The Linguistic Atlas of the Upper Midwest.* Vol. 3. Minneapolis: Univ. of Minnesota Press.

American Languages. 2009. "American Languages: Our Nation's Many Voices." Univ. of Wisconsin Digital Collections. http://digital.library.wisc.edu/1711.dl/AmerLangs.

Andersen, Henning. 1988. "Center and Periphery: Adoption, Diffusion, and Spread." In *Historical Dialectology: Regional and Social,* ed. Jacek Fisiak, 39–83. Berlin: Mouton de Gruyter.

Anderson, Bridget. 2005. "The ɑ/ɔ Merger in Suburban Atlanta as a Case of Phonological Leveling." Paper presented at the 34th annual conference on New Ways of Analyzing Variation (NWAV 34), New York, Oct. 20–23.

Anderson, Robert Charles. 1993. "The Great Migration Study Project." *William and Mary Quarterly,* 3rd series, 50: 591–93.

Anderson, Virginia DeJohn. 1991. "The Origins of New England Culture." *William and Mary Quarterly,* 3rd series, 48: 231–37.

Baayen, R. H., D. J. Davidson, and D. M. Bates. 2008. "Mixed-Effects Modeling with Crossed Random Effects for Subjects and Items." *Journal of Memory and Language* 59: 390–412.

Bailey, Guy, Thomas Wikle, and Lori Sand. 1991. "The Focus of Linguistic Innovation in Texas." *English World-Wide* 12: 195–214.

Bailey, Guy, Tom Wikle, Jan Tillery, and Lori Sand. 1993. "Some Patterns of Linguistic Diffusion." *Language Variation and Change* 5: 359–90.

Banks, Charles Edward. 1930. *The Planters of the Commonwealth: A Study of the Emigrants and Emigration in Colonial Times.* Boston: Houghton Mifflin.

Baranowski, Maciej. 2007. *Phonological Variation and Change in the Dialect of Charleston, South Carolina.* Publication of the American Dialect Society 92. Durham, N.C.: Duke Univ. Press.

Bates, Douglas, Martin Maechler, and Bin Dai. 2008. "lmer: Linear Mixed-Effects Models Using S4 Classes." R software package. Version 0.999375-27. http://cran.r-project.org/web/packages/lme4/index.html.

Bauman, John, and Brent Culligan. 1995. "General Service List." http://www.jbauman.com/gsl.html.

Bernstein, Cynthia. 1993. "Measuring Social Causes of Phonological Variation in Texas." *American Speech* 68: 227–40.

Bloch, Bernard. 1935. "The Treatment of Middle English Final and Preconsonantal *R* in the Present-Day Speech of New England." Ph.D. diss., Brown Univ.

Bloomfield, Leonard. 1933. *Language.* New York: Holt.

Boberg, Charles. 1997. "Variation and Change in the Nativization of Foreign (a) in English." Ph.D. diss., Univ. of Pennsylvania.

———. 2000. "Geolinguistic Diffusion and the U.S.-Canada Border." *Language Variation and Change* 12: 1–24.

———. 2001. "The Phonological Status of Western New England." *American Speech* 76: 3–29.

———. 2006. "Sex, Gender and the Phonetics of Canadian English." Paper presented at the 35th annual conference on New Ways of Analyzing Variation (NWAV 35), Columbus, Ohio, Nov. 9–12.

Boberg, Charles, and Stephanie M. Strassel. 1995. "Phonological Change in Cincinnati." In "Proceedings of the 19th Annual Penn Linguistics Colloquium," ed. Rajesh Bhatt, Susan Garrett, Chung-Hye Han, and Roumyana Izvorski. *University of Pennsylvania Working Papers in Linguistics* 2.2.

Bresnan, Joan. 2007. "Is Syntactic Competence Probabilistic? Evidence from English Dative Constructions." Plenary address at the 33rd annual meeting of the Berkeley Linguistics Society, Berkeley, Calif., Feb. 9–11.

Campbell, Lyle. 2004. *Historical Linguistics: An Introduction*. 2nd ed. Cambridge, Mass.: MIT Press.

Carver, Craig M. 1987. *American Regional Dialects: A Word Geography*. Ann Arbor: Univ. of Michigan Press.

Census Bureau. 1994. "Census 1990 Special Tabulation: Census Tract of Work by Census Tract of Residence (STP 154)." http://mcdc2.missouri.edu/cgi-bin/uexplore?/pub/data/stp154.

———. 1995. *1990 Census of Population and Housing: County-to-County Migration Flow Files*. Special project 312. CD. Washington, D.C.: U.S. Dept. of Commerce.

———. 2003. *Census 2000 Migration Data*. DVD. Washington, D.C.: U.S. Dept. of Commerce.

———. 2004. "Census 2000 Special Tabulation: Census Tract of Work by Census Tract of Residence (STP 64)." http://www.fhwa.dot.gov/ctpp/tract.htm.

Chambers, J. K. 1992. "Dialect Acquisition." *Language* 68: 673–705.

———. 1998. "Myth 15: TV Makes People Sound the Same." In *Language Myths*, ed. Laurie Bauer and Peter Trudgill, 123–31. London: Penguin.

Chase, Margaret Taft. 1935. "The Derivatives of Middle English Short *o* in the Speech of New England." Master's thesis, Brown Univ.

DARE. Dictionary of American Regional English. 1985–. Ed. Frederic G. Cassidy and Joan Houston Hall. 4 vols. to date. Cambridge, Mass.: Belknap Press of Harvard Univ. Press.

DeCamp, David. 1958. "The Genesis of the Old English Dialects: A New Hypothesis." *Language* 34: 232–44.

Dillard, J. L. 1995. "American English in the English Diaspora." In *New Approaches to American English*, ed. Zoltán Kövecses, 3–18. Budapest: Dept. of American Studies, Eötvös Loránd Univ.

Dobson, E. J. 1957. *English Pronunciation, 1500–1700*. 2 vols. Oxford: Clarendon.

Downes, William. 1998. *Language and Society*. 2nd ed. Cambridge: Cambridge Univ. Press.

Eckert, Penelope. 1989. *Jocks and Burnouts: Social Categories and Identity in the High School.* New York: Teachers College Press.

———. 2008. "Where Do Ethnolects Stop?" *International Journal of Bilingualism* 12: 25–42.

Evanini, Keelan. 2009. "The Permeability of Dialect Boundaries: A Case Study of the Region Surrounding Erie, Pennsylvania." Ph.D. diss., Univ. of Pennsylvania.

Feagin, Crawford. 1993. "Low Back Vowels in Alabama: Yet Another Merger." Poster presented at the 22nd annual conference on New Ways of Analyzing Variation in English (NWAVE 22), Ottawa, Oct. 14–17.

Fischer, David Hackett. 1989. *Albion's Seed: Four British Folkways in America.* New York: Oxford Univ. Press.

———. 1991. "Albion and the Critics: Further Evidence and Reflection." *William and Mary Quarterly,* 3rd series, 48: 260–308.

Foulkes, Paul, Gerry Docherty, and Dominic Watt. 1999. "Tracking the Emergence of Sociophonetic Variation." In *ICPhS 99: Proceedings of the 14th International Congress of Phonetic Sciences, San Francisco, 1–7 August 1999,* 1625–28. Berkeley: Univ. of California.

Fridland, Valerie. 1998. "The Southern Vowel Shift: Linguistic and Social Factors." Ph.D. diss., Michigan State Univ.

———. 2004. "The Spread of the *cot/caught* Merger in the Speech of Memphians: An Ethnolinguistic Marker?" Paper presented at the 3rd conference on Language Variety in the South (LAVIS III), Tuscaloosa, Ala., Apr. 15–17.

Garde, Paul. 1961. "Réflections sur les differences phonétiques entre les langues slaves." *Word* 17: 34–62.

Gordon, Matthew J. 2006. "Tracking the Low Back Merger in Missouri." In *Language Variation and Change in the American Midland: A New Look at "Heartland" English,* ed. Thomas E. Murray and Beth Lee Simon, 57–68. Philadelphia: Benjamins.

Grandgent, C. H. 1891. "English Sentences in American Mouths." *Dialect Notes* 1: 198–204.

Guy, Gregory R. 1990. "The Sociolinguistic Types of Language Change." *Diachronica* 7: 47–67.

Hägerstrand, Torsten. 1953. *Innovationsförloppet ur korologisk synpunkt.* Lund: Gleerupska univ.-bokhandeln. Trans. Allan Pred as *Innovation Diffusion as a Spatial Process.* Chicago: Univ. of Chicago Press, 1967.

Hall, David D. 1990. Rev. of *Albion's Seed: Four British Folkways in America,* by David Hackett Fischer. *New England Quarterly* 63: 657–61.

Hall, Robert A., Jr. 1950. "The Reconstruction of Proto-Romance." *Language* 26: 6–27.

Hall, Stephanie A., Rachel I. Howard, Francesca McLean, John Vallier, and Ross Gersten, comps. 2002. American Dialect Society Collection (AFC 1984/011), Archive of Folk Culture, American Folklife Center, Library of Congress, Washington, D.C. Revised by Marcia K. Segal, 2004. Encoded by Judy Ng, 2006.

Harris, John. 1985. *Phonological Variation and Change: Studies in Hiberno-English.* Cambridge: Cambridge Univ. Press.

Herold, Ruth. 1990. "Mechanisms of Merger: The Implementation and Distribution of the Low Back Merger in Eastern Pennsylvania." Ph.D. diss., Univ. of Pennsylvania.

———. 1997. "Solving the Actuation Problem: Merger and Immigration in Eastern Pennsylvania." *Language Variation and Change* 9: 165–89.

Herzog, Marvin I. 1965. *The Yiddish Language in Northern Poland: Its Geography and History.* Special issue, *International Journal of American Linguistics* 31.2.

Hock, Hans Heinrich. 1986. *Principles of Historical Linguistics.* Trends in Linguistics: Studies and Monographs 34. Berlin: Mouton de Gruyter.

Irons, Terry Lynn. 2007. "On the Status of Low Back Vowels in Kentucky English: More Evidence of Merger." *Language Variation and Change* 19: 137–80.

Johnson, Daniel Ezra. 2000. "The Acoustic Correlates of Lip Rounding." Unpublished MS.

———. 2009. "Getting Off the GoldVarb Standard: Introducing Rbrul for Mixed-Effects Variable Rule Analysis." *Language and Linguistics Compass* 3: 359–83.

Kerswill, Paul. 1996. "Children, Adolescents, and Language Change." *Language Variation and Change* 8: 177–202.

Kilpatrick, Rachel S. H. 1937. "The Speech of Rhode Island: The Stressed Vowels and Diphthongs." Ph.D. diss., Brown Univ.

Kurath, Hans. 1928. "The Origin of the Dialectal Differences in Spoken American English." *Modern Philology* 25: 385–95.

Kurath, Hans, Marcus L. Hansen, Bernard Bloch, and Julia Bloch. 1939. *Handbook of the Linguistic Geography of New England.* Providence, R.I.: Brown Univ.

Kurath, Hans, and Guy S. Lowman, Jr. 1970. *The Dialectal Structure of Southern England: Phonological Evidence.* Publication of the American Dialect Society 54. University: Univ. of Alabama Press.

Kurath, Hans, and Raven I. McDavid, Jr. 1961. *The Pronunciation of English in the Atlantic States: Based upon the Collections of the Linguistic Atlas of the Eastern United States.* Ann Arbor: Univ. of Michigan Press.

Labov, William. 1963. "The Social Motivation of a Sound Change." *Word* 19: 273–309.

———. 1991. "The Three Dialects of English." In *New Ways of Analyzing Sound Change,* ed. Penelope Eckert, 1–44. San Diego, Calif.: Academic Press.

———. 1994. *Principles of Linguistic Change.* Vol. 1, *Internal Factors.* Oxford: Blackwell.

———. 2001. *Principles of Linguistic Change.* Vol. 2, *Social Factors.* Oxford: Blackwell.

———. 2002. "Driving Forces in Linguistic Change." In *Proceedings of the 2002 International Conference on Korean Linguistics.* Seoul: Seoul National Univ. Available at http://www.ling.upenn.edu/~wlabov/Papers/DFLC.htm.

———. 2003. "Pursuing the Cascade Model." In *Social Dialectology: In Honour of Peter Trudgill,* ed. David Britain and Jenny Cheshire, 9–22. Philadelphia: Benjamins.

———. 2007. "Transmission and Diffusion." *Language* 83: 344–87.

Labov, William, Sharon Ash, and Charles Boberg. 2006. *The Atlas of North American English: Phonetics, Phonology and Sound Change.* Berlin: Mouton de Gruyter.

Labov, William, Malcah Yaeger, and Richard Steiner. 1972. *A Quantitative Study of Sound Change in Progress.* Philadelphia: U.S. Regional Survey.

Ladefoged, Peter. 1960. "The Value of Phonetic Statements." *Language* 36: 387–96.

LANE. Linguistic Atlas of New England. 1939–43. Director, Hans Kurath. 3 vols. Providence, R.I.: Brown Univ.

Leonard, Clifford S., Jr. 1978. Review of *Proto-Romance and Sicilian,* by Michael L. Mazzola. *Language* 54: 180–86.

Lusk, Melanie. 1976. "Phonological Variation in Kansas City: A Sociolinguistic Analysis of Three-Generation Families." Ph.D. diss., Univ. of Kansas.

Maguire, Warren. 2008. "What Is a Merger, and Can It Be Reversed? The Origin, Status and Reversal of the 'NURSE-NORTH Merger' in Tyneside English." Ph.D. diss., Newcastle Univ.

Majors, Tivoli. 2005. "Low Back Vowel Merger in Missouri Speech: Acoustic Description and Explanation." *American Speech* 80: 165–79.

Malkiel, Yakov. 1984. "Revisionist Dialectology and Mainstream Linguistics." *Language in Society* 13: 29–66.

Martinet, André. 1955. *Économie des changements phonétiques: Traité de phonologie diachronique.* Berne: Franke.

McDavid, Raven I., Jr. 1981. "Low-Back Vowels in Providence: A Note in Structural Dialectology." *Journal of English Linguistics* 15: 21–29.

McLoughlin, William G. 1978. *Rhode Island: A Bicentennial History.* New York: Norton.

McNair, Elizabeth DuPree. 2005. *Mill Villagers and Farmers: Dialect and Economics in a Small Southern Town.* Publication of the American Dialect Society 90. Durham, N.C.: Duke University Press.

Metcalf, Allan A. 1972. "Directions of Change in Southern California English." *Journal of English Linguistics* 6: 28–34.

Mills, Carl. 1980. "The Sociolinguistics of the /ɑ/ ~ /ɔ/ Merger in Pacific Northwest English: A Subjective Reaction Test." *Research on Language and Social Interaction* 13: 345–88.

Moulton, William G. 1968. "Structural Dialectology." *Language* 44: 451–66.

———. 1990. "Some Vowel Systems in American English." In *Studies in the Pronunciation of English: A Commemorative Volume in Honour of A. C. Gimson,* ed. Susan Ramsaran, 119–36. New York: Routledge.

Mufwene, Salikoko S. 1995. "The Founder Principle in Creole Genesis." *Diachronica* 13: 83–134.

Nycz, Jennifer. 2005. "The Dynamics of Near Merger in Accommodation." In *Proceedings of ConSOLE XIII,* ed. Sylvia Blaho, Luis Vicente, and Erik Schoorlemmer, 273–85. Leiden, Netherlands: Dept. of General Linguistics, Univ. Leiden. Available at http://www.hum2.leidenuniv.nl/pdf/lucl/sole/console13/console13-nycz.pdf.

————. 2010. "Mergers and Acquisition: Linguistic and Social Factors Underlying Herzog's Principle." Ph.D. diss., New York Univ.

O'Brien, Meredith. 1992. "Linguists Criticize Accent Position." *Springfield* (Mass.) *Union-News,* July 10: 1.

Orbeck, Anders. 1927. *Early New England Pronunciation as Reflected in Some Seventeenth Century Town Records of Eastern Massachusetts.* Ann Arbor, Mich.: Wahr.

Orton, Harold, et al., eds. 1962–71. *Survey of English Dialects.* B: *The Basic Material.* 4 vols., each of 3 parts. Leeds: Arnold.

Payne, Arvilla C. 1976. "The Acquisition of the Phonological System of a Second Dialect." Ph.D. diss., Univ. of Pennsylvania.

————. 1980. "Factors Controlling the Acquisition of the Philadelphia Dialect by Out-of-State Children." In *Locating Language in Time and Space,* ed. William Labov, 143–78. New York: Academic Press.

Pinheiro, José C., and Douglas M. Bates. 2000. *Mixed-Effects Models in S and S-PLUS.* New York: Springer.

Pop, Sever. 1950. *La dialectologie: Aperçu historique et méthodes d'enquêtes linguistiques.* 2 vols. Louvain, Belgium: Chez l'Auteur.

Richards, Eric. 2004. *Britannia's Children: Emigration from England, Scotland, Wales and Ireland since 1600.* London: Hambledon and London.

Sankoff, Gillian. 2004. "Adolescents, Young Adults, and the Critical Period: Two Case Studies from 'Seven Up.'" In *Sociolinguistic Variation: Critical Reflections,* ed. Carmen Fought, 121–39. Oxford: Oxford Univ. Press.

Smith, Jennifer, Mercedes Durham, and Liane Fortune. 2007. "'Mam, My Trousers Is Fa'in Doon!': Community, Caregiver, and Child in the Acquisition of Variation in a Scottish Dialect." *Language Variation and Change* 19: 63–99.

Terrell, Tracy D. 1976. "Some Theoretical Considerations on the Merger of the Low Vowel Phonemes in American English." In *Proceedings of the Second Annual Meeting of the Berkeley Linguistics Society, February 14–16, 1976,* ed. Henry Thompson, Kenneth Whistler, Vicki Edge, Jeri Jaeger, Ronya Javkin, Miriam Petruck, Christopher Smeall, and Robert D. van Valin, 350–59. Berkeley: Berkeley Linguistics Soc., Univ. of California.

Thomas, Erik R. 2001. *An Acoustic Analysis of Vowel Variation in New World English.* Publication of the American Dialect Society 85. Durham, N.C.: Duke Univ. Press.

Trudgill, Peter. 1974. "Linguistic Change and Diffusion: Description and Explanation in Sociolinguistic Dialect Geography." *Language in Society* 3: 215–46.

————. 1986. *Dialects in Contact.* Oxford: Blackwell.

————. 2004. *New-Dialect Formation: The Inevitability of Colonial Englishes.* Edinburgh: Edinburgh Univ. Press.

Trudgill, Peter, and Tina Foxcroft. 1978. "On the Sociolinguistics of Vocalic Mergers: Transfer and Approximation in East Anglia." In *Sociolinguistic Patterns in British English,* ed. Peter Trudgill, 69–79. London: Arnold.

Wakelin, Martyn F. 1988. "The Phonology of South-Western English, 1500–1700."
   In *Historical Dialectology: Regional and Social*, ed. Jacek Fisiak, 609–44. Berlin:
   Mouton de Gruyter.

Weinreich, Uriel, William Labov, and Marvin I. Herzog. 1968. "Empirical Founda-
   tions for a Theory of Language Change." In *Directions for Historical Linguistics:
   A Symposium*, ed. W. P. Lehmann and Yakov Malkiel, 97–195. Austin: Univ. of
   Texas Press.

Wells, J. C. 1982. *Accents of English*. 3 vols. Cambridge: Cambridge Univ. Press.

Wetmore, Thomas H. 1959. *The Low-Central and Low-Back Vowels in the English of the
   Eastern United States*. Publication of the American Dialect Society 32. University:
   University of Alabama Press.

Wright, Joseph. 1905. *The English Dialect Grammar: Comprising the Dialects of England,
   of the Shetland and Orkney Islands, and of Those Parts of Scotland, Ireland and Wales
   Where English Is Habitually Spoken*. Oxford: Frowde.

Yang, Charles. 2009. "Selectionist Forces in Language Change." Paper presented at
   the 33rd Penn Linguistics Colloquium, Philadelphia, Mar. 27–29.

Zelinsky, Wilbur. 1973. *The Cultural Geography of the United States*. Englewood Cliffs,
   N.J.: Prentice-Hall.

INDEX

accommodation, 75, 92, 111, 140, 144, 180, 192, 211, 220, 222

acoustic analysis, 3, 13, 34, 36, 97; of principal low vowel systems, 106–9, 111, 129, 131, 136, 154, 192, 205, 221

adolescence, 60, 77, 88, 203

Allen, Harold, 8

allophony, 8, 23, 108, 138, 140, 181, 183, 211; allophonic conditioning, 76, 108–9, 112, 126, 136, 138, 181, 183. *See also* merger, conditioned

Andersen, Henning, 96, 222

Anderson, Bridget, 194, 214

Anderson, Robert, 16

Anderson, Virginia, 16, 215

Ash, Sharon, 7–11, 13, 33–34, 41, 43, 45, 49, 51, 84, 107, 214, 217

Assonet, Mass., 100–101, 103–6, 146, 149, 192, 204, 210

Atlas of North American English, 7–11, 13, 33–34, 41, 43, 45, 49, 51, 84, 107, 214, 217

Attleboro, Mass.: family study in, 149–54, 190–201, 205, 220–21; geographic study in, 100–101, 129; in history, 19–21; pilot study in, 41; school study in, 48–76, 82–93, 218. *See also* South Attleboro, Mass.

auditory analysis: of Hanley recordings, 33–38; of geographic study, 99–107; compared to acoustic, 108, 117, 119, 121, 129, 131, 132, 152

Baayen, R. Harald, 52

Bailey, Guy, 8

Banks, Charles, 14–16, 215

Baranowski, Maciej, 5, 8, 107

Barlow family, 179, 183, 186

Barrington, R.I., 20, 21, 103, 192, 204, 220

baseline (in regression), 55–57, 60–61, 71–72, 81, 217

Bates, Douglas M., 52, 217

Bauman, John, 136

Belfast (Northern Ireland), 111, 127

Bellingham, Mass., 20, 41, 98, 104, 219. *See also* South Bellingham, Mass.

Berkley, Mass., 20, 200–202

Bernstein, Cynthia, 8

Blackstone, Mass., 20–21, 41, 100, 195, 210

Bloch, Bernard, 18, 39

Bloomberg family, 179

Bloomfield, Leonard, 11

Boberg, Charles, 7–11, 13, 22, 33–34, 41, 43, 45, 49, 51, 84, 107, 213, 214, 217

Boston, Mass., 13–40, 48, 52, 57, 74, 95–105, 137–45, 151, 190–203, 213, 218–21

boundary (dialect), 6–8, 145–46, 209–11, 214, 222; between ENE and MAIN systems, 10–12; in family study, 149, 151, 178, 191–93, 195, 198, 204, 206, 207; in geographic study, 95–97, 99–101, 103, 106, 131, 143–44; in history, 13, 17, 21, 29, 33–34, 40, 41; in school study, 45, 48, 54, 84, 89–90

boundary (political), 18–19, 21, 33

Bresnan, Joan, 52

Bristol, R.I., 19

Bristol County, Mass., 18, 28, 33, 202

British English, 18, 22–24, 60, 213

broad *a*, 107, 117, 216

Brookline, Mass., 48, 49, 51, 54–58, 65–76, 82–93, 218

Brooklyn, N.Y., 66–68, 74, 217, 218. *See also* New York City

Burlington, Vt., 31, 34

Burrillville, R.I., 20–21, 33

California, 7, 8

Cambridge, Mass., 16, 28, 36, 38

Campbell, Lyle, 1

Canada, 34, 44, 55, 84, 194, 213–14, 217

Carver, Craig, 33

Census Bureau, U.S., 48, 105, 145, 179, 199–202, 206, 211

Central Falls, R.I., 20, 98

Chambers, J. K., 44, 93, 194, 204, 217

Champagne family, 177–78

change, external, 2, 5, 96, 203–4, 211, 222

change, internal, 2, 7, 96, 204, 209, 219

Charleston, S.C., 5, 8

Chase, Margaret, 29, 30, 32–33, 216

cohort, 90, 178, 195–98, 222

college, 30–31, 49, 53–54, 76, 82, 84, 86, 137, 139, 181

Columbus, Ohio, 9–10

commuting, 105, 195, 201–2

Connecticut: in history; 13–15, 17–18, 28–31, 33, 34, 40; in family study, 153–54, 181, 190, 200–201, 215; in geographic study, 97–98, 100, 102, 145; in school study, 49, 55

cousin, 145, 180, 220

Culligan, Brent, 136

Cumberland, R.I.: in family study, 145, 151–52, 177–79, 193, 204–5, 220; in history, 18, 20–21, 41

Current Peers. *See* peer group, current

Dai, Bin, 52

Dana, Henry Wadsworth Longfellow, 36–38

Dartmouth, Mass., 19–21, 41, 98, 142, 144, 200–202, 219

Davidson, D. J., 52